This Is How We Teach Reading... And It's Working!

The what, why, and how of teaching phonics in K-3 classrooms
✲ A week-by-week, step-by-step instructional guide ✲

HEATHER WILLMS

GIACINTA ALBERTI

Pembroke Publishers Limited

© 2022 Pembroke Publishers
538 Hood Road
Markham, Ontario, Canada L3R 3K9
www.pembrokepublishers.com

Library and Archives Canada Cataloguing in Publication

Title: This is how we teach reading...and it's working! : the what, why, and how of teaching phonics in K-3 classrooms / Heather Willms, Giacinta Alberti.

Names: Willms, Heather, author. | Alberti, Giacinta, author.

Identifiers: Canadiana (print) 20220177546 | Canadiana (ebook) 20220187045 | ISBN 9781551383576 (softcover) | ISBN 9781551389585 (PDF)

Subjects: LCSH: Reading—Phonetic method—Study and teaching (Early childhood)

Classification: LCC LB1573.3 .W55 2022 | DDC 372.46/5—dc23

Editors: David Kilgour, Alison Parker
Cover Design: John Zehethofer
Typesetting: Jay Tee Graphics Ltd.

Printed and bound in Canada
9 8 7 6 5 4 3 2

To my Elissa. There is no doubt that your educational journey would have been very different if we had known about Structured Literacy. It has been your hard work and tenacity that have made you a reader and it brings me great joy to know that you continue to read for knowledge and pleasure. *Heather*

To my husband, Spencer, and our sweet beagle, Doolin: your love and encouragement carry me through life. To my parents, thank you for the millions of big and little things that you have done, and continue to do, to support me; your help has got me to where I am and keeps me going. Finally, to the rest of my family and friends: I'm so grateful to have you all in my life. *Cinta*

Contents

Introduction

To You, the Teacher

Heather asked a retired grade 1 teacher who had taught for thirty-five years, how had she managed to stick with the demands of the classroom for so long? She worked with a very diverse population — families struggling with poverty, newcomers to Canada, and parents with low literacy skills. Her answer: "When students come to me, they don't know how to read. Some of them don't even know how to hold a book. By the time they leave me, they can all read. It's magical!"

If you are holding this book in your hands, it could mean several things. It could be that you have become aware of in-depth reading inquiries like the United States' National Reading Panel of 2000 and the recent Ontario Right to Read inquiry report of 2022, or the current focus on years of reading research that directs teachers toward a return to explicit phonics instruction. You may be aware that phonics is one of the "Big 5" of reading instruction according to the **Science of Reading,** but you have never explicitly taught phonics and do not know where to start and how to get the job done. Perhaps you were never introduced to phonics instruction in your teacher training and wonder if you have missed something. You may be skeptical about the return of phonics, as you do not want to be drilling your students on phonics rules, which you have been taught are not an effective approach to reading instruction. Of course, you could be here for an entirely different reason. Whatever your reason for picking up this book, we are glad you are here.

Why Phonics?

With dropping reading scores in the United States at the turn of the century, the National Reading Panel of 2000 was mandated to look at reading instruction and figure out what was necessary for effective reading instruction in schools. Educators and researchers began conversations that really had not taken place prior to the panel. Before this work, educators taught reading in a way that seemed best, and on a parallel track, neurological researchers worked to discover what was happening in the brain as children/adults learned to read. The panel recommended five necessary components to reading instruction, often referred to as the Big 5: phonemic awareness, phonics, vocabulary, fluency, and comprehension (Armbruster et al., 2001). While reading instruction over the past thirty or more years had embraced comprehension, fluency, and vocabulary, educators were not aware of the role of phonemic awareness, and phonics had essentially been placed on the shelf as perhaps an outdated way to teach reading.

Reading is a human invention. There is no part of the brain that is specifically designed for reading; therefore, the reading process essentially uses areas of the brain designed for other functions. Neuroscientists researching reading have found that specific areas of the brain are engaged in the reading process. Through fMRI brain scans, researchers noted that these areas of the brain were engaged with efficient readers but were not in adults and children with reading difficulties. However, after instruction with a structured, synthetic phonics approach, brain scans of students with reading difficulties paralleled those of efficient readers.

The information that neurological researchers shared with the panel in 2000 was not new. Although we now have the technology to implement brain scans while students are reading, as well as before and after they learn to read, these visuals only confirmed what researchers have known all along.

A second important discovery by neurological researchers is that there is a timeline for when children's brains have the highest plasticity for learning to read. An exploration of the research is beyond the scope of this book, but in short, it is easiest for children to learn to read before the age of eight, when the ventral visual system is still undergoing reorganization (Dehaene, 2021). After this sensitive period, students are still able to learn to read, but it will be more difficult and most likely take longer. This is to say that if you are teaching children between the ages of six and eight, there is an urgency in teaching them to decode and that is done best through explicit synthetic phonics instruction.

It is not uncommon for educators learning about the Science of Reading (SOR) to be quite frustrated when they learn that this shift could have happened a long time ago and changed the educational trajectory for countless students.

This book focuses on **one** of the Big 5: phonics. Of course, reading is such a complex task that we cannot talk about phonics without referring to the other four, so you will see phonemic awareness, vocabulary, fluency, and comprehension showing up on the following pages in varying degrees. Although all five components appear throughout the book, as you build a comprehensive phonics program, it is critical that you embed the other four into your practice to ensure you are delivering a well-rounded reading program.

We are a district reading support teacher (Heather) and a learning support teacher (Giacinta) who, like many of you, are concerned about the growing number of students arriving in the reading support room because they are struggling with reading. We are concerned that for many children, the introduction to explicit phonics instruction is happening in the support room rather than the classroom, which means there is no time for additional practice of these newly acquired skills. We are also concerned about the number of students receiving reading support year after year and yet not moving ahead in their reading journey. What educators have not understood until now is that explicit phonics instruction benefits all readers. Although explicit phonics instruction has been seen as an intervention in the past, we now know that it is critical for all students. Consider the adage, "A rising tide floats all boats." If we teach all students well through a Structured Literacy approach, every student benefits.

Structured Literacy

Structured Literacy is reading instruction that is **systematic, explicit, engaging, and success-oriented.** This is a shift from a balanced literacy approach, which focuses on guiding, sharing, and independent reading. **Systematic** means that the teacher follows a scope and sequence or learning progression for introducing each skill, with ongoing review of skills previously taught and mastered. With **explicit** instruction, the teacher provides clear and precise instruction of each concept. Activities are multimodal and encourage active participation (**engaging**) of all students at their level. **Success-oriented** instruction sees the teacher providing corrective feedback when errors occur. In Structured Literacy, the teacher spends a significant amount of time in instruction and coaching, with a minimal amount of time when students are learning on their own. Structured Literacy instruction is based on ongoing assessment, with continual adjustments made in response to the progress of the students being taught.

There are strong parallels between teaching math and teaching reading, with concepts building on those that have been previously taught and teachers continuously providing instruction and modeling. We would never consider discontinuing math instruction after grade 2, but for some reason, reading instruction is sometimes considered to be complete at that point.

What Teachers Are Asking

We have introduced explicit, systematic phonics instruction to classroom teachers and schools, working alongside educators as they screen, prepare, and deliver lessons that target the needs of the students who are seated before them. As teachers began to shift their practice, they started asking us the same questions, questions that have been asked not only within our district, but by teachers and schools Heather has worked with across Western Canada.

- "What are the phonics building blocks that my students need and what strategies are the most effective in moving my students forward as readers?"
- "Is there a scope and sequence or reading progression that I can follow to ensure I cover all the phonics concepts my students need to become strong readers?"
- "What do **I** (as an educator) need to know to teach phonics explicitly? I was not taught these concepts as a student or a teacher in training."

Since there has been a limited amount of targeted, explicit phonics instruction at the classroom level over the past fifty years, it can be difficult to find resources that align with the reading research that has taken place over the same period. This book is a response to the requests of many, many dedicated teachers committed to offering their students the most effective strategies and instruction in phonics.

What We Would Like to Share with You

We are excited to share this approach with you because these are the structures and strategies that we have seen work in our own schools, classrooms, and reading support rooms. We have seen that when teachers explicitly teach phonics in the classroom, the reading support teacher is able to offer the extra support and practice some students need to "break the code" and develop foundational reading skills. We are seeing fewer students requiring reading support outside the classroom, we are seeing students in grades 4, 5, 6, and beyond learning to read for the first time, and we are seeing students moving out of targeted reading support groups because they now have the knowledge and skills they need to access text in a powerful way. The doubters are becoming enthusiastic converts because of what they are seeing in their students and their schools.

This Is How We Teach Reading breaks down four years of phonics instruction into weekly lessons (with ongoing review), with flex weeks that follow the rhythms of busy, and often interrupted, school schedules. It contains sample lesson plans, word lists, and a compilation of evidence-based strategies that will move students along in their reading journey. By following the blueprints and concept descriptions and using the lesson plan structure and the high-impact activities suggested, educators will be able to confidently offer students structured, evidence-based, explicit instruction in phonics.

We think it is important to begin with sharing a summary of how students learn to read. Linguist and educator Louisa Moats (2020) states, "Informed teachers are our best insurance against reading failure. While programs are very helpful tools, programs don't teach, teachers do." Understanding how students learn to read empowers you, the educator, to make the decisions necessary to support your students. Your knowledge will guide your instruction toward evidence-based practices and resources, and away from those that are less effective in reading instruction.

We share how we set up our lessons, ensuring that we cover all the components necessary for a strong, synthetic phonics approach. It is not possible to cover all the components of a well-developed phonics program in one lesson, but by working from a lesson plan that addresses key aspects of phonics instruction, students will have the opportunity to practice and learn a skill over several days, without missing critical activities because there was no game plan in place.

While this is **not a full-boxed phonics program**, we do want to share with you the evidence-based strategies and high-impact activities that we know and have seen to be powerful in teaching decoding and encoding. With busy days and diverse learners, educators do not have time to devote to preparing and delivering lessons and activities that make little impact on learning. These strategies are broken down into two components: decoding and encoding. You will see that manipulating is a common thread that runs through these activities, because students who work within words and learn to manipulate letters and sounds develop a foundational understanding of how words are put together.

Finally, we share four sets of blueprints for how to cover four years of foundational concepts from kindergarten to grade 3. This is a **flexible structure that can be adapted and changed** to meet the needs of your students. The key understanding when approaching these blueprints is that no matter what grade is being taught, educators start where their students are (which will be evident through the screening process) and move forward from there. Is the structure too fast? Slow the progression of concepts to the pace that works for your students. Are concepts introduced too slowly? Then move to the next week's concept without spending a week practicing skills that are already in place. This is not a fast scope and sequence because we have seen that many students have not had a solid understanding of foundational concepts before the next concept was introduced.

Unfortunately, there are currently many students in grades 4 and beyond with gaps in their phonics knowledge. If you are teaching above grade 3 and have students lagging in reading and/or spelling skills, this adaptable approach can be used to target concepts needed to fill those gaps. Teachers can screen their students and move to the appropriate lessons and word lists in the blueprints. These strategies and blueprints are also appropriate for the reading support room, since effective intervention involves additional practice of the explicit phonics instruction taught in the classroom. Parallel concepts and word lists, along with additional practice and time, is all some lagging students need to learn and implement these concepts.

Once this foundational work is complete, students will possess the building blocks needed to move further into multisyllable work, morphology (the internal structure of words), and etymology (where words come from) in grades 4 and beyond.

Of course, as educators we would not leave you without structured lesson and high-impact activity templates, word lists, resources, and recommended supplemental materials. Our hope is that due to the flexibility of this structure, you will add your own evidence-based practices as you discover them, so that *This Is How We Teach Reading* will remain the guide you keep close at hand, rather than a book you read and then leave on your shelf.

Two Words of Caution

First, as you discover how the brain learns to read and the strategies and steps that support that process, it is easy to look back and feel badly about not teaching this way in previous years. Rather than spending time feeling disappointed about what you did not know and therefore were unable to do, we hope you will look forward and be excited about what is ahead.

Second, as educators, we are always working to provide our students with the most effective instruction possible. As you learn more about the Science of Reading and evidence-based practices, you may be tempted to toss aside all current practices and revamp your entire reading program over the next few months. We strongly encourage you to be gentle with yourself as you shift to practices that align with what neuroscience is telling us about how students learn to read. There are many demands on a teacher's time and heart, so as you start following the blueprints at the end of this book, choose one or two strategies at a time and slowly adjust your practice. As you begin to master strategies and concepts, you can then add the next piece that you would like to embed into your teaching. There is only one of you, so be kind to yourself as you enter this exciting time in education when we are finally witnessing reading scores rising rather than falling!

How Children Learn to Read — The Science of Reading

The Simple View of Reading and Scarborough's Reading Rope

The **Simple View of Reading** (Tumner & Gough,1986) is a very good place to start when it comes to understanding how students learn to read. For students to read **and** understand, they must have the skills to decode a passage and the language to understand it. Both are required to read with understanding, which is our goal.

This model is further expanded in Scarborough's Reading Rope (Scarborough, 2001), which shows the micro skills that make up language comprehension and word recognition. Under language comprehension, Scarborough addresses micro skills such as background knowledge, language structures, and vocabulary, and under word recognition, she includes phonological awareness, decoding, and sight recognition. Hollis Scarborough created the rope as a visual to explain to parents the skills students need to become proficient readers. Her early models were made out of pipe cleaners so that parents had a clear visual of how the rope is built and strengthened.

From an intervention perspective, this model is very helpful. If a child is struggling with reading, finding out if it is a decoding or language concern can help direct supports that are needed. If you are teaching English Language Learners (ELLs), it is critical to explicitly teach both decoding and language comprehension to support both their language development and emerging literacy skills.

After the Simple View of Reading (SVR), it is important to know and understand the Big 5 of Reading (phonemic awareness, phonics, vocabulary, fluency, and comprehension) and their role in reading instruction. As you work with the phonics lessons and activities found within this book, you will notice that we are constantly enfolding the other Big 4 into our phonics lessons. This is very intentional as a rich interplay between the Big 5 contributes to powerful, effective instruction and growing strong readers.

Phonemic Awareness

You may have heard the terms "phonemic awareness" and "phonological awareness" used interchangeably when talking about reading instruction, but they are not the same thing. **Phonological awareness** is an umbrella term that addresses the ability to recognize and manipulate the spoken parts of sentences and words. It includes rhyming, onset and rime, syllables, and phonemes.

A phoneme is the smallest unit of speech (e.g., /s/, /ă/, /ch/) and therefore **phonemic awareness** is the ability to recognize and manipulate the smallest units of a spoken word (the phoneme). The English language is made up of forty-four phonemes and it is important that children can identify and manipulate them in order to match these sounds with letters on the page. Explicit practice with phonemic awareness, activities that require students to isolate and manipulate phonemes and ultimately attach them to graphemes (letters), builds a strong knowledge base for decoding and an understanding of how words are put together for encoding (spelling). Strong phonemic awareness skills enable readers to isolate and flex sounds when they come across new words and seek to match them with the words they have heard and/or spoken.

Phonics

A simple way of describing phonics is that words are made up of sounds, and letters represent those sounds. When addressing phonics, students begin by learning the names of the twenty-six letters of the alphabet and their sounds. Since there are forty-four phonemes and only twenty-six letters, we deal with some of the extra phonemes by combining letters to represent sounds. This is an oversimplification, but it makes sense to students and helps them to understand the code of our English language.

When children learn to read by matching sounds to letters and begin to decode, we often say they have "broken the code." They have made the connection that the marks on the page (which represent sounds), can be combined to match the words that they speak (the **alphabetic principle**), and that's really what reading is all about. A grade 1 colleague shared with us that a student exclaimed, "The letters are talking," when they realized that the letters matched the words they spoke. They clearly understood the connection between speech and text.

While some children may learn to read with broad literacy instruction, a deep understanding of how our language is put together comes from explicit instruction in phonics (which benefits all learners). Reading and writing are linguistic work, as students are learning the English language system that they use every day.

Vocabulary

Vocabulary is the recognition and understanding of the meaning of words. Students who recognize, understand, and can use a large bank of words are considered to have a large or broad vocabulary (orthographic lexicon), whereas students who have a small or limited vocabulary recognize, understand, and use a small bank of words.

There are three tiers of vocabulary:

Tier 1: words students use and understand in day-to-day speech (e.g., "house," "man," "you")
Tier 2: words that are used across curriculums (e.g., "contrast," "drenched," "flitting")
Tier 3: words that are curriculum-specific (e.g., "metamorphosis," "sphinx," "assassination")

As educators, we want to intentionally build Tier 2 vocabulary, so that students recognize and understand these types of words when encountering them across content areas, in speech, and in texts.

Strong phonics instruction will include lessons and activities that explore and teach the meaning of words. The larger a student's lexicon, the more words they will be able to recognize in print. This contributes to a greater understanding of the text.

Fluency

Fluency is the ability to read quickly, accurately, and with expression. When students read with expression, it indicates that they understand what they are reading. Strong fluency skills are an indicator that all is well in the decoding and comprehension world for a student.

Students who read fluently can see through the text to the story behind it. Students who are not fluent end up using so much mental desk space to decode that they are not able to see through to the story beyond the text.

The bank of stored words that a student brings to a text (their orthographic lexicon) impacts their fluency skills. For students to move beyond constantly decoding as they read, it is critical that they have a bank of stored words that they recognize accurately and instantly. This is not done by memorizing words by sight but through orthographic mapping (see below).

Comprehension

Comprehension, or understanding what a text is communicating, is the goal of reading and is the reason we read. While there are several important pieces that contribute to comprehension (for example, background knowledge and knowledge of the text structure), the other Big 4 are also building blocks of comprehension. It is not uncommon for teachers to choose to teach comprehension skills (main idea, inferring, sequencing, etc.), which have been found to have minimal impact on reading comprehension (Shanahan, 2018), without realizing that a lack of fluency, decoding skills, and vocabulary may be the factors that are impeding a student's comprehension.

If students cannot hear that words are made up of sounds, they will not be able to recognize them in text. If students are not able to decode, they will not be able to understand what is on the page (phonics). If students do not understand the words they are reading, even though they can decode them, they will not be able to comprehend (vocabulary). Finally, if students are not able to read quickly and accurately, they will have trouble moving past the text to the message the author is trying to convey (fluency).

Orthographic Mapping

Ortho = straight **Graphy** = writing

It is important to look at orthographic mapping (OM) before we move on, because it plays a significant role in word storage and retrieval. If this is your first introduction to OM, you may want to look at other reliable sources that provide more detail (Kilpatrick in Reference Section, page 264).

OM is the process of forming sound-to-letter connections in order to combine and recall the spelling, pronunciation, and meaning of words (Kilpatrick, 2016). It is a process where children learn to read words at a glance, spell from memory, and develop and store vocabulary. As children store words for instant retrieval, they build a bank of words they can instantly draw from — an orthographic lexicon.

Respected reading researcher Linnea Ehri (2014) states, "Orthographic mapping (OM) involves the formation of letter-sound connections to bond the spellings, pronunciations, and meanings of specific words in memory. It explains how children learn to read words by sight, to spell words from memory, and to acquire vocabulary words from print." In other words, strings of letters are attached to sounds, which form words, which have meaning.

Words are stored in memory: orthographically in spelling; phonologically in pronunciation; and semantically in meaning. Once students begin to map (matching letters to appropriate sounds for meaning) and store words, their reading ability takes off. With this process in place, they can map and store new words through one to four exposures in text.

All of this is to say that practice with decoding, manipulating words, and word play contribute to the storing of words. This is quite different than previously held theories that proposed reading as a visual process. In fact, words are not stored visually, but are stored in the much larger oral filing system (Kilpatrick, 2016).

This brings us back to fluency. As a student engages with texts and practices using the phonics concepts that have been explicitly taught, their brain begins mapping and storing words. This reading growth allows them to move to much more complex phonics concepts because they are building on the knowledge of words and their concepts that have been previously stored.

Many reading support teachers work with older students (grades 4 and up) who are still decoding every word on the page. A sign that orthographic mapping is not in place is when a student decodes a word in text and then needs to decode the same word on the next page, and then again on the next. These students may not need a specialized intervention program, but more practice with the evidence-based activities that are listed in this book — more additive blending, more manipulating of letters and sounds, more reading practice with decodable texts — so that they begin to build the neurological pathways that lead to the mapping process. While typically developing readers may need one to four exposures to a word in order to map and store it, struggling readers may need eight, twelve, or even twenty exposures. This does not mean the work cannot be done, it just takes more time and more exposures to a word.

2

Assessment for Instruction

Reading assessment can be a tricky piece for educators. An important component of reading assessment is the teacher sitting one-on-one with a student listening to them read. We understand that this can seem almost impossible in complex and busy classrooms. As challenging as this is, how will teachers know where their students are in their reading journey if they do not listen to them read?

Traditionally, many teachers have done a benchmark that assesses reading fluency and comprehension, often confirming what the teacher already knows about the student's general reading ability. While this is a good starting point, screens that look at phonics word reading, phonemic awareness, and spelling allow teachers to dig down into foundational skills and reveal exactly where the gaps are. This information is invaluable, as educators are then able to teach to the needs of the students before them.

The Why, What, and When of Screening

The Why

Screens provide a teacher with a snapshot of a student's skills in a variety of areas. Not only can teachers use these screens to assess skills at the beginning of the school year, but they can rescreen at several points throughout the year to ensure that instruction is supporting student growth, especially where there are lagging skills.

The data that a teacher gathers from screens supports scaffolding lessons within the classroom. Word choices, the amount and type of materials used, as well as partnering and grouping for activities, can be made more effective because the teacher is knowledgeable regarding the skills of the readers they are working with.

Screens are extremely important when creating small groups for targeted reading instruction within the classroom. When using just a benchmarking system, you may have two students at the same reading level, but that does not necessarily mean that they need the same targeted instruction to move forward. If we think back to the Simple View of Reading (SVR), one student may need work with decoding, while the other student may need work with language. A classroom may have four or five students who are struggling with vowel teams, but they are all reading at different levels! By screening students, we will know what skills are not yet developed and can target those skills, regardless of the reading "level."

Screens will also go a long way when working with the reading support teacher in your building. Approaching them with data and a knowledge of the skills that your students are missing (even though they have been explicitly taught and practiced) will help the reading support teacher plan targeted intervention groups more effectively. Screens are often the starting place for rich conversations with the reading support teacher, parents, and administrators. When school-wide, consistent screening takes place, it provides an overview of the needs and strengths of all students. It can guide class placement, intervention schedules, funding allocation and services, and school goals.

The What

Phonemic Awareness (PA) Screens

Since we know that PA is a reliable predictor of reading success in K–1 (Kilpatrick, 2016), it is critical that we screen for PA in these early years. If students are struggling with PA, the sooner intervention begins, the more opportunity teachers have to build these critical skills.

For kindergarten and grade 1 students, we use a simple **PA screen** to see if students can identify beginning, end, and medial sounds; can break apart and blend words at the phoneme level; and do simple addition and deletion of sounds.

In grades 2 and 3, it is important to identify a student's ability to add, delete, and substitute sounds if they are struggling with reading. If PA is a concern for students beyond grade 1, reading support teachers are often already involved in supporting growth in this area and will be able to share information with the classroom teacher. If your reading support teacher is not engaged in this type of work, or you do not have support from a reading support teacher, we would encourage a PA screen for students who are lagging in decoding and also appear to be struggling with spelling.

Letters and Sounds

Attaching sounds to letters and learning the names of the letters is a significant part of reading instruction in kindergarten and grade 1. Screening for letter names and sounds can begin as early as kindergarten and continue until the end of grade 1. Students who are still struggling with letter names and sounds at the end of grade 1 may require time with the reading support teacher to help solidify these foundational skills through additional instruction and practice.

Tricky Words Screens

Although the terms "high-frequency" and "tricky" are often used interchangeably, high-frequency words are words that occur most often in English texts whereas tricky words are words where there isn't a direct sound-to-symbol correlation in part of the word. Tricky words can be difficult to decode in the early years when students have had limited exposure to phonics instruction. After tricky words have been explicitly taught, teachers can screen to check that students are retaining and able to apply their knowledge of high-frequency and tricky words. Automatic recall of these words is important because not all words in texts will be decodable. There are a variety of screens that can be used, including a simple one we have included on page 245.

Benchmarking

At the end of grade 1, if students have "broken the code" and are decoding, we begin using a leveled benchmark or equivalent comprehension/fluency screen. There are several important takeaways from a leveled benchmark/fluency comprehension screen.

- It is a way to hear how fluently students read authentic texts and/or passages.
- It allows a teacher to check for reading comprehension.
- It allows a teacher to catch idiosyncrasies and nuances in student reading that might not be picked up on in the classroom setting (e.g., dropped suffixes, mispronounced letter sounds, strategies when approaching unknown words, etc.).
- With benchmarking and comprehension/fluency screens being leveled, teachers can measure reading growth.
- It provides the teacher one-on-one time to listen to each student read.

A WORD OF CAUTION REGARDING BENCHMARKS

Benchmarking can be a valuable tool in the hands of a knowledgeable educator. While there are benefits to a benchmarking system, there are also pitfalls that must always be kept in mind.

- The first several levels of a benchmarking system are pattern-based texts, which do not align with emergent decoding. Students need to be able to recognize and decode several tricky words in order to get onto the benchmarking system. Many early-level benchmarking books include words and phonics patterns that students have never seen (e.g., "I see a tractor," "I see a giraffe"). A student who is confidently reading with decodable texts may not pass a level 1 benchmark. According to the benchmarking system, the student is not reading, yet they are! This may cause unnecessary concern for teachers and administrators. On the other hand, a student may pass the first few benchmark levels because they have a few stored tricky words and are very good at guessing the book pattern or guessing words by looking at the pictures (rather than decoding). The benchmark says they are reading when we all know they are not. Benchmarking an emergent reader will not yield accurate data unless the benchmarking system begins with decodable texts.
- When we use a benchmarking system, we do not use the three-cueing MSV system that is included on most running record sheets. MSV stands for meaning, syntax, and visual, and represents strategies a reader may use to understand the text. This system **does not align** with what researchers are telling us about how students learn to read, and therefore it is not a valuable data-gathering tool.
- Once a student is decoding well and reading widely, benchmarking will no longer provide teachers with valuable data for classroom instruction. At this point, it is more beneficial to continue to work with phonics word reading and spelling screens to assess what students know and what concepts need additional instruction.

Phonics and Word Reading Screens

A good phonics or word reading screen will provide lists of concept-based words (including nonsense words) for students to read. These lists are typically grouped by phonics pattern — vowel teams, Vowel-Consonant-e (VCe), inflected endings, etc. Once phonics concepts have been taught and students are engaging with the concepts in print, these screens are incredibly valuable. They will show teachers which concepts need explicit instruction and/or further review. Some educators shy away from nonsense words, but if students can apply a phonics concept to a nonsense word, it indicates that the skill is fully understood.

Spelling Screens

Decoding and encoding go hand in hand in reading instruction. When students spell correctly, it shows that they understand how words are put together. When teachers say that their students are reading well, our next question is always, "How is their spelling?" Many times, the response is that their spelling is very concerning. When students read, the letters are provided for them, but when they spell, they must generate the correct letters for each word.

Spelling screen results will often align with the information gathered from phonics and word reading screens, but not 100 percent of the time. Students who struggle with reading vowel teams will often have a difficult time using them in their writing. Spelling screens will also catch readers who have strong decoding skills but do not understand when and where to use certain phonetic patterns or rules. For example, a student may know that when reading, "ai" makes the /ā/ sound, but when writing the word "airplane," they are unsure whether to write "plane," "plain," "plan," "plein," or "playn." At this point, they often resort to their visual memory to decide what "looks right."

There are many excellent spelling screens available (see resources, page 260). The most important component of a spelling screen is not that it indicates which words are spelled correctly, but that it focuses on the types of errors students are making. It should indicate which phonics concept the student is struggling with — for example, errors with short vowels, vowel teams, complex consonants, inflected endings, etc. With this information, educators can teach explicitly to the gaps that show up on the screen. Once the concept has been taught, they can rescreen to check that students now understand and use the concept correctly.

One of the perks of this type of assessment is that you can administer it to the whole class at once.

Progress Monitoring

Progress monitoring, or formative assessment, is a key component of working with the concepts in the blueprints we provide in chapter 5. Teachers can quickly see if students understand concepts by monitoring their progress when working on independent activities. A class list on a clipboard for teacher notation is all that is needed to record a student's understanding of concepts being practiced.

The When

Since assessments and screens provide teachers with a snapshot of the skills that students have acquired, they can be used as an initial assessment, especially if a teacher does not have access to previous screening data. Ideally, screens from each year would be stored and passed on to a student's new teacher in the following year, but this requires a school-wide system of collection and storage. Once an initial screen has been completed, teachers can teach targeted concepts and then rescreen to see if those concepts have been mastered by their students.

If you would like to use the blueprints included in this book but do not know where to start, or if you are unsure if your students have the skills that were targeted in a previous grade, screening will show you which concepts require quick review and which concepts require explicit instruction.

In intervention, screening and rescreening are an integral part of instruction and this should be true in the classroom as well. As interventionists, we rescreen every six weeks and listen to our students read independently each week, because if students are not applying the targeted instruction we are providing, we need to change tactics and activities. It would not make sense to screen in the fall, teach all year and rescreen in the spring only to discover that instruction has not been effective all year. Although rescreening does not take place as often in the classroom setting, screening several times throughout the year, along with progress monitoring, provides insight into how students are responding to the instruction the teacher is providing.

A few things to consider:

- An effective screen should be quick and targeted, taking no more than ten to fifteen minutes per student.
- When rescreening, start where students had trouble. Do not go back and rescreen concepts at which students are proficient.
- If initial screening tells you that a student can do all that is required of them at your grade level, do not continue rescreening that student. In your work with that student, challenge them with complex texts, tasks, and rich conversations.
- Students in grades 2 and 3 who are lagging significantly in their skills are probably already working with the reading support teacher. Reading support teachers often screen on a regular basis and are happy to share their data with you. We still encourage you to read one-on-one with these students, as it is important that you, their teacher, hear them read.

Heather remembers doing spelling screens three times a year with her grade 5 students. Not understanding the potential value of a good spelling screen, she gave the screen, counted the number of words correct, and then compared it to a norms list that showed a grade level equivalent for each score. The tool did not break down the words by concept, which a good spelling screen will do. The screen revealed nothing to pinpoint or guide further instruction for her students.

K–3 Screening Timeline

Kindergarten	Grade 1
Fall: • oral language checklist • concepts of print • phonemic awareness screen **Midyear:** • recheck all fall screens *for at-risk/bubble students* • progress monitoring **Spring:** • phonemic awareness screen • uppercase & lowercase letter names • letter sounds • decoding screen (VC/CVC)	**Fall:** • phonemic awareness screen • developmental spelling • letter names & sounds • decoding screen (VC/CVC) **Midyear:** • phonemic awareness & letter names & sounds *for at-risk/bubble students* • progress monitoring • decoding screen (blending vc & cvc words, short phrases, decodable text) • tricky words screen **Spring:** • phonemic awareness & letters & sounds *for at-risk/bubble students* • decoding screen *for at-risk/bubble students* • benchmark or fluency/comprehension screen • developmental spelling screen • tricky words screen

Grade 2	Grade 3
Fall: • letters & sounds *for at-risk/bubble students* • tricky word screen *for at-risk/bubble students* • phonics word reading screen • spelling screen • benchmark or fluency/comprehension screen **Midyear:** • progress monitoring • spelling *for at-risk/bubble students* • benchmark or fluency/comprehension *for at-risk/bubble students* **Spring:** • phonics word reading screen • spelling screen • benchmark or fluency/comprehension screen	**Fall:** • spelling screen • phonics word reading screen • benchmark or fluency/comprehension screen **Midyear:** • progress monitoring • spelling *for at-risk/bubble students* • benchmark or fluency/comprehension *for at-risk/bubble students* **Spring:** • spelling screen • phonics word reading screen • benchmark or fluency/comprehension screen

Some of our favorite screens can be found on page 260.

3

Explicit Phonics Instruction

Structure of a Phonics Lesson

The following phonics lesson plan structure is intended to address multiple target areas for explicit phonics instruction. It is not meant to be taught in one lesson but over several days. Although we recommend specific activities in the weekly lesson plans as a **starting point,** the expectation is that teachers will choose a variety of high-impact activities (from this book or from their own practice) to engage with the concept throughout the week. The pacing of the lesson is dependent on the students being taught. Some classes may move quickly through the lessons each week, while others may require extra time for teacher-led and independent practice. Progress monitoring by the teacher will guide the pacing of the lesson components. It is more important that students understand the concepts being taught than that they complete the blueprint. With each set of blueprints, the year begins with a thorough review of the concepts introduced in the previous year. If teachers do not complete all the concepts covered in the year, those final concepts will be addressed in the following year of instruction.

Lesson Plan

Target Concepts: _____	
1	**Warm-up/review:** 2–5 minutes Review concept from the previous week. Once the new concept is introduced, it becomes part of the warm-up and review. This time could also be used to cover concepts from previous weeks that require ongoing instruction and review. For example, if you have taught Vowel-Consonant-e (VCe) and students continue to omit the "e" in long vowel words, then this is an appropriate place to embed review of this concept.
2	**Introduce new concept(s) (I Do):** 5 minutes This is an introductory overview of the new concept to be taught. It is a short explanation of the concept by the teacher, followed by teacher examples and modeling. Spoken words, letter tiles, and word lists in print can all be used to model the concept.

3	**Phonological awareness:** 3–5 minutes A short oral/auditory activity that focuses on the phonemes (sounds) of the concept being taught. Phonological awareness can be used for introducing and/or reviewing concepts, as well as for guided practice. Teachers can embed it into any part of the lesson structure.
4	**Teacher-led guided practice with new concept (WE Do):** 10–15 minutes Teacher and students work through an activity together, reinforcing the concept being taught. Word ladders, reading word lists, giant flash-card activities, etc. are all appropriate activities for guided practice. As the week progresses, teachers will likely spend less time on guided practice and more time engaged in individual, extended practice activities. When initially introducing the concept, teachers may not get further than teacher-led guided practice.
5	**Extended/independent practice activities to apply new concept (YOU Do):** 15–20 minutes Students are engaged in independent and small-group activities that practice and reinforce the concept being taught. It is important that a variety of multimodal activities are included. Independent activities can include word sorts, vocabulary work, games, worksheets, etc. These can be scaffolded to meet the needs of all learners. This is an opportunity for progress monitoring. The teacher can walk around with a clipboard and a class list and check individual understanding and application of the concept to determine which students still have unfinished learning.
6	**Tricky words:** 10 minutes Follow word list progression. We have provided sequential lists to ensure that each of these words is explicitly taught in kindergarten and grade 1. Teachers can embed these words into their concept lessons or address them separately in mini-lessons during the week. Starting in week 29 of kindergarten, there are sets of tricky words to introduce, practice, and review. Word lists, games, spelling/mapping, flash cards, and finding them within text can all support this learning.
7	**Decoding with text (YOU Do):** 15–20 minutes Students begin to apply the newly learned concept(s) through reading text. Text(s) should include previously taught skills in addition to the current concept being taught. Various tricky words will also be included in the text, but most of the words should be decodable with a focus on the targeted concept. Texts may include phrases, short passages, or books. See recommended decodable text resources on pages 262–63.
8	**Encoding (YOU Do):** 15 minutes Students begin to apply the newly learned concepts to writing. Word lists for encoding should be cumulative, including previously taught concepts. Activities may include explicit spelling (phoneme-to-grapheme spelling), dictated phrases, paper or whiteboard activities, letter tiles, etc.

9	**Intervention**: 10–15 minutes 3–4 times/week Intervention activities could include small-group work with the teacher in the classroom, targeted practice activities in the students' individual reading bags, activities students have mastered sent home for home reading and word play, or targeted intervention with a reading support teacher.
10	**Extending**: included as part of 5 above Optional activities for students who quickly and firmly grasp the concept being taught. These activities include more complex concepts and/or materials.

Tricky Words

We teach tricky words in the classroom and during reading support. When beginning a tricky words activity, one student exclaimed, "These aren't 'tricky' words anymore, they're 'easy' words!"

One of the biggest criticisms of the English language is that it is not phonetically consistent. There is an inaccurate perception that there are so many words that do not follow a pattern or rule that it is not worth the time or energy to teach phonics to children. While there are words that are not fully decodable and therefore require special attention, more than 80 percent of English words either align, or closely align, with a pattern or rule. Words that do not align are sometimes viewed as containing phonetic errors when, in fact, they are simply taking on a different and often more complex role, and are therefore temporarily irregular. The words that do not align with common phonics patterns are often high-frequency Anglo-Saxon words (e.g., "the," "is," "his") that need to be added to a child's orthographic lexicon in order to access even simple texts. Once these complex phonics patterns are explicitly taught, many tricky words are no longer considered tricky.

These difficult-to-decode words have been given a variety of names over the years: sight words, heart words, jail words, red words, misbehaving words, etc., but we prefer to call them tricky words. These are not to be confused with high-frequency words, which contain both decodable and tricky words, since the criterion is not how the words are constructed and decoded but simply how often they show up on the page. With good decoding skills, students can decode many high-frequency words, but tricky words require special attention and explicit instruction.

Traditionally phonics instruction suggested that readers needed to visually memorize tricky words, but we disagree. While these words contain challenges for decoding, they almost always contain portions that are decodable (an exception would be a word like "of" where both the "o" and the "f" take on new sounds). Through explicit instruction, students can learn to read and store these words for automatic retrieval.

Intervention within the Classroom

While this is not a book about reading intervention, we know that students do not all learn at the same pace. Even in kindergarten, students do not come to school with the same experiences and exposure to text. Some students come to us knowing all their letters and sounds, and a small number of students may already be reading. Other students may have had minimal exposure to text and know nothing about speech sounds and the letters that represent them. While we have addressed struggling readers throughout this book, we want to take a bit of time to address them specifically, before moving on to strategies and curriculum blueprints.

One of the critical components of successful intervention for struggling readers is that they receive explicit reading instruction in the classroom along with their peers. Broad reading instruction is not enough for many students and, as mentioned earlier, everyone benefits from explicit, sequential reading instruction. When it becomes evident that, even with explicit phonics teaching, a student needs additional instruction and practice, the support outside the classroom should be devoted to practice rather than introducing concepts for the first time. There are few "magical tricks" that are performed with the reading support teacher: struggling readers simply need more of the sequential, explicit instruction that is happening in the classroom!

Strategies like using pictures rather than words, pictures paired with words, an adult supporting independent group practice, etc., will provide exposure to new concepts without causing frustration to struggling readers.

Small-Group Instruction

As teachers engage in periodic screening, progress monitoring, and explicit instruction, they will be able to identify students who require further instruction and extra practice. The first step is to try to provide additional practice and instruction through targeted small-group instruction in the classroom. During independent activities, teachers can organize small groups of students to work on specific skills. It's important to note that if there is more than one adult supporting the classroom, the most skilled adult (usually the teacher) works with the most vulnerable learners and supporting staff works with stronger readers.

Small-group targeted classroom instruction can easily be confused with a balanced literacy approach to reading, where students spend more time with independent activities than they do engaged in explicit instruction with their teacher. The model of centers, where students rotate through stations (one of which might be working with the teacher), is not a hallmark of Structured Literacy. As noted earlier, one of the distinctive elements of Structured Literacy is that students spend significantly more time in explicit instruction with the teacher than they do practicing and exploring activities on their own. This is not to say that we should not have literacy centers, it just means that the bulk of targeted instruction and practice is with the teacher.

Once teachers have done all they can to support struggling readers at the classroom level, it is time to begin conversations with the reading support teacher, as some students require targeted small-group support outside the classroom setting. It is not uncommon to choose to take students out of the classroom during literacy blocks because the material being presented in class is too challenging or requires foundational building blocks struggling readers do not have. While this appears to be a logical step, it puts students who need additional instruction and practice in a situation where they will need to receive **all** their reading instruction from a reading support teacher and therefore do not get the additional time and instruction that they require. If these students remain in the classroom, and the teacher scaffolds the lessons based on their skill set, they receive exposure to each concept and, as much as possible, the chance to practice and engage with the concept at their level. Time spent outside the classroom, which may be necessary for reading growth, can then be devoted to additional practice and instruction.

This leads to the question, "When should students be pulled from the classroom?" For intervention to be effective and for students to move forward, it is ideal to have forty-five to sixty minutes, four times a week. We know that this is not possible in many situations, and we have seen significant progress made with thirty-five minutes four or five times a week. What does not work is thirty minutes twice a week or fifteen minutes three times a week, as reading support teachers then are simply "stabilizing the boat." If this time can be drawn from a variety of classes, students will not miss a large portion of any one topic. Gym, art, and music are not recommended times to pull struggling readers, as these subjects allow students a break from the rigor of academic classes and often these are subjects where they have a chance to shine. We realize that schedules and support times are rarely this ideal, but it is a noble goal to strive for.

Silent Reading

The role of silent reading is a curious one. Advocates of silent reading view it as an opportunity for students to practice their developing reading skills. While this appears to be an excellent idea, there are several troubling pieces to consider.

- What typically happens during silent reading is that good readers read, and poor readers either pretend to read (to look like their peers) or look at pictures in nonfiction books. The net result is that students who do not need extra practice reading practice their reading, and students who need the practice do not get it.
- Students who struggle with reading will often choose books beyond their skill level in an attempt to fit in with their peers. They do not want to be seen reading "easy" or "little kid" books and therefore pretend to engage with texts that they are not able to read (see suggested resources on pages 262–63).
- Silent reading time may be one of the few times in the day when the classroom is quiet and teachers can address difficulties arising from recess or lunch, take a few minutes to collect their thoughts, and/or gather materials for the next stretch of teaching. It may be used as an opportunity for students to settle back into the classroom and self-regulate after high-energy activities. These are valid reasons for students to pull out books and read for short periods of time but reading practice must then be addressed in another way.
- If the teacher takes this time to work with struggling readers in small groups while other students read, when do these students independently practice their skills in text?

While the beloved silent reading time may not be an effective time for reading practice, it is an exceedingly difficult time block to move away from because it offers so much more than reading practice. In a system where it is challenging to cover all the material teachers are tasked with delivering, coupled with the challenges of living and working with class sizes of up to thirty or more, there really is not time to spend on activities that are not effective or equitable for all students, such as silent reading. This is one of the many pieces of classroom life where teachers must critically examine practices and decide whether they serve their intended function. If this block is important for reasons other than reading practice, then it should stay, but alternative times are needed to address reading practice.

Classroom Materials

As teachers work with students who are above or below the reading skills of their grade level, it is important that they have access to the materials required to do this work. A trip to the library or the classroom of a colleague is often enough to access reading material that is above grade level, but this is not so simple for struggling readers.

Decodable texts with characters and themes that are age-appropriate are important. They do not need to be glossy, high-tech publications, but should contain topics that interest students at their skill level. Class book bins and/or book bags must include material that is appropriate for struggling and advanced readers. Additional references to decodable texts can be found on page 49 and suggested books are listed on pages 262–63.

It is important to organize all your phonics materials so that accessing and using them is easy and efficient. In chapter 5 we detail how to set up a phonics box for your K–3 program (see page 66).

Accessing Additional Support

Human resources are a challenge in the classroom setting. We realize that not all teachers even have access to a reading support teacher and therefore the classroom teacher must find time to do this work. Often creativity rules the day when extra humans are needed to support students who need additional reading practice. A few suggestions include:

- **Big buddies to listen to students read.** This, of course, must be balanced with the needs and rights of older students who are coming to school to learn. Often there are older students who are very skilled when working with younger students and who need opportunities to flex their leadership muscles and/or build confidence through the recognition that comes from helping others.
- **Peer reading with an educational assistant.** Small groups of struggling readers can often practice reading with an educational assistant who is attached to one of the students in a classroom. This type of peer engagement can often be beneficial for students who struggle with building relationships or staying focused in the classroom context.
- **Fluency apps and technology programs where students are recorded while reading.** Tools like Reading Progress in Microsoft Teams are engaging ways for students to practice reading and provide teachers with the opportunity to check recordings after school or later in the week. These are also excellent for tracking progress, sharing with parents (both concerns and successes), and using in e-portfolios and/or online reporting. One word of caution is that we want to place our most vulnerable learners with our most skilled adults. Using fluency apps and programs should be for all students and not used to replace explicit reading instruction and support from the classroom or reading support teacher.

Reading Instruction and English Language Learners

English Language Learners (ELLs) are a unique group of learners in our classrooms. When referring to the SVR, they need explicit instruction and support with both decoding and language comprehension. It is important to keep in mind that each student comes to us with unique experiences with literacy, language, and formal schooling. Bilingual does not mean biliterate, and students who grow up in dual-language homes may come to us with different language skills than students who learned one language and then a second before arriving in our classrooms.

ELLs who begin schooling in English in either kindergarten or grade 1 will get explicit reading instruction along with their peers. Sounds and letters, decoding, and concepts of print should all be explicitly taught in these grades and therefore oral language will be the unique focus of working with ELLs at this level.

In higher grades, oral language and explicit phonics instruction should be a focus of support. When students have literacy skills in their first language, it provides them a structure to work with when learning English. For others, especially students who have fled their home country and spent years in intermediary countries, there may be few or no literacy skills to build upon.

Refugees who have spent years moving from country to country before settling may have a smattering of educational experiences in several languages, which can be confusing. They may also come to their current classroom with negative experiences around school and literacy. Some of our students have shared that in intermediary countries they were ignored by their teachers or shamed in front of their peers. It can take time for such students to build trust and a positive attitude toward reading and writing.

Older students will need to start with letters and sounds, even if their home language uses the same alphabet. The Roman alphabet is not attached to all the same phonemes in other languages and therefore this must be explicitly taught. While teachers sometimes hesitate to start with sounds and letters because it seems too young ("I don't want to take them back to grade 1!"), it is important to look at this from a linguistic perspective. Share with students that this is the alphabet used for English, and these are the sounds that are attached to these letters. Instruction in the forty-four English phonemes is important, as there are phonemes that are unique to English and the forty-four found in English will not include all the phonemes of a student's home language.

If students come to school with literacy skills in their home language, it is important to encourage continued reading growth in that language. Speaking with parents and ensuring that students have adequate and appropriate reading material for home reading in their first language not only supports developing readers but opens important literacy communication with parents. Immigrant services, inter-library loans, and community centers, all provide means to source appropriate books in a student's home language. Encouraging students to bring these books to school for reading periods or to share with their classmates creates opportunities for rich discussions about literacy, culture, and community. Many English-speaking students have never seen books that start from right to left, or texts in an alphabet other than the Roman alphabet.

Reading instruction for ELLs means more of the explicit, structured teaching that is happening in the classroom. Unlike reading intervention, though, we target both decoding **and** language comprehension. English learners need explicit instruction and practice with oral language and language comprehension as well as decoding, with ample opportunities to practice their developing skills.

Supporting Reading at Home

Strategies for Parents

As society continues to change and shift, the ability of families to support home reading practice is shifting as well. Even with limited time, there are many strategies that can be implemented at home to support a child's reading journey. Sharing this list of strategies provides families with a variety of reading activities to choose from.

- Engage in back-and-forth conversations. Oral language development plays a significant role in learning to read. Conversations can take place almost anywhere and help children with learning vocabulary, narrative storytelling, and listening for meaning. Parents can help their child tell or retell stories and events in a way that makes sense to the listener. A wonderful tool for helping students organize narrative storytelling is the Story Grammar Marker produced by MindWing Concepts.
- Read to children (see below). Before reading to them, do quick story walks. Read the title and then discuss the pictures in the book and what might or might not happen in the story as you flip through the pages.
- When children are reading at home, practice the five-finger rule. As they read the first few pages, if there are five or more words on a page that they need to stop and decode, the book is too challenging for independent reading. Teachers and librarians can help ensure children have the appropriate books for home reading practice.
- Play with language through word games, silly poems, and tongue twisters. Any activity that explores language and focuses on the sounds of words supports the reading journey. Older students enjoy playing with languages like Pig Latin and Ubbi Dubbi, which focus on breaking apart words and inserting nonsense syllables.
- If students are picking up pencils and pens at home, encourage the proper formation of letters. Teachers can share letter formation guides that will help support this emerging skill. It is exceedingly difficult to change incorrect printing habits once they have been used for extended periods of time.

Reading to Children

Many children come home tired after a long day at school and reading aloud to children is an excellent way to support developing readers. There are many important benefits that come from parents reading aloud to their children and this activity should never be underrated. Reading aloud:

- exposes children to how written language is put together. Written language is very different from the way we speak and reading aloud helps children become familiar with the rhythms and structures of written language.

- helps children develop sustained attention in one direction. As children listen and engage in a story, they are developing stamina to pay attention for a sustained period of time. With the speed of technological devices, busy family lives, and a waning focus on conversation, children do not always have the opportunity to develop this skill in our current culture.
- helps build vocabulary. A rich vocabulary enables children to recognize words in conversation, as well as in print when they are reading independently. Encourage parents to take time to pause and talk about new and unusual words when reading with their children.
- provides exposure to new ideas, genres, and types of text. We have been made aware of a link between declining empathy in children and declining engagement with story. As children read, or are read to, they enter into the lives of others, gaining access to their thoughts and feelings. This provides children with the big idea that not everyone feels the same way they do or experiences events in the same way (Rymanowicz, 2017).
- engages adults and children in story together. The physical act of sitting side by side, with a book, and sharing a story builds relationships. It contributes to the development of a positive attitude toward books and reading. It reveals the worlds contained within books and the pleasure and the anticipation of wondering, *what will happen next?*

There is much more that can be said about how children learn to read, assessment, and phonics instruction. If you are interested in learning more about these topics, or the Science of Reading, we encourage you to check the recommended reading list on pages 263–64. With this foundational knowledge in mind, we would like to turn to the high-impact activities that will support the work of explicit phonics instruction.

Evidence-Based, High-Impact Activities

In busy classrooms, educators do not have time to engage students in activities that will not have significant impact on their learning. It is important to find and use activities and strategies that have a proven track record of providing ongoing growth in readers. What does "evidence-based" mean when talking about reading strategies? It is easy to say that a strategy or data is "research-based," because anyone can take two groups of students, test them, engage one group of students in a specific activity, and then test all students again to see if there is a difference between the outcomes of both groups. While this is not how good research is done, one could slap "research-based" on the activity because there was a pretest, a control group, an activity, and a post test. Voila, research! In a world where educators are looking to what neurological researchers have to say about how children learn to read, research has become a wonderful marketing tool for resources and reading strategies. Unless we know what research has been done and by whom, and that it is peer-reviewed by other experts in the field, we are very cautious with the term "research."

Let's look at evidence-based instead. In education, evidence-based means that a strategy is aligned with what neuroscience, psychology, and cognitive science tell us will be effective in instruction **and** it shows consistent, measurable success in the classroom.

The following strategies meet the criteria above and we have seen significant and rapid growth in our students by using these activities in reading instruction. While there is overlap in the benefits of each activity, we have grouped them according to whether they are decoding or encoding activities. For each activity, variations are presented from most scaffolded to least scaffolded. If you have students who are struggling with accessing or retaining concepts, this allows you to start with a more scaffolded variation of an activity when working with them in small groups or one-on-one.

Mapping

In many of the activities described in this book, we use the term "mapping." By this, we mean an activity in which students match the letters used to construct a word with the sounds that are attached to those letters. This is known as the alphabetic principle, and while it seems obvious to us as proficient readers, it must be discovered by students learning to read. Mapping, which can also be called coding, includes both encoding (spelling) and decoding (reading). This is not to be confused with orthographic mapping, which is the process whereby strings of letters on a page are attached to the sounds in speech and their meaning, and stored in the brain for quick retrieval when reading and writing.

Decoding

Learning Letters and Sounds Activities

According to Catts et al. (2015), one predictor of later reading success is a solid knowledge of letter names and sounds in kindergarten. You will notice that we do not have a long list of activities directed at explicitly learning letters and sounds. What we have found is that once students have been introduced to each letter and sound, this knowledge is reinforced in meaningful ways by engaging in the high-impact activities below.

Key Words and Kinesthetic Actions

Many phonics programs attach a word and picture to each letter to support students in remembering and storing the proper pronunciation of a letter (e.g., "a" — "apple"). These are often posted in the room for students to refer to when needed. When introducing and reviewing letters, the teacher says the letter sound, the letter name, and the key word (/ă/ — "a" — "apple" or /b/ — "b" — "bat").

A kinesthetic action also helps students remember and store letter names and sounds, as well as engaging them in activities. When introducing and reviewing sounds, have students do the hand movement associated with each letter. For example, with the letter "i," the teacher says "/ĭ/ — 'i' — 'itchy'" while pretending to scratch their arm. The programs Itchy's Alphabet and Jolly Phonics offer good kinesthetic actions associated with learning letter sounds.

Spell Off

When building words with letter tiles or magnetic letters, have students say the letter sounds or letter names as tiles are returned to their place at the top or bottom of their board. This simple activity keeps students engaged in the learning process and provides additional review for students who still struggle with their letter names and sounds. This can also be done as the teacher builds words on the board either with letter tiles or with a dry erase pen.

Alphabet Arc

The alphabet arc is helpful in teaching letter shape recognition, orientation, sequencing, names, and sounds. Arcs can be printed in both uppercase and lowercase letters. You can download free arcs from the Florida Center for Reading Research.

Suggestions for using alphabet arcs:

- When starting with the alphabet arc, work with the first half of the arc (a–m). Once students are confident with these letters, continue with the second half of the arc, and then move to using the entire arc.

- Arcs can be used for singing the alphabet song and pointing to the letters. If you are using the tune "Twinkle, Twinkle, Little Star," we suggest starting the tune midway through the song ("Up above the world so high") as students tend to memorize the beginning of the song without attaching it to specific letters.
- Students can match plastic letters or letter cards/tiles to the arc while saying the letter names and sounds.
- Students can match uppercase letters on a lowercase arc and vice versa.
- Students can be asked to find letters before and/or after a target letter.
- Students can be asked to find letters by either their name or their sound.
- Games:
  - **"Find the Closest" game:** The teacher tells students two letters or sounds and asks which letter/sound is closest to "z" or "a."
  - **"I Spy" game:** The teacher says a letter or a sound and students find it on the arc.
  - **"What's in the Middle?" game:** The teacher says two letters and students find letter/s that are between them.
  - The teacher points to a letter on the arc and students say its name and sound. The teacher asks students to think of as many words as they can that begin with that letter. Students can also lead this activity.

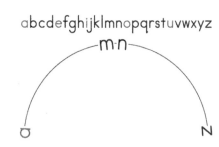

Picture Cards and Small Objects

Picture cards and small objects can be used for learning letters and sounds. Well-chosen images (e.g., "egg" is not a good example of the /ĕ/ sound, whereas "edge" is) can be used for a variety of activities to reinforce letters and sounds. For example, items/cards that begin with the same letter/sound can be sorted into one pile or container, with items/cards for nontarget sounds into another. Cards and items can be sorted by beginning sound and/or end sound depending on the skill level of the students you are working with.

Sound Walls

As teachers have begun to move to a speech-to-print approach to reading, sound walls are replacing word walls. The word wall is problematic as it is difficult for students to find words when they are organized by their initial letters. For example, the word "of" starts with the letter "o" but makes the schwa sound /uh/. If a student is wondering how to spell "of," they would have a hard time finding it on a word wall because it would not be found under "u," it would be found under "o." Sound walls consist of the organization and display of phonemes. Letters of the alphabet are typically divided into consonants and vowels. A vowel valley is organized by jaw/mouth position and this board will include diphthongs, schwa, and vowel-r. Consonants are organized by their phoneme group (stops, fricatives, glides, etc.) and by their voiced and unvoiced sounds. Each letter often has a photo of a mouth, showing the position of the lips and tongue used for pronouncing the letter it is attached to.

There are many examples of sound walls on educational websites, in webinars, and on SOR resource sites. If you are interested in sound walls, invest the time in learning how they can be used most effectively.

A few suggestions for using sound walls:

- If using pictures of mouths on the wall, take pictures of your students' mouths, assigning each student to a letter or letters.
- If you have limited wall space, consider a digital sound wall that you can project on a whiteboard when needed.
- Add concepts as you teach them; if you have a finished or digital sound wall, cover concepts not yet explicitly taught and "unveil" them as you introduce them. Some creative teachers build their sound wall in black and white and then cover the concepts in colored cards once they have been explicitly taught.
- Students and teachers can refer to the sound wall when reviewing concepts and looking for specific spelling patterns or sounds.
- A sound wall is worth putting up only if it is going to be used for instruction and review. If it is not a teaching tool, it simply adds visual clutter to the classroom.

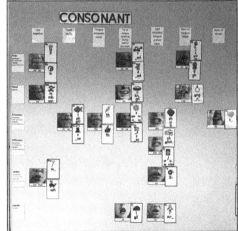

Photographs courtesy of Leslie Nielsen

Word Lists and Nonsense Words

Word lists are one way to practice blending, as well as to address new letters and/ or concepts. We have included many word lists in this book. They can be used in high-impact activities but also as lists on their own. You will also notice that we have included nonsense words, which can be found in phonics word reading screens.

- If a student is able to apply a concept appropriately in a nonsense word, it shows they have a firm understanding of that concept.
- Nonsense words are helpful for struggling readers, as short nonsense words can be easier to read than longer real words.
- Nonsense words can be parts of larger words, preparing students for multisyllable work.

Additive Blending

When using additive blending activities, words should contain only concepts previously and explicitly taught or currently being introduced.

Additive Blending with Letter Tiles: Highly Scaffolded Additive Blending
This additive blending activity using a tile board can be modeled by the teacher but allows children to engage in the process independently once they are familiar with the task. It works well one-on-one or with a small group of students who need additional support with blending. The steps below are for the word "sip"; be sure to move through the process quickly, especially as students become more proficient.

- The teacher places an "s" tile on the board and asks, "What is the sound of this letter?" The students respond with /s/.

  s

- The teacher then adds an "i" tile to the board. It is placed to the right of the first tile but a little distance away from the "s." The teacher asks, "What is the sound of this letter?" The students respond with /ĭ/.

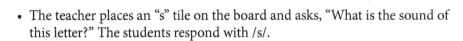

- Next the teacher moves the "i" next to the "s" and says, "Let's blend these sounds." The teacher and students blend the sounds, /sĭ/.

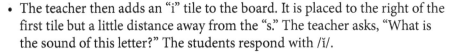

- The "p" is the final letter to be added to the tile board and is placed next to "si" but a short distance away. The teacher asks, "What is the sound of this letter?" The students respond with /p/.

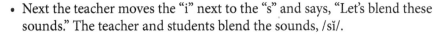

- The "p" is now moved to join the "si" and the teacher says, "Let's review these sounds /sĭ/ and /p/. Let's blend the sounds."

- Teacher and students blend the sounds. The teacher asks, "What is the word?" and the students respond with "sip."

This is the most scaffolded form of additive blending because each letter sound is reviewed before adding it to the word. It also allows the students to physically move the letter as they add the sound.

Conventional Additive Blending Part 1
Materials: whiteboard and erasable pen

- The teacher writes a word on the board.
- If students do not know their letter sounds, before blending, review each of the letter sounds in the word. If the word is "sip," review /s/, /ĭ/, and /p/.
- Starting with the first letter in the word, the teacher puts a dot under the letter "s" and the teacher and students say the sound. For "sip," they would say /s/.

| teacher writes | s i p | students say | /s/ |

- Now add the /ĭ/ sound to the /s/ by joining both letters from beneath with a whiteboard pen, so that students now say /sĭ/.

| teacher writes | s i p | students say | /si/ |

- Continue for the remainder of the word, adding one sound each time.

| teacher writes | s i p | students say | /sip/ |

When students begin confidently blending, teachers can add digraphs, complex consonants, vowel teams, etc. When practicing words with digraphs or vowel teams, identify the digraph or vowel team before blending. For example, for the word "crunch," have students identify the digraph "ch" before starting to blend. Draw a small bracket under the diagraph so that students know the two letters work together to create one sound, and don't sound them out individually when they reach this point in the blending process.

| crunch |

Conventional Additive Blending Part 2
Once students are blending with confidence, the second step is to have them blend quietly "in their heads" while the teacher moves through the word with the whiteboard pen, joining the letters while the students silently blend. After silently blending the word, the teacher asks students to say the word all together. A very curious thing happens once students are blending independently. We asked a

group of students to go back to Part 1, where the teacher directs the blending, because we were making a video to support teachers. These struggling readers had a terrible time doing the step-by-step blending once they were confidently blending on their own. We put a word on the board, and they would say, "It's 'sip.'" We would ask them to pretend they did not know but they continued to just tell us the word before we could model the blending process. We finally gave up and complimented the students on their excellent skills!

The Additive Blending Game

To keep students engaged and excited about blending, teachers can make a game with the activity. If students blend accurately and can decode the word, they get one point, but if they are not able to blend accurately, the teacher gets one point.

The greatest challenge for students is to avoid saying the individual letter sounds partway through the word. For example, if the word is "crunch," students may blend it /c/, /cr/, /crŭ/, /n/, without returning to the beginning of the word when adding the "n." Students become very careful if they know that there are points involved and it creates a lively game for everyone. Our one caution with the game is to watch for students who are hesitant to blend because they might make a mistake and lose a point for their team, and therefore they do not say anything at all. Mistakes are welcome and sometimes the teacher likes to get a few points too!

Choosing Words

When beginning to blend with students, be sure to choose words where there is a one-to-one correspondence between the phoneme (sound) and the grapheme (letter). Avoid words with vowel-controlled "r," silent "e," tricky words, etc., where letter sounds are impacted by other letters in the word.

Why Additive Blending?

There are several reasons why additive blending is helpful for students:

- Additive blending keeps the letter sounds in order as students blend. If students sound out one letter at a time, by the time they reach the end of the word, they can sometimes forget what sounds were at the beginning of the word. This creates very unusual pronunciations.
- Additive blending lightens the cognitive load of remembering all the sounds in the correct order. By carrying the sounds along with the decoding process, students can focus on each new sound without worrying about keeping everything together and in order.
- Additive blending provides a significant amount of practice for sounds, blends, digraphs, and vowel teams. In a word like "chin," for example, by the time the student reaches the end of the word, they have read the digraph /ch/ three times.
- Something happens when sounds are blended that can be slightly different than when they are in isolation. By using additive blending, students hear each sound blended with the sounds on either side, making the reading process more natural. They hear the correct pronunciation of the word as they decode.
- When most of the class is blending, teachers can move on to continuous blending but continue to do additive blending when working with small groups of struggling blenders who need additional practice with this skill.

Continuous Blending

Many children blend by breaking a word into individual sounds. Then they speed it up, saying each sound until they are able to blend and recognize the word. Stop sounds (plosives) like "d," "p," and "g" are challenging to blend because often students (and adults) will put an /ŭ/ sound at the end of them (/dŭ/, /pŭ/, /gŭ/). This interferes with the following vowel, making it more challenging to identify a word. For example, a student might say /dŭ/-/ŏ/-/g/ rather than the blended /dŏ/. Mark Seidenberg, in his book *Reading at the Speed of Sight*, uses an excellent example of this when describing Elmo decoding on *Sesame Street*. As he runs back and forth, faster and faster, he starts to "flex," or adjust, the letter sounds to blend them smoothly. We can do this flexing from the start with continuous blending.

Continuous blending is less scaffolded than additive blending, in that it encourages students to move from one sound to the next without ending the previous sound. For example, with the word "sip," students place their finger under the "s" and start to blend as they move from one letter to the next. It sounds like /sssssiiiiip/. For some students, after learning additive blending, they find this second scaffold helpful for blending words quickly. When working with tricky stop sounds, the reader must move directly to the second sound to maintain a continuous flow of sound (/tiiiiinnnnn/).

Continuous blending is parallel to how skilled readers approach a new word. A skilled reader will slowly start with the first sound and continuously blend the sounds until they reach the end of the word. The speed at which a reader does this is governed by how complex the word is and how familiar it is to the reader. If the word does not align with what the reader has heard or spoken, they begin to flex or adjust the sounds, searching for a pronunciation that they recognize.

Continuous blending does not support remembering the order of sounds the way that additive blending does. Students who are not able to remember the sounds at the beginning of the word when blending benefit from being taught the more scaffolded additive blending first.

Addressing Tricky Words

Tricky words need special attention and often they are addressed as sight words with a focus on visually memorizing the whole word as a unit. It is much more effective to break the word down and look at the portions that can be decoded and then memorize ("learn by heart") the letters that fall outside of the phonics knowledge young readers possess.

Some tricky words follow their own pattern and are a bit easier to teach. For example, when "s" comes at the end of short Anglo-Saxon words, it often says /z/ rather than /s/. This is true in words like "is," "his," "has," and "was." "Use" follows this tricky pattern even though the VCe remains in place. Some words are more complex.

In kindergarten and grade 1, we have provided a plan to address the tricky words listed below. If students in grades 2 and up are still struggling with these words, it is important to take the time to review each word and how to approach it in print.

An effective way to explicitly teach tricky words is to carefully look at the construction of the word. Help students to identify which portion of the word is decodable and which portion needs to be "learned by heart." This can be done by using letter tiles, writing on a whiteboard, or using large word cards. This is an example of word mapping.

For example, "said" is a very common tricky word. Teachers can show students that the /s/ and the /d/ are decodable. Once these two letters have been addressed, move to the "ai" in the middle of the word. Ask students what it should say; if they do not know, tell them that "ai" makes the sound /ā/. Then tell them that, in fact, the "ai" in this word says /ĕ/. Very tricky!

We like to put the spoken sound **under** the tricky letter(s) so that students can reference it when decoding and working with the tricky word. We also like to put a heart over these same letters to indicate that this is the portion of the word that needs to be "learned by heart." Explicit instruction and review of these words helps all students learn to decode and recognize them in print. We like to have these words posted (with the heart and correct sounds) in the room, perhaps on a tricky word bulletin board, so that students can refer to them when reading and writing.

For example:

said   ♥
/ĕ/   said
              /ĕ/

A similar example of how to decode tricky words is to have the words written on cards or listed on paper and scored the following way:

- A green dot under the letters/parts that are decodable or make their "known" sound.
- A yellow dot under letter(s) that follow a common phonetic pattern, but which students have not yet been explicitly taught.
- A red dot under letter(s) that do not make a regular phonetic sound (the part that has no known pattern to be taught and will always need to be learned by heart).

● (red)   = STOP! The letter(s) do not make the regular sound.
○ (yellow) = SLOW DOWN! The letter(s) makes a regular sound, but it might be a sound students haven't learned yet.
◐ (green) = GO! The letter(s) makes the regular sound.

Set 1	
t h e ○ ○	i s ● ○
o f ○ ●	h i s ● ● ○
a s ● ○	w a s ● ○ ○
h a s ● ● ○	t o ● ●
d o ● ●	

Variations to This Activity

Put one word at a time on a flashcard.

w a s ● ○ ○

Trace over each letter with red, yellow, or green.

w a s

Once these words have been explicitly taught, they can be practiced using a variety of activities, such as flash cards, games, searching for them in text, etc. We use the following sets of tricky words when teaching reading. The lists below are embedded in the kindergarten and grade 1 blueprints. Each week, one to three words are introduced and practiced. The progress monitoring checklist in the Resources section (page 245) can be used to track progress after each set of tricky words has been explicitly taught.

Tricky Word List

Set 1	Set 2	Set 3	Set 4
the	her	all	where
of	you	one	who
as	your	from	only
has	are	have	very
is	use	live	any
his	come	give	put
was	some	or	many
to	said	what	two
do	there	they	old

Set 5	Set 6	Set 7	Set 8
were	mother	goes	world
because	father	word	over
want	been	school	people
other	every	open	enough
their	work	move	carry
love	again	eyes	answer
would	once	close	above
could	great	watch	most
should	does	idea	kind

Heather was working with a small group of students in the photocopy room one morning (yes, we will work anywhere we have to) and one student with complex behaviors had chosen to crawl under a large desk rather than join the other three students for the lesson. Heather was introducing this group of grade 2/3 nonreaders to tricky words. She began the lesson by talking about words that are tricky and mentioned that some of the letters in the words were quite naughty. From under the desk came a little voice that said, "I do things that are naughty! I like naughty." He then crawled out from under the desk, settled on the floor with his peers, and began engaging with the lesson!

Blending Boards

Blending boards are an excellent way for students to independently practice blending and working with specific phonics concepts. They are easy and inexpensive to make and can be customized to fit the skills already covered through explicit instruction. We make our boards using letter cards with the same font as the magnetic letters the teacher uses on the board for teaching, and students use on individual magnet boards. The vowels are red and the consonants are black. Once individual letters have been taught, cards with digraphs and blends can be added to the boards, as well as vowel teams, diphthongs, and vowel-r in grade 2.

When building blending boards, use a green button below the first letter set, so students who struggle with direction know where to start. We are very careful with the letters we choose and their placement on the blending board. When making two-letter words, boards can be set up with the vowels on the first ring and consonants in the second ring and vice versa for CV words. When making three-letter words, vowels are always placed in the middle. We do not use "r" in the final ring card set until vowel-r has been explicitly taught.

Using a Blending Board

When using a blending board, students tap the buttons below each letter while saying the letter sound. They then place their finger on the string at the bottom of the board and blend the sound while running their finger from left to right along the string. Cars, planes, and critters can be used to move along the blending string, instead of students using their finger. Students then choose a letter to change by flipping it up to reveal the letter beneath it. A wide range of words and nonsense words can be read with just a few letters on each binder ring. Blending boards work well in centers and small-group activities, as well as for independent practice.

Blending Lines

Blending lines (Blevins, 2017) are an excellent addition to reading word lists. They are a quick and easy activity that can be read aloud as a class, in partners, and independently. Blending lines consist of strings of words that have minimal spelling differences so students must analyze each word as they read. This is different from word families, where the first letter changes for each word. Blending lines are a decoding activity that corresponds well with encoding word ladders (where students are generating word chains), which can be found in the encoding section later in this chapter.

Remember when creating blending lines that the most scaffolded lines are those in which the beginning letter of the word changes, then those in which the final letter changes; it is most difficult for students to work with medial letter changes. Lines can consist of words that review previous concepts learned, as well as phrases and short sentences, so that students see new concepts in the context of meaningful print. The word lists in this book will help you create your own blending lines.

Sample blending lines for short a /ă/:
Line 1 (initial sound): cat, mat, sat, hat, pat
Line 2 (final sound): can, cat, cap, bat, bad, bag
Line 3 (medial sound): bit, bat, but, bet, bed, bad
Line 4 (mixed set target skill): bat, fan, lad, sap, pan, sad
Line 5 (challenge words): span, chat, glad, slam, staff, grand
Line 6 (connected to text): The fat cat sat on a bag.
Line 7 (connected to text): The fat cat sat on a bag with a pan on his lap.

Sample blending line for vowel team ai /ā/:

Line 1 (initial sound): pail, nail, snail, stain, train, main

Line 2 (final sound): pain, paint, brain, braid, maid, mail

Line 3 (medial sound): gain, grain, sail, snail, wait, waist

Line 4 (mixed set target skill): drain, jail, faith, remain, wait, stain

Line 5 (review words for mastery): plan, tame, crunch, scrap, find, going

Line 7 (challenge words): dainty, remainder, ailment, reclaim, complain, mislaid

Line 8 (connected text): The snails wait in the pail.

Line 9 (connected text): I was detained, so had to wait for the main train.

Word Sorts

Word sorts are a popular classroom activity used to reinforce and review instruction in phonics concepts. Students, or groups of students, receive a stack of cards with one word printed on each card, as well as heading cards. Heading cards will either have the target concept written on them (e.g., "hard c" and "soft c") or a sample word for each sorting pile (e.g., "candy" and "city"). The task is for students to sort the cards into rows, columns, or piles, dividing them into groups where the same concept is present in each word in the group.

The use of word sorts can be a bit of a cautionary tale when it comes to teaching phonics. They have the potential to be a powerful activity for analyzing words and reinforcing a phonics concept being taught. On the other hand, if all phonics teaching and review is done through word sort activities or if students short-circuit the process by simply looking at the words and visually sorting the cards, it will do very little to build targeted skills. Programs that suggest you can teach your entire phonics program through word sorts are worthwhile only if used as one activity among many in your teacher's toolbox.

The Word Sort Process

THE SORT PART 1

By using decks of word cards rather than paper/pencil sorts, sorting and categorizing words becomes multimodal and much more engaging for students.

Have students shuffle and place word cards upside down on the table or floor. Partners take turns drawing a card, reading the word, and placing it in the correct row, column, or pile under a heading card. Both partners see each card and support one another in this process.

THE SORT PART 2

We like to have students play a second part of the game.

Once the word cards have been sorted into piles, rows, or columns, students take turns giving their partner a clue to the meaning of one of the words in the sort. For example, if students are sorting hard and soft "c" and "g" word cards, Student 1 may say, "It's another name for ashes." Student 2 then looks at all the cards and guesses the word "cinder." If correct, students remove the "cinder" card from the sort. Student 2 then looks at the remaining cards and gives a clue to the meaning of a word. Student 1 guesses the word. This activity can also be done with more than two students.

It can be very challenging for some students to generate questions and it may take extensive practice and modeling to build this type of flexible thinking. Part 2 will build and reinforce vocabulary for new words and words whose meaning students do not clearly understand. We also use challenging and possibly unknown words in the sorts, as long as they are decodable.

Scaffolding for a Range of Skill Levels

We like to make several sorts for one concept, using words that range from simple to more complex. One set of cards may use simple CVC words or words that are short and decodable, the second set of cards uses grade-level words, and the final set of cards contains challenging, complex words. We copy sort cards onto the same color paper, with the same layout, and the same font. For students, it looks like everyone has the same sort, but, in fact, there are three sorts created for students at different points in their reading journey. The teacher can tell which sorts are which (since they all look the same) by using different words for the sort's heading cards.

Highly scaffolded sorts will have pictures on the heading cards and may even use picture cards instead of words for emergent readers.

Open and closed sorts can also be used for scaffolding. When the teacher tells students how they will be sorting the cards, it is called a closed sort. Using the target concept hard and soft "c" for example, students are told they are to sort the word cards into two rows, columns, or piles, one for hard "c" and one for soft "c." An open sort, on the other hand, has a stack of word cards and no directions as to how they are to be sorted. Students must look at all the cards and decide the best way to sort them. This requires an understanding of a wide range of phonics concepts and the ability to identify patterns in an assortment of words.

Making the Most of Word Sorts

- Use sorts sparingly and alongside other high-impact activities. If you choose a few concepts where you would like to add word sorts, you will not be burdened with hours of laminating and cutting in front of the TV at night.
- Add nonsense words to the sort. When engaging in the Sort Part 2, students can be left with nonsense words at the end of the question time.
- Add rule breakers to the sort. There can be an alternative place to put words that do not fit the heading cards or follow the phonics concept being taught.
- Have the sort heading cards copied on a different color of paper or in a different color of text than the words to be sorted to identify them as heading cards. To support struggling readers, use pictures as the heading cards. For extending, use multisyllable words as the heading cards, rather than naming the concept ("giraffe" rather than "soft g").

Fluency Phrases

While we have discussed fluency as one of the Big 5, working on this skill while teaching phonics is an excellent example of how the Big 5 should not be taught in isolation. Fluency activities provide opportunities for students to practice and reinforce what they have learned regarding decoding.

For beginning readers, working with short phrases is a powerful scaffold for moving toward text passages. Two- to five-word phrase cards allow students to build confidence and practice reading text. When first introduced to fluency phrases, it is not uncommon for students to begin the reading process by memorizing the cards. This is not initially concerning because as the teacher builds knowledge through explicit instruction, and students practice, there are more cards than they are able to memorize. Phrases are one of our favorite places to start building fluent reading.

Once students can decode the words on a card by pointing to each word or running their finger below the text as they read, the fluency work begins. If the student reads the phrase card in a halting manner, have them reread the phrase until it is fluent. You can have the student read, look at you, and repeat the phrase and then read it again in the same fluid manner. The goal is for students to read aloud at the pace of speaking, and it is important that we tell students that this is the goal, as some students believe that faster is better. Continuous prompting to read aloud at a speaking rate deters students from zipping through or chanting a memorized phrase.

As students grow in their decoding abilities, more complex phrases can be added. The program Letters and Sounds (Resources, page 261) has wonderful sets of emergent fluency phrases. This is where we start. Once students have mastered these emergent phrases, we move them to the 600 Fry Phrases found on Tim Rasinski's website (Resources, page 261). These phrases not only contain a continuum of increasingly complex words, but also include punctuation. Rasinski, a professor of literacy education at Kent State University, is one of our gurus when it comes to fluency, and we encourage you to check out his work and resources.

Punctuation

Punctuation is an important component of reading fluency. Many teachers bemoan the fact that students read right through punctuation, ignoring or oblivious to its existence on the page. Punctuation must be explicitly taught as it plays a vital role in fluent reading.

An example of explicitly teaching punctuation is specifically addressing the **question mark.** Do students know that when there is a question mark, the pitch of their voice rises? Students enjoy practicing this skill and will often exaggerate the rise of their voice when reading a phrase with a question mark. We love this fun exaggeration that students often engage in, because over time it settles in to become an embedded practice.

The question mark, along with other punctuation, offers a wonderful opportunity to talk with ELLs about their home language. Does a question in their language mean that the speaker raises the pitch of their voice at the end of the sentence or phrase? Often the answer is no, and not only do English speakers find this fascinating, but it can lead to a rich conversation about the home language of a student learning English.

Using Fluency Phrases in the Classroom

There are a variety of ways phrases can be used in the classroom.

- Copy phrases onto strips of paper and laminate. As students learn to read the phrase strips fluently, they can be ringed, along with the student's name, and stored in reading bags, on hooks, or in desks.
- Place sets of laminated strips on rings and add to class book bins, along with books that are at the equivalent skill level. Students can choose to read a book or a set of rings during reading practice times.
- Copied and laminated strips can be ringed and sent home for additional practice.

- Teachers or other adults in the room can use the phrase strips for small-group instruction.
- In partners or small groups, play the Fluency Phrase Game.

The Fluency Phrase Game

This engaging game can be played in pairs or with small groups of students. Although it is a simple game, beginning readers ask to play it again and again.

- Take three to eight fluency strips that students are working on and place them face down on the floor or a table.
- Students take turns flipping over one strip at a time. The group reads the strip together and then repeats the phrase at the rate of speaking. If students are confident with the set of phrases they are using, the person who turns over the strip can read it while teammates check that it has been read correctly.
- Once all the strips have been turned over, they can be shuffled, and the game begins again.
- If there is an adult engaged in this activity, the game can be extended. Once students have taken turns turning over and reading strips, the adult can then read a strip and ask students which strip they have read. When the correct strip is identified, it is removed from the remaining strips and the adult reads another strip aloud. The game continues until all the strips have been removed from the table.

Fluency Passages

Fluency passages are short passages of text that focus on one or more phonics concepts. Some of the benefits of fluency passages are that they are short (which makes them excellent for repeated readings), they can be marked up, there are no pictures for guessing, and they are inexpensive (unlike decodable texts).

You will notice in the following lesson plans that every phonics concept is taken to text so that students engage with the words in an authentic way. When selecting passages, ensure that while the passage focuses on the concept being taught, it does not include words with concepts that have not yet been taught. Passages where most of the text is decodable are preferred because additional time and energy are not spent on words that do not fall into the focus concept. Finding decodable fluency passages can be quite challenging, but there are several great sources on pages 261–62.

Using Fluency Passages in the Classroom
- When introducing passages, read them aloud together (choral) as a class.
- After introducing and working with a new concept, give each child a short passage that contains several words that include the target concept. Have students find and highlight all the words that contain the new concept. Practice reading the passage as a class and individually with the highlighted words. The highlights provide a scaffold that alerts students to pay particular attention to these words. Once students become fluent with the passage (this may take several days), provide them with unhighlighted copies to practice with.
- Passages can be used for small-group instruction.
- Students can practice reading the passages in pairs. They can switch readers with every sentence or whenever one of the concept words is read.

- Once students become fluent with passages, the passages can be sent home for practice and celebration.
- Passage fluency can be used for progress monitoring.

Decodable Books

Decodable books are books with a strong phoneme-grapheme alignment, which makes them easier to decode. Typically, these books are available in a series where each book builds on the phonics skills introduced and practiced in previous books. For example, an emergent series of decodable books will start with one short vowel (usually /ă/), a few consonants in VC and simple CVC words, and one or two tricky words. Subsequent books add another short vowel and a few more consonants and continue this way until all the short vowels have been added. Once short vowels and consonants have been addressed, they move on to other phonics concepts. The progression of phonics concepts can vary from one series to the next, but the concepts addressed are indicated on the back of the book or inside the back cover. This information helps teachers fit the book into the scope and sequence they are using. One indicator of a good series of decodable texts is that the concepts are laid out in a clearly defined way, with new concepts building on those addressed in previous books.

With a shift to Structured Literacy, there are many new decodable books on the market. If you are looking for decodable books, do not be swayed by pretty pictures and lovely colors. Decodable texts are all about word selection based on targeted phonics concepts and, from a student perspective, they do not need highly engaging pictures. One of our favorite sets of decodable books, Primary Phonics, is an old series with simple black-and-white drawings. A teacher once picked them up and commented on how no child would ever want to read them, whereas we have seen students love the series because they are the first books they have ever truly read.

What decodable books and passages are:
- opportunities for students to practice specific phonics concepts.
- a tool for students to build confidence as readers.
- a tool for students to show that they can read. As noted earlier, benchmark systems begin with pattern books, which are not decodable. A student reading decodable books may not be able to get onto the benchmarking system because they do not know enough tricky words, even though they can successfully decode.
- exciting for students. While we might consider them mind-numbingly boring, struggling readers do not feel this way. They love the fact that they are reading rather than guessing, and they are proud of the growing stack of books they can read.

What decodable books and passages are not:
- "Great literature." Decodable books and passages are teaching tools. They are not meant to be read out loud for pleasure or used for exposure to big ideas and rich vocabulary, because none of those things can be found in a decodable book.
- essential for every reader. Some readers will move to leveled texts or rich texts quite quickly, while other students require the scaffold and practice that decodable books offer. Teachers shouldn't insist that all students read

Heather was working with a group of grade 2 boys who were not reading. At the beginning of her time with them, one of the boys, in frustration, told her he had never read a book. After doing a significant amount of PA, word building with letter tiles, letter and sound manipulation, and phrase reading, she introduced the book *Mac and Tab* from the Primary Phonics series. After several days of working through the book, the boys walked into the reading support room and saw the book on the table. The boy who had never read a book exclaimed, "*Mac and Tab*! I love *Mac and Tab*." Although his enthusiasm for the book was heartwarming, he wasn't saying he loved the book *Mac and Tab*; what he was really saying was that he loved the fact that he could READ *Mac and Tab*.

Heather was reading with a grade 2 student who was reading for the first time. When he finished the book, he turned to her and proudly said, "I didn't guess for any of them." He understood that instead of guessing (as he had in the past), he was reading every word.

decodable texts, but they should be available for those who need them and/ or want to use them.

Things to Consider before Purchasing or Downloading Decodable Texts
- Check the phonics progression of the texts. If the authors add too many complex concepts too early in the series, they may not serve your struggling readers.
- Consider the themes, ages of the characters, and the age of the reader. Do they align with the students you are working with?
- Find out whether the series provides enough practice before moving on to the next phonics concept. If a series moves too quickly, you will need to purchase multiple series to provide enough practice for young readers (especially those who need a significant amount of practice with each concept).
- Cost. There are some very good free and inexpensive decodable books available. It is not worth paying large amounts of money for a series that has high shipping costs, exchange rates, or price tags because the pictures are colorful and the paper is glossy! Trust us when we say that this will be more important to you than the struggling reader who finally has a book that they can read.
- Consider downloadable purchases so that you can print on demand. This allows you to send black-and-white copies home and you do not need to worry about a few books getting lost or ruined along the way.

How to Use Decodable Texts and Passages
The most valuable feature of decodable books (besides the fact that students can read them) is that they align with the explicit phonics concepts taught in the classroom. When introducing concepts, it is important that students see and practice them in meaningful text, as opposed to exclusively in isolation, such as single words and items on word lists.

There are a variety of ways to implement decodable texts in the classroom, as shown in the lesson plans in this book. They are excellent for small-group work, partner reading, and independent practice. They are short enough to be appropriate for home reading. Students will enjoy reading books they have mastered again and again, because they help support fluent reading and build confidence.

We have shared our favorite decodable texts on pages 262–63.

Decoding Multisyllable Words

Multisyllable words are words that are made up of more than one word part (syllable). Each syllable contains a vowel (or vowel sound). There are three simple steps that you can teach students to help them tackle long, multisyllable words.

1. Identify all prefixes and suffixes. When practicing breaking words into syllables, circle or underline them.
2. Count the vowels (excluding silent "e") to determine how many syllables there are.
3. Determine where to break the syllables apart and identify the vowel sounds (long or short) by using the Six Syllable Rules.

For short multisyllable words, such as "cabin," "picnic," etc., you can start with step 2.

The Six Syllable Rules

1. **Open Syllables.** When a syllable ends with a vowel, the vowel says its long sound (e.g., "o•bey").
2. **Closed syllables.** When a syllable ends in a consonant (the vowel is followed by a consonant) and is therefore "enclosed," the vowel makes its short sound (e.g., "in•dex").
3. **VCe.** When a vowel is followed by a consonant and the letter "e," the vowel makes its long sound and the "e" is silent (e.g., "face"). This letter team does not get separated when breaking multisyllable words into syllables for decoding.
4. **Vowel teams.** Two or more letters that make one vowel sound (long or short). Vowel teams may contain vowels (e.g., "oa") or a combination of vowels and consonants ("ough"). Vowel teams do not get separated when breaking multisyllable words into syllables for decoding.
5. **Vowel-r.** When a vowel is followed by "r," the "r" works with the vowel to create a new sound ("ar" says /ar/, "or" says /or/, and "er," "ir," "ur" say /er/) Vowel-r teams are not separated when breaking multisyllable words into syllables for decoding.
6. **Consonant-le.** When a consonant is followed by the letters "le," they form a syllable. The "e" is silent and a voiced schwa (/ə/) is heard, even though there is no letter to represent this sound (e.g., "maple," /mā•pəl/).

The Six Syllable Rules help students with decoding. Typically, two consonants are divided unless another rule is at play (e.g., blends and trigraphs stay together). Students may need to break up letters in a variety of ways to determine the correct syllable units.

For example: "observe."

- "Observe" has two syllables because it has two vowels (the second "e" is silent).
- It has two consonants back-to-back so division would be between the "b" and the "s": "ob-serve." It would not be logical to break the word into "o-bserve" since "bs" does not start any English words. "Obs-erve" could work but a typical division is between two consonants where possible.
- "Ob" is a closed syllable, so the vowel is short and "serve" has a vowel-r sound, which is also covered by one of the Six Syllable Rules.

As each of these concepts is covered in the blueprints, a short reference will be made to its role in helping students break apart multisyllable words for decoding. Continue to talk about and practice strategies for decoding these words when they are encountered.

Syllable Boards

Learning about syllables helps students decode larger words and supports vocabulary knowledge by understanding the meaning of smaller word parts. Syllable boards (small whiteboards, approximately 3" x 5") can be used for teaching students how to accurately identify and write the syllables in a multisyllable word. The student taps or claps the correct number of syllables and writes each syllable on a separate board, paying attention to the accurate spelling of each syllable. Boards are then placed in a row to form the completed word. Attention given to each syllable and its spelling supports encoding skills. Syllable boards can be purchased or made by cutting magnetic dry-erase sheets to the desired size.

ACTIVITIES:

- Show students a multisyllable word written either on paper or on a whiteboard. Students must break the word into syllables and write them on syllable boards.
- Provide students with a variety of word parts written on syllable boards. Students must arrange the syllable boards to create meaningful words.
- Write a variety of prefixes and/or suffixes on syllable boards. Students write a base word on a larger whiteboard and then add and delete syllable boards to create new words.

These same activities can also be done with index cards, but whiteboards allow for easy changes and corrections.

Encoding

Letter Formation

Letter formation is an important component of teaching letters and sounds and should not be underestimated. Proper formation supports the brain in recognizing and storing the shapes of letters. Teaching and reinforcing proper letter formation, grip, and pressure are critical in kindergarten and grade 1. If these habits are not well established in these years, children will develop their own unique habits, which can impact their written output in later years and be difficult to correct. There are many creative and engaging ways to teach letter formation.

- Finger tracing on uppercase and lowercase letters (on paper or felt/textured letters).
- Tracing laminated letters with a dry erase pen.
- Creating letters in sand with a tool or your finger.
- Sky writing — students draw letters in the air. When sky writing, it is important to teach anchor points. For example, attic/main floor/basement or hat line/belt line/shoe line. As the teacher guides students through the letter, they reference each position. For example, for a lowercase "h" the teacher might say, "Start at the hat line, then move through the belt line and down to the shoe line. Now draw up to the belt line, over the hill, and down to the shoe line." Students can stand while sky writing which gives them a chance to stretch and move.
- Table writing — this can be done with either fingers or a dry erase pen on the desk or tabletop.
- Use modeling clay, sensory bags (gel with glitter), arranging small objects, pipe cleaners, Wikki Stix, etc., to create letter shapes.
- Use any of the excellent paper/pencil programs available, such as Handwriting without Tears, and Printing like a Pro.

Elkonin Boxes

While the use of Elkonin boxes is a stand-alone PA activity that helps students hear and understand that words are made up of sounds, we have included them here as a highly scaffolded approach to the beginning of the encoding process. This tool should be used in both ways with emergent and struggling readers.

Elkonin boxes, or cubes, are used to represent phonemes (sounds) rather than letters. They are named after the Russian psychologist D.B. El'konin, who used them in the 1960s to help students break words into phonemes and then blend them back together. For students who are struggling with the phonemic awareness aspect of reading, the boxes allow them to focus solely on the sounds in words without being distracted by letter symbols. This extremely scaffolded approach allows students to work with a wide range of words without requiring them to know all the phoneme-to-grapheme correspondences.

There are a variety of ways that Elkonin boxes can be used effectively.

Identifying Phonemes in Words

Materials: Each student and the teacher will need a ziptop bag with some type of counters (small cubes/blocks, pebbles, or tiles) in various colors and a piece of paper with a small graph to place their markers on (diagram below and in resources on page 238). Students will need one more counter than the longest word they will be working with. If you are working with three-letter words, for example, provide each student with a graph with four boxes and four counters. This will ensure that students will have to make a decision regarding how many counters to use.

Placement paper

I Do (teacher modeling):
- The teacher points to their graph and explains that students will listen for the sounds in a word and then move one counter onto one box on the paper for each sound they hear.
- The teacher models with the word "in." The teacher says the word and then taps the sounds on their fingers (touching the thumb to first the pinkie finger, and then the ring finger), or taps on the table to identify the sounds in the word, /ĭ/ /n/.
- The teacher taps and says the sound /ĭ/ and moves one counter into the first box on the paper.
- The teacher then taps and says the sounds /n/ and moves a second counter onto the paper beside it.
- The teacher checks the two sounds by tapping on the first counter and saying /ĭ/ and then on the second counter, saying /n/. The teacher then places a finger under the first box and slides it to the right, saying the word "in."

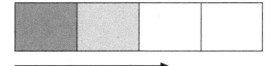

WE Do (guided practice):
- Students and teacher do several words together using the steps above.

Note: Select words that can be easily broken down into phonemes. We avoid words that contain vowel-controlled r, diphthongs, etc.

For emergent readers, start with words containing two sounds and build up to more sounds over several days.

YOU Do (independent practice):
- The teacher continues to provide words while moving around the room to observe students while they use the Elkonin boxes to segment sounds and then blend them into words.

Intervention: When doing this activity with struggling readers, use words that contain letters and sounds that have already been introduced and explicitly taught.

Extending: This activity can be extended by using sticky notes for each sound. Once the word is created with the correct number of sticky notes, students can write the correct grapheme on each one.

Identifying Specific Phonemes in Words

Once students can hear the correct number of sounds in words and can add the correct number of counters to represent those sounds, you can move a step further by having them indicate when they hear sounds that are the same.

Materials: Each student and the teacher will need a ziptop bag with counters of various colors and a paper with a small graph to place their counters on. It is important that there be two or more counters of the same color.

I Do (teacher modeling):
- Follow the same steps as above, but use words with three or more sounds and that contain two of the same sound (e.g., "pop," "dad," "mom," "baby," "trait"). For example, the teacher models with the word "dad." The teacher says the word and then taps the sounds on their fingers or taps on the table to identify the sounds in the word.
- The teacher taps and says the sound /d/ and moves one counter into the first box on the paper.
- The teacher then taps and says the sounds /d/ /ă/ and asks students if the second sound is the same or different than the first sound. By going back to the /d/ before adding the /ă/, the teacher provides ongoing review and comparison for students who struggle with remembering the first sound, as well as context for the second sound.
- When students respond that it is a different sound, the teacher moves a counter of a different color onto the paper beside it.
- The teacher taps and says the sounds /d/ /ă/ /d/ and asks students if the third sound is the same or different from the first two sounds. When students respond that it is the same as the first sound, the teacher moves a counter that is the same color as the first counter onto the paper.
- The teacher checks the three sounds by tapping on the first counter saying /d/, on the second counter saying /ă/, and on the last counter saying /d/. The teacher then places a finger under the first box and slides it to the right, saying the word "dad."

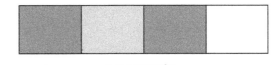

WE Do (guided practice):

- Students and teacher do several words together using the steps above.

Note: Select words that can be easily broken down into phonemes. We avoid words that contain vowel-controlled r, diphthongs, etc.

For emergent readers, start with two-sound words and build up to more sounds over several days.

YOU Do (independent practice):

- The teacher continues to provide words while moving around the room to observe students while they use the Elkonin boxes to segment and then blend words.

Phoneme-to-Grapheme Spelling

Ask any teacher how they feel about the way their students spell and you will rarely hear that all is well. There have been many theories and strategies for teaching spelling over the past few decades — everything from inventive spelling to the GUM strategy (Give it a try, Underline it, Move on) to not teaching spelling at all. It is not uncommon for good spellers (students and adults) to tell us they spell in a way that "looks right" rather than relying on any specific skills or strategies. Thankfully this can be avoided by teaching students phoneme-to-grapheme spelling.

If decoding really is looking at a string of letters on a page and matching them to the sounds that we speak and hear, then encoding should be approached the opposite way. What are the sounds that we speak or hear, and what are the matching letter(s) required on the page?

We use phoneme-to-grapheme spelling early in the encoding or spelling process. The class has the opportunity to spell many words together, so that students become comfortable with the process. Struggling students, and those who are hesitant to make a mistake, know that they can copy what the teacher has modeled on the board, providing an opportunity for every student to succeed. This process helps students to "lock in" the concept that each sound in a word needs one or more letters to represent it. Older students who consistently omit letters and sounds when they spell will benefit from this activity as well.

Materials: Provide graph paper for students to engage in this activity.

- We use graphs with large squares and laminate them for reuse (pages 231–36). For students with fine-motor challenges, you can use very large graphs or letter tiles, so that they are choosing letters rather than printing them. In the blackline masters included in this book there are graphs, as well as split grids, for this activity. Split grids have less visual information, and by separating each graph line, students can practice correct letter formation as it allows space for letters that move below the line (e.g., "p," "g," "j"). See template on pages 231–36.
- We had our school district print shop make large, dry erase, magnetic graph charts for teacher modeling. These are split grids for visual clarity

and there is a large, open space at the end of each graph line for students to print the graphed word to see what it looks like in print.

c	a	p			cap

g	o	t			got

Split Grid for Phoneme-Grapheme Mapping (up to 5 sounds)

The Phoneme-to-Grapheme Spelling Process
1. The teacher says the word and students repeat it — for example, "sip."
2. Teacher and students count the sounds together either by tapping the sounds on the table or by touching their thumb to fingertips. Students can also put their hands together, palms facing and touching each other, and "chop" the sounds from left to right. Regardless of the movements students use to break apart the word by phonemes, the goal is to always move in the same direction as reading text (left to right). While it may seem like a small detail, for many students it does matter, because it transfers to directionality when they read and write.

    Note: just a reminder that the teacher will need to mirror students, so that what the teacher does is the correct direction for the student facing them (e.g., right-handed teachers hold their hand with their palm open toward students and touch their thumb to their pinkie first because that will be left to right for students).
3. When the class agrees that there are three sounds, or phonemes, in "sip," they tap out three boxes in the grid and underline them.

s	i	p			

4. The teacher then finger-taps the first sound and asks students, "What is the first sound in 'sip'?"

5. Students respond with /s/ and the teacher asks, "What letter makes the /s/ sound?" For students who are still struggling with letter sounds, this is excellent review.
6. The teacher and students write an "s" in the first box.
7. Repeat for the remaining letters in the word.
8. Once you have worked together to write "s," "i," and "p," it is time to check.
9. The teacher asks students to put their finger under the first box, while modeling on the board. The teacher asks, "What letter is in the first box?" Students respond with "s" /s/. "What letter is in the second box?" Students respond with "i" /ĭ/, etc.
10. Once all letters have been checked, students put their finger under the "s" and slide their finger from left to right while saying "sip."
11. The teacher and/or students can then write the word at the end of the graph if there is a box provided for this activity.
12. Once students become confident in the process, emergent readers can be guided through the first two letters of the word and then asked to fill in the last letter on their own, gradually releasing students to work independently. The teacher can also share a word, have the students repeat it, and then ask students which letter they think will be in the first box. Students can then try the first letter on their own. It is easiest for students to hear the first sound in a word, so this would be a logical place to start independent practice.

Samples of student work:

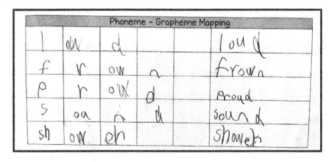

For some students, learning to spell through phoneme-to-grapheme spelling is not enough to support the transfer of correct spelling to their daily writing. One of the ways we support the transfer is to have students spell in phrases. If students are spelling a word in a short phrase, they are less inclined to focus just on the word they are working with. You will notice in our lesson plans that we recommend practicing each word in a phrase that consists of several short decodable words along with the target word. For example, if students are learning VCe and the word is "late," ask students to write "I am late." They will then be approaching and practicing the VCe word in an authentic writing way.

Once students become confident at phoneme-to-grapheme spelling, have them write a short phrase in the long box at the end of each row, rather than the single word.

l	a	te			I am late

Scaffolding Phoneme-to-Grapheme Spelling with Letter Tiles

This strategy is excellent for struggling readers or students with fine-motor-skill challenges. Use the exact same stepwise process as the phoneme-to-grapheme spelling strategy, but rather than writing the letters in a grid, have students select and arrange magnetic tiles on a tile board.

Why do both phoneme-to-grapheme spelling **and** letter tile building when they are essentially the same task? Spelling graphs require students to write the letters, which adds the skills of letter formation and letter retrieval, since there are no letters provided. We teach and use letter tile word building before introducing phoneme-to-grapheme spelling since a selection of letters is provided for word building.

Setting Up and Using Tile Boards

Our print shop makes student-sized (approximately 1" x 2") magnetic letter tiles for us. These tiles match the larger magnetic tiles teachers use on their whiteboards. Tiles can also be purchased from a variety of sources. Any magnetic whiteboard will work for these activities. Using whiteboards, rather than a metal surface, provides the option of having students print words with dry erase pens once they have been built.

There are a few tricks to using and storing magnetic tiles and boards that will make them easier to manage in the classroom setting.

- Some classes have a tile board for every student. These can be stored in magazine file boxes with each student's name written on masking tape on the back of the board. They also store well in flat student mailboxes. When there are not enough boards for the entire class, they can be loaded with a variety of tiles and used for small-group work. For example, there might be four boards with one vowel and four consonants, and another four boards loaded with all the vowels and a larger selection of consonants.
- We do not have all the letters of the alphabet on our magnetic tile boards when working with early readers. Tile boards can be loaded with one vowel and the first four consonants introduced to students. As students grow in

their knowledge and use of letters, more tiles can be added to the board. It can be very confusing and visually overwhelming for early readers to have to look through twenty-six letters to find the one they are looking for.

- We ask students to keep the vowels (in red) at the side of the board and the consonants along the top (or vice versa). This keeps the boards organized and helps students find the letters they are looking for. After building a word, tiles are returned to their respective homes so that they are ready for the next activity.

- Extra tiles store well in tackle boxes. Each letter, digraph, or vowel team can be stored in its own compartment, so that teachers can simply take a stack of tiles and distribute them to students without having to look for particular tiles. Some whiteboards are magnetic on both sides, which allows for storage of extra letters on the back of the board, making them easily accessible for other students.

- We have seen teachers make letter tiles out of paper and place them in ziptop baggies for their students. This works if you do not have access or funding for tiles and boards.

Magnetic Letter Tiles and Intervention

We have found it is very important that magnetic boards with letter tiles contain the number of tiles a child can manage. Tile boards that are full of letters are overwhelming for students who are just learning to decode and encode. Some of the Wilson tile boards, which are designed to fold and allow for a large surface area, have a grid with the letters printed right onto the board. Even with the grid free of tiles, we have worked with children who have found the printed graph visually distracting and overwhelming. White magnetic boards with no markings enable teachers to load the boards with tiles in a way that is appropriate for each student, using only letters students have been explicitly taught.

Scaffolding with Elkonin Box Tiles

We have magnetic letter tiles that are colored squares (Elkonin boxes, see also page 53). For students who are struggling with the phonemic awareness aspect of reading, the colored tiles can be used as a bridge to letter tiles. Teachers can say a word, students can count the sounds in the word, and then place a colored square on the tile board to represent each sound. This scaffolded activity allows students to focus solely on the sounds in the word without requiring them to know all of the phoneme-to-grapheme correspondences needed to encode the word. Once the colored squares are in place, they can find the letter tiles that represent the sounds for each square.

Scaffolding the Encoding Process Using Letter Tiles and 10-Frames

10-frames (on magnetic whiteboard material) from math make an excellent scaffold for the encoding process. They can be ordered through educational companies and online businesses like Amazon, or teachers can make them with magnetic erasable sheets (example of a 10-frame below).

1. Teacher says the target word and students count the sounds in the word. Students place the appropriate number of colored squares in the top row of the 10-frame.
2. Students and teacher tap out the sounds to ensure that the number of squares is correct.

3. Students tap the first square, say the first sound in the word, and select the appropriate letter tile. Students repeat for each sound in the word.
4. Students and teacher check the sounds by tapping each letter and saying the sound.
5. Students put a finger under the first letter tile and slide their finger to the right while blending the word.
6. Students write the word in the bottom row of the 10-frame using a whiteboard pen.
7. Students put a finger under their first written letter and slide their finger to the right while blending the word.

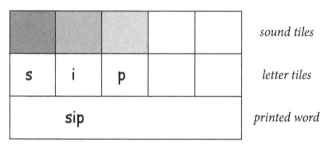

sound tiles

letter tiles

printed word

sound tiles
letter tiles
printed word

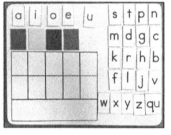 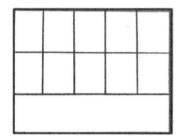 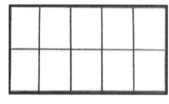

Encoding Using Whiteboards

Whiteboard encoding is an activity that students enjoy. It is great for short blocks of time in the day, either at the end of a period or before a break. The process of using whiteboards is similar to that of letter tiles.

Materials: student whiteboards, whiteboard pens, and erasers
The process:
1. Students tap (on their fingers or on the tabletop) the number of sounds in the word — for example, "sip."
2. Students draw three horizontal lines on their whiteboard.
3. Students tap the first sound /s/ and the teacher asks what letter makes the /s/ sound. Students say "s" and write it on the first line of their whiteboard.
4. Students tap the first two sounds /s/ /ĭ/, the teacher asks what the second sound is, and students say /ĭ/. The teacher asks what letter makes the /ĭ/ sound, and students say "i" and write the letter on the middle line of their whiteboard.
5. Students tap all three sounds /s/ /ĭ/ /p/, the teacher asks what the third sound is, and students say /p/. The teacher asks what letter makes the /p/ sound, and students say "p" and write the letter on the third line of their whiteboard.
6. Students tap each letter on their board while saying the sounds to check that they are correct.
7. Students put their finger under the "s" and slide to the right while blending the word.

For students who might struggle with drawing lines on their board, permanent lines can be added to a select number of whiteboards, or painter's tape can be used to create lines on the board.

Manipulating Phonemes

As previously stated, when students are able to manipulate letters and sounds, it shows us they have a clear understanding of how words are built. The previous word-building activities are important, but when they lead to sound and letter manipulation, there is a tremendous impact on reading progress. Magnetic letter tiles are among the best tools for doing this work!

The Phoneme Manipulation Process with Letter Tiles
This work is easiest when done in a small group setting as the teacher is able to quickly check and provide corrective feedback.

- Using the phoneme-to-grapheme spelling strategy listed above, have students build the word "sip."
- Review the sounds in the word by having students put their finger on each letter in the word and say the sound. Then have them put their finger under the "s" and run their finger under the word while saying "sip."
- Ask students what they need to do to change the word "sip" to "lip." Have students finger tap, table tap, or *chop* the new word "lip."
- Ask students to put their finger on the letter that needs to be changed. If students are having trouble finding the correct sound, tap, or *chop* the word "sip" and then the word "lip."
- Ask students to remove the "s" tile and place it at the top/side of the board where consonants are stored. Now ask them which tile needs to replace the /s/ sound.
- Students take the "l" from the top/side of the board and place it in front of the "i" and "p."
- Check the new word all together by having students place their finger on each letter to say the sound. Then have them put their finger under the "l" and run their finger under the word while saying "lip."
- The teacher can then move to a new word ("tip" for example), or clear the board and begin again with a new word.
- This work can be done with many phonics concepts (blends, digraphs, "magic e," vowel teams, etc.). This is very powerful when working with initial blends, as emergent readers often struggle to hear the second sound in a blend, skipping it and moving directly to the vowel. It is important to remember that students find it easiest to identify the beginning sound, then end sound, and finally medial sound. When starting this work with students, manipulate beginning sounds first, then end sounds, and finally medial sounds.
- **Extending:** Some students will catch on to this activity quickly and will have the word built while you are supporting the class in locating the sound and letter to be changed. For these students, once they have built the correct word, have them use a whiteboard pen and build other words where the same sound is manipulated ("tip," "rip," "dip," etc.). They will not be able to do this with letter tiles as there is only one tile for each letter.

The Phoneme Manipulation Process with Whiteboards

The process is the same with whiteboards, but students write and erase letters rather than move them in and out of place manually.

Word Ladders and Word Chains

Word ladders are another highly engaging tool that provides students with opportunities to generate words and manipulate letters and sounds. This is an activity that we do not introduce until students are able to build words and manipulate sounds and letters with whiteboards or letter tiles. We recommend two different word ladder activities.

STUDENT-GENERATED WORD LADDERS

Materials: word ladder sheets, dry erase pens, and erasers

We have included a ladder template for you to copy and use with your students (see page 230). We like to laminate these for ongoing use. They can also be put into plastic sleeves and used with whiteboard markers in the same way.

TEACHING THE WORD LADDER PROCESS

1. The teacher draws a word ladder on the board. Choose a word that contains the focus concept and write it on the bottom rung of the ladder. If the focus concept is short vowel "o" /ŏ/ the word could be "top"; if it is /l/ blends, the word could be "flat"; and if it is VCe, it could be "gate," etc.

2. The teacher asks students what letter could be changed to create a new word. Students offer suggestions. The teacher takes one suggestion and writes the new word on the second rung from the bottom. If the first word is "top," the new word might be "mop."

3. The teacher and students continue to generate new words and add them to the rungs on the ladder ("top," "mop," "lop," "lot," "log," "leg," etc). Once they reach the top, the ladder is complete. Take the time to read all the words on the ladder before moving on to a new one.

4. As we have seen, it is easiest for students to identify and manipulate the first letter of the word, so it is important that the teacher model manipulation of beginning, end, and middle sounds in that order. For students who struggle with PA, changing the first letter and sound might be all they are able to do the first few times they work with ladders.
   - The teacher and students might do several ladders together, even over several days, before students create them independently.
   - Once students are ready to work independently, they are given a word to write on the bottom rung and are asked to work up the ladder, generating new words on their own.

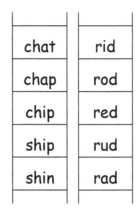

chat	rid
chap	rod
chip	red
ship	rud
shin	rad

Examples of word ladders

Intervention and Extending: Our print shop has created a template with three ladders for one side of the page and a large ladder on the back. This sheet automatically sets up a scaffold for students. If students struggle with fine-motor skills, they can work on the large ladder on the back. If students work quickly, they can be asked to complete all three ladders on the page, whereas other students may have done excellent work by completing one ladder correctly.

WORD CHAINS

Word chains work the same way that ladders do. Students start with one word written on a piece of lined paper or a whiteboard. By changing one letter/sound in the word, they create a new word and write it after the first word. The activity continues as students build a long "chain" of words on the line. An example might be "maid — main — chain — rain."

WORD LADDER GAMES

Another effective way to use word ladders is to give students a word and then a clue as to what a new word will be. Tim Rasinski is a master at creating these ladders and has published several books containing them. He also offers free ladders through his email and Twitter account. These ladders can be copied and distributed for meaningful extending activities and are excellent to do once a week as a class.

Giant Flash Cards

Giant flash card activities are an engaging and interactive way to practice blending and phonics concepts. Flash cards can be made with 8 1/2" x 11" cardstock (in portrait layout) and laminated for durability. We use the same font as we do for our letter tiles and other materials, with all letters in lowercase and vowels in red.

Students come to the front of the room and are each given one letter to help form a word. The rest of the class acts as the "directors" of the letters. The teacher tells the class the word and the students with flash cards must sort themselves into the correct order. Cards must be held with two hands so that they are upright and visible to the class. The students with letters can discuss how they should arrange themselves, with the support of the class directors. If several directors begin to monopolize the conversations, rules can be adjusted so that each director is allowed one comment per word.

Once everyone agrees on the order, the word is read aloud by the class. New letters are handed out to different students and the process begins again. This activity can be used for simple, decodable words, as well as teaching and reviewing digraphs, vowel teams, vowel-r, etc.

This activity can be **extended** by adding more than the necessary letters for any given word. For example, if the word is "short," the teacher can hand out "sh," "ch," "or," "er," and "t" cards. Students must organize themselves into the word "short" and decide which letter cards are not required. This works very well with vowel teams where two teams make the same sound, for example "ai" and "ay." When working with "ai" and "ay," the necessary letters can be handed out and students with the "ai" and "ay" cards can stand at the side. Students must decide which team is needed according to where /ā/ is in the word. If the word is "play," the "ay" card will be needed, but if the word is "maid" the "ai" card will be used.

5

Blueprints, Concept Pages, and Lesson Plans

Scope and Sequence

Teaching phonics is not a "once and done" approach to teaching. Concepts are explicitly taught, reviewed, and then embedded in the language of the classroom. After a concept is taught, it is important that educators continually refer to it when it is discovered in print and review it when correcting errors in student work. Only through such reinforcement does a concept become effectively mapped and stored in the brain.

We now turn to the blueprints for K–3, with week-by-week plans. Each year's blueprint reviews the previous year's concepts before moving on to new material. The school year begins in review, with new concepts introduced starting in late fall. This provides the opportunity for enrichment activities for students who understand the concepts being covered, as well as time to "catch up" for students who are lagging or have missed key instruction from the previous school year. It also allows for times when teachers were not able to complete the previous year's lessons. It is more important to teach each concept well than to complete the blueprint. Any concepts that you do not cover will be reviewed or covered by your students' teacher the following year.

Each concept page contains a combination of the following information: introduction to the concept to be taught, key strategies, phonics information that the teacher must keep in mind, word lists (including nonsense words and extending words), sample word chains, and, for kindergarten and grade 1, a tricky word sequence. There are a variety of phonics concepts covered in these K–3 blueprints, so the information each concept page contains may look different according to what is needed to teach it. Within the blueprints there are also many references to correct spelling and sound correlation. To provide clarity on pronunciation, we have included Letters-to-Sounds Correlation Charts on pages 251–53.

With highly engaging lessons, it has been our experience that once students know the "rule" or "pattern," they often share when they discover it in print or ask many questions when they discover departures from what they have been taught. This sharing can lead to interesting and engaging conversations about language, reading, and writing.

There are many ways to approach a phonics scope and sequence. For example, some educators like to move from letters and sounds to blends, because with a blend, each individual sound is heard. Some educators like to move from letters and sounds to digraphs, as you see here, because like letters, they have one sound. One methodology is not necessarily better than the other, but what is important is that whatever approach is chosen, it needs to be explicitly introduced to students and taught with fidelity.

The Scope and Sequence Overview that follows provides a broad picture of the phonics concepts taught in our K–3 blueprints. For a more detailed summary and quick reference for what is taught when, see the Summary of Concepts and Tricky Words Sets Taught in K–3 on pages 266–69.

Scope and Sequence Overview

Kindergarten					
• phonological awareness	• 26 uppercase & lowercase letter names	• 26 letter sounds	• blending skills • (VC & CVC)	• tricky words (set 1)	• printing (letter formation) & phoneme-grapheme correspondence

Grade 1					
• review all kindergarten concepts	• digraphs • initial and final consonant blends	• open & closed syllables (short/long vowel sounds)	• VCe • inflected endings	• schwa • floss rule • 3-letter initial blends	• tricky words (all sets)

Grade 2			
• review all grade 1 concepts	• complex vowels (vowel teams, diphthongs, & r-controlled vowels)	• hard & soft c & g • the many jobs of y	• complex consonants (silent letters) • inflected endings • past-tense verbs

Grade 3			
• review all grade 2 concepts	• possessive plurals • common contractions • soldier rule • consonant-le	• doubling rule • common suffixes & prefixes • homonyms & homophones • irregular plurals	• complex vowel teams • sh, si, ti, ci • endings: ture & sure • additional sounds of ch

Creating a Phonics Box

Before you start your phonics instruction with the blueprints below, an excellent way to organize your materials and lighten the workload for your teaching team is to create phonics boxes. The teaching team that developed this idea wanted their school to work with the same scope and sequence (the one included in this book) to ensure comprehensive phonics instruction from K–3. Each teacher will have a box that is ready for phonics instruction for the school year, along with a tool kit that contains teaching items such as letter tiles, fluency phrase rings, 10-frames, etc. When we shared the idea with other teachers in the district, everyone was interested and wanted to create them for their schools. We now have phonics boxes popping up across our district and teachers are sharing their best activities with colleagues in other schools.

Box Contents

- 1 copy of *This Is How We Teach Reading…and It's Working!*
- 1 plastic legal file box (approximately 17 by 14 by 10 inches)
- 37 file hangers (one for every week of instruction)
- Approximately 50 file folders, one for each new concept
- A set of file pockets for storing assessment material like screens, progress monitoring, checklists, etc.
- A box or tote for storing teaching tools (whiteboards, 10-frames, blending boards, tricky word rings, letter tiles, etc.)

Building the Box

1. Using the blueprints as a guide, label file hangers with the weeks of instruction for the school year. For example, grade 1 has thirty-seven weeks of instruction so will require thirty-seven file hangers. File hangers are added for review and flex weeks as well, as a place to store assessments and extra material for instruction and review.
2. In each weekly file hanging, add file folders with the following items:
   - a copy of the weekly concept page and any assessments required for progress monitoring
   - flash cards
   - word sort masters
   - decodable phrases
   - decodable passages
   - a copy of the cover, or a list, of all decodable texts available within the school that align with the concept being taught
   - activities that support teaching that concept (e.g., word wheels, worksheets, games)
   - reproducible tricky-word flash card masters (if appropriate)

Helpful Hints

- You will be surprised how much material you already have on hand that fits neatly into the box.
- It is important that teaching teams decide together what goes into their grade-level boxes. If the team does not agree that an activity or strategy aligns with SOR, it does not get added to the box.
- When creating K–3 phonic boxes for the first time, it is important to note that you will be building two-and-a-half years of instruction over four years since the last half of one grade becomes the first half of the box in the following grade. For example, the new material taught after the winter break in grade 1 becomes the review material in the fall of grade 2.
- Digital material can be stored the same way. Create one file for each phonics grade level, and then within that file, create a file for each instructional week.
- Rather than put decodable books into the boxes, copy the cover of the book so that you know which specific book addresses the concept being taught. This frees up books for ongoing use (especially for teachers in the following grade who will be reviewing these concepts before you begin teaching them).
- Most of our boxes at this point belong to the school, so that if a teacher leaves, their box is available to the next teacher who comes.
- Visit our "This Is How We Teach Reading…" Facebook page for more ideas for reinforcing concepts.

When we first created these boxes, the very clever teachers put a three-year plan in place:

Year 1: build the box framework, add lesson concept pages from this book, word lists, decodable books/passages, and instructional material that has already been created.

Year 2: add activities for whole-class instruction, independent practice, and small-group intervention (word sorts, word wheels, blending boards, games, etc.). Check for lessons where there is insufficient material and find adequate resources to fill those files.

Year 3: create home reading material (books, passages, and activities) for each concept to be taught. Rome wasn't built in a day, and neither are phonics boxes.

Kindergarten Blueprint

This is our way of approaching the phonics and decoding skills that are covered over the course of the kindergarten school year. The following structure begins with 19 weeks of introducing the names and sounds of the letters of the alphabet. This is followed by several flex weeks of review and then explicit instruction of tricky words starting in week 29. Students may have been exposed to these words before week 29 but were not ready for explicit instruction in tricky words since their letters and sounds were not firmly in place. We realize that the pacing of these concepts may need to be flexed according to the needs of the students you are working with. For example, in some regions and countries, letters, sounds, and beginning blending happen in prekindergarten. If this is true for you, move to the grade 1 blueprint. As a professional who knows your students, you will use your expertise to adjust the pacing of introducing and reviewing concepts. This may mean speeding up or slowing down the progression of instruction. Once a concept has been taught, it should be continuously reinforced and applied through conversation, practice activities, and instruction. This work is cumulative; each new letter set is added to previous letter knowledge and continues to be practiced and reinforced.

Full lesson plans for weeks 4 and 5 are presented here. They can be used as models for many other lessons.

This K–3 scope and sequence is set up so that all new concepts introduced in each grade are reviewed at the start of the following year. This allows teachers to take the time required to introduce, teach, and practice each new concept. If you do not complete all the lessons in this year, rest assured that they will be covered again for your students in the fall, and next year's teacher may need to take a little more time with concepts that were not completed in the scope and sequence.

A note about intervention. When concepts have been explicitly taught and you have provided adequate opportunities for practice and review, but a student is not retaining the concept or is unable to apply it, that's when it is appropriate to begin conversations with your school support teacher(s) regarding intervention. Since concepts are being introduced for the first time in kindergarten, pull-out intervention would be unlikely before the spring. Intervention at that time could be for additional practice with letters and sounds and blending.

At the end of kindergarten, our hope is that students will have all of their letter names and sounds, be able to blend sounds to read VC and CVC words, be able to print graphemes to spell VC and CVC words, and have had exposure and engagement with the first nine tricky words (set 1).

The kindergarten phonics blueprint addresses only one of the strands of the Big 5 in classroom reading instruction and assumes parallel instruction in fluency, vocabulary, phonemic awareness, and comprehension. You will notice that we suggest the Heggerty resource (see Resources We Recommend on page 262) for phonemic awareness activities in the Kindergarten Blueprint. Any explicit phonemic awareness resource can be used for teaching and strengthening these skills, along with poetry, singing games, and other activities that involve word play.

Kindergarten Letters and Sounds Progression

Almost every week new letters are added to the progression (these are highlighted in bold type). When a new vowel is introduced, previously taught vowels are omitted so students can focus on the new vowel sound using consonants that have been previously taught. The following week, previously taught vowels are added back into the progression.

Weeks 1–3	Early literacy exploration
Week 4	**a, s, t**
Week 5	a, s, t, **p, n**
Week 6	**i,** s, t, p, n
Week 7	a, i, s, t, p, n
Week 8	a, i, s, t, p, n, **c, d**
Week 9	**o,** s, t, p, n, c, d
Week 10	o, a, i, s, t, p, n, c, d
Week 11	o, a, i, s, t, p, n, c, d, **g, m**
Week 12	**e,** s, t, p, n, c, d, g, m
Week 13	e, a, i, o, s, t, p, n, c, d, g, m
Week 14	e, a, i, o, s, t, p, n, c, d, g, m, **k, r**
Week 15	**u,** s, t, p, n, c, d, g, m, k, r
Week 16	a, e, i, o, u, s, t, p, n, c, d, g, m, k, r
Week 17	a, e, i, o, u, s, t, p, n, c, d, g, m, k, r, **h, b**
Week 18	a, e, i, o, u, s, t, p, n, c, d, g, m, k, r, h, b, **f, l**
Week 19	a, e, i, o, u, s, t, p, n, c, d, g, m, k, r, h, b, f, l, **j, v**
Week 20	a, e, i, o, u, s, t, p, n, c, d, g, m, k, r, h, b, f, l, j, v, **w, x**
Week 21	a, e, i, o, u, s, t, p, n, c, d, g, m, k, r, h, b, f, l, j, v, w, x, **y, z**
Week 22	a, e, i, o, u, s, t, p, n, c, d, g, m, k, r, h, b, f, l, j, v, w, x, y, z, **q/qu**

	WEEK 1	WEEK 2	WEEK 3	WEEK 4
SEPTEMBER	√ concepts of print √ discovering letters & words in environment √ establishing learning routines √ phonemic awareness activities (Heggerty, rhyming, etc.)	√ concepts of print √ discovering letters and words in environment √ establishing learning routines √ phonemic awareness activities (Heggerty, rhyming, etc.)	√ screening week: phonemic awareness & concepts of print √ discovering letters & words in environment √ establishing learning routines √ phonemic awareness activities (Heggerty, rhyming, etc.)	√ letter names & sounds (**a, s, t**) √ identifying letter names & sounds √ VC & CVC blending & letter formation √ phonemic awareness activities (Heggerty, rhyming, etc.)

	WEEK 5	WEEK 6	WEEK 7	WEEK 8
OCTOBER	√ letter names & sounds (previously taught sounds & **p, n**) √ identifying letter names & sounds √ VC & CVC blending, word building & letter formation √ phonemic awareness activities (Heggerty, rhyming, etc.)	√ letter names & sounds (excluding a, including previously taught sounds & **i**) √ identifying letter names & sounds √ VC & CVC blending, word building & letter formation √ phonemic awareness activities (Heggerty, rhyming, etc.)	√ letter names & sounds (previously taught sounds with a, i) √ identifying letter names & sounds √ VC & CVC blending, word building & letter formation √ phonemic awareness activities (Heggerty, rhyming, etc.)	√ letter names & sounds (previously taught sounds & **c, d**) √ identifying letter names & sounds √ VC & CVC blending, word building & letter formation √ phonemic awareness activities (Heggerty, rhyming, etc.)

	WEEK 9	WEEK 10	WEEK 11	WEEK 12
NOVEMBER	√ letter names & sounds (excluding a, i, including previously taught sounds & **o**) √ identifying letter names & sounds √ VC & CVC blending, building, & manipulating, letter formation, spelling & reading in context √ phonemic awareness activities (Heggerty, rhyming, etc.)	√ letter names & sounds (previously taught sounds with a, i, o) √ identifying letter names & sounds √ VC & CVC blending, building & manipulating, letter formation, spelling & reading in context √ phonemic awareness activities (Heggerty, rhyming, etc.)	√ letter names & sounds (previously taught sounds & **g, m**) √ identifying letter names & sounds √ VC & CVC blending, building & manipulating, letter formation, spelling & reading in context √ phonemic awareness activities (Heggerty, rhyming, etc.)	√ letter names & sounds (excluding a, i, o, including previously taught sounds & **e**) √ identifying letter names & sounds √ VC & CVC blending, building & manipulating, letter formation, spelling & reading in context √ phonemic awareness activities (Heggerty, rhyming, etc.)

DECEMBER

WEEK 13
- ✓ letter names & sounds (previously taught sounds with a, i, o, e)
- ✓ identifying letter names & sounds
- ✓ VC & CVC blending, building & manipulating, letter formation, spelling & reading in context
- ✓ phonemic awareness activities (Heggerty, rhyming, etc.)

WEEK 14
- ✓ flex/review

(winter break)
- ✓ winter break

JANUARY

WEEK 15
- ✓ letter names & sounds (previously taught sounds & **k, r**)
- ✓ mini lesson on rule for when to use c/k when spelling
- ✓ identifying letter names & sounds
- ✓ VC & CVC blending, building & manipulating, letter formation, spelling & reading in context
- ✓ phonemic awareness activities (Heggerty, rhyming, etc.)

WEEK 16
- ✓ letter names & sounds (excluding a, i, o, e, including previously taught consonants & **u**)
- ✓ identifying letter names & sounds
- ✓ VC & CVC blending, building & manipulating, letter formation, spelling & reading in context
- ✓ phonemic awareness activities (Heggerty, rhyming, etc.)

WEEK 17
- ✓ letter names & sounds (previously taught sounds with a, i, o, e, u)
- ✓ identifying letter names & sounds
- ✓ VC & CVC blending, building & manipulating, letter formation, spelling & reading in context
- ✓ phonemic awareness activities (Heggerty, rhyming, etc.)

WEEK 18
- ✓ letter names & sounds (previously taught sounds & **h, b**)
- ✓ mini lesson on b vs. d
- ✓ identifying letter names & sounds
- ✓ VC & CVC blending, building & manipulating, letter formation, spelling & reading in context
- ✓ phonemic awareness activities (Heggerty, rhyming, etc.)

FEBRUARY

WEEK 19
- ✓ letter names & sounds (previously taught sounds & **f, l**)
- ✓ identifying letter names & sounds
- ✓ VC & CVC blending, building & manipulating, letter formation, spelling & reading in context
- ✓ phonemic awareness activities (Heggerty, rhyming, etc.)

WEEK 20
- ✓ letter names & sounds (previously taught sounds & **j, v**)
- ✓ identifying letter names & sounds
- ✓ VC & CVC blending, building & manipulating, letter formation, spelling & reading in context
- ✓ phonemic awareness activities (Heggerty, rhyming, etc.)

WEEK 21
- ✓ letter names & sounds (previously taught sounds & **w, x**)
- ✓ identifying letter names & sounds
- ✓ VC & CVC blending, building & manipulating, letter formation, spelling & reading in context
- ✓ phonemic awareness activities (Heggerty, rhyming, etc.)

WEEK 22
- ✓ letter names & sounds (previously taught sounds & **y, z**)
- ✓ identifying letter names & sounds
- ✓ VC & CVC blending, building & manipulating, letter formation, spelling & reading in context
- ✓ phonemic awareness activities (Heggerty, rhyming, etc.)

MARCH

WEEK 23
- ✓ letter names & sounds (previously taught sounds & **q/qu**)
- ✓ identifying letter names & sounds
- ✓ VC & CVC blending, building & manipulating, letter formation, spelling & reading in context
- ✓ phonemic awareness activities (Heggerty, rhyming, etc.)

WEEK 24
- ✓ screening week:
- ✓ recheck all fall screens *for at-risk students*
- ✓ progress monitoring

WEEK 25
- ✓ flex/review

- ✓ spring break

APRIL

WEEK 26
- ✓ review short vowel sounds e, a
- ✓ targeted review of letter sounds based on March summative assessment
- ✓ blending sounds to read words
- ✓ phonemic awareness activities
- ✓ building words/manipulating sounds
- ✓ writing graphemes & words
- ✓ printing letter formation

WEEK 27
- ✓ review short vowel sounds o, i, u
- ✓ targeted review of letter sounds based on March summative assessment
- ✓ blending sounds to read words
- ✓ phonemic awareness activities
- ✓ building words/manipulating sounds
- ✓ writing graphemes & words
- ✓ printing letter formation

WEEK 28
- ✓ practice & reinforce all letter sounds & blending skills
- ✓ blending sounds to read words
- ✓ phonemic awareness activities
- ✓ building words/manipulating sounds
- ✓ writing graphemes & words
- ✓ printing letter formation

WEEK 29
- ✓ practice & reinforce all letter sounds & blending skills
- ✓ blending sounds to read words
- ✓ phonemic awareness activities
- ✓ building words/manipulating sounds
- ✓ writing graphemes & words
- ✓ printing letter formation
- ✓ introduce tricky words, set 1 (**the, of**)

MAY

WEEK 30
- ✓ practice & reinforce all letter sounds & blending skills
- ✓ blending sounds to read words
- ✓ phonemic awareness activities
- ✓ building words/manipulating sounds
- ✓ writing graphemes & words
- ✓ printing letter formation
- ✓ introduce tricky words set 1 (previously taught + **as, has**)

WEEK 31
- ✓ practice & reinforce all letter sounds & blending skills
- ✓ blending sounds to read words
- ✓ phonemic awareness activities
- ✓ building words/manipulating sounds
- ✓ writing graphemes & words
- ✓ printing letter formation
- ✓ introduce tricky words set 1 (previously taught + **is, his**)

WEEK 32
- ✓ practice & reinforce all letter sounds & blending skills
- ✓ blending sounds to read words
- ✓ phonemic awareness activities
- ✓ building words/manipulating sounds
- ✓ writing graphemes & words
- ✓ printing letter formation
- ✓ introduce tricky words set 1 (previously taught + **was**)

WEEK 33
- ✓ practice & reinforce all letter sounds & blending skills
- ✓ blending sounds to read words
- ✓ phonemic awareness activities
- ✓ building words/manipulating sounds
- ✓ writing graphemes & words
- ✓ printing letter formation
- ✓ introduce tricky words set 1 (previously taught + **to, do**)

WEEK 34	WEEK 35	WEEK 36	WEEK 37
✓ screening week: ✓ phonemic awareness screen ✓ uppercase & lowercase letter names ✓ letter sounds ✓ decoding screen (VC & CVC words)	✓ play with letters, sounds, words ✓ targeted review of concepts based on assessments	✓ play with letters, sounds, words ✓ targeted review of concepts based on assessments	✓ play with letters, sounds, words ✓ targeted review of concepts based on assessments

JUNE

Weekly Concept Pages with Full Lesson Plans in Weeks 4 and 5

Kindergarten Weeks 1–3 Target Concept: early literacy exploration

(see blueprint, page 71)

Description of Concept

The first few weeks of kindergarten are focused on emotional well-being; building connections, relationships, and trust; learning routines; and understanding what it is like to be at school. Specific targeted instruction can begin with a focus on introducing phonological awareness activities, concepts of print, and discovering letters/sounds/words in the school and classroom environment.

Week 3: Screening of students' early literacy skills is also an important part of the beginning of kindergarten. The following screens are recommended in the fall of kindergarten:

- oral language checklist
- concepts of print
- phonemic awareness screen

Kindergarten Week 4 Target Concept: "a," "s," "t"

(see blueprint, page 71)

Description of Concept

Letter names: **a, s, t**
Letter sounds: **/ă/, /s/, /t/**

Teaching letters and sounds is cumulative work; lessons and word lists include only the letter sounds that have been explicitly taught. When introducing more than one sound in a week, you may introduce them at the same time or individually.

Including a kinesthetic movement and key word to go with each sound helps children to retain the sounds and commit them to memory.

Explicit teaching and practice of letter formation is an important part of introducing new letter names and sounds.

Keep in mind that the lesson plan below is intended to be taught over a 5-day span.

Lesson Plan

Target Concepts: a, s, t
1	**Warm-up:** 1–5 minutes Review: books and stories are made up of words, words are made up of letters. "When you read books and words, you start at the left and move to the right (demonstrate on the board, chart paper, or with a book)."

2	**Introduce new concepts (I Do):** 5 minutes "We will begin learning some letter names and sounds so that we can learn to read." A fun and engaging way to begin introducing letters and sounds to children is to create a tray (bag or box) of items that all start with the sound of the new letter being introduced. The tray can be covered with a cloth to create curiosity. The teacher takes off the cloth and shows each item while emphasizing their beginning sound. Students guess what the new sound is (and its corresponding letter). If introducing all three letters at once, you could have three or more items for each sound, but only introduce items with one sound at a time, and have students guess the sound/letter and then move to the next set of items. Once all new sounds and letters have been determined, show students these letters on the board/chart paper/poster or "unveil" them on a sound wall display if you have one.
3	**Phonological awareness:** 3 minutes Start with the letter "a" and its sound /ă/. Repeat the following quick activity with "s" and "t." 1. "The /ă/ sound is made by the letter "a." (Teacher may show a kinesthetic movement of their choice to represent this sound.)" Students repeat the sound after the teacher and copy the movement to go with the sound. Repeat several times, asking for a couple of students to demonstrate. Ask students to notice the position of their mouth (mirrors can be used), whether it is a voiced sound, and how the air flows when they say the letter. Our key word for the letter "a" and sound /ă/ is "apple." The word "apple" starts with /ă/. 2. "Some other words that start with this sound are: 'ant,' 'alligator.'" (Emphasizing the /ă/ sound.) Can you hear the sound /ă/ at the beginning of these words?" (Give more examples as needed.) 3. "I'm going to say some words that start with the sound /ă/ and some that don't; every time you hear that sound, show me the /ă/ movement." (Mix words that start with /ă/ with words that start with other sounds (not other vowel sounds.) 4. "Can you think of any words that start with the sound /ă/?" *Later in the week when students have a good grasp of these sounds, repeat some of these phonological awareness activities but choose words where the target sound is found in the middle and/or ending sounds in words. If you have a letter song, introduce it here. Possible follow-up activities for practice and reinforcement: – giant flash card activities – "I spy with my little eye, something that starts with /ă/, /s/, or /t/." – Elkonin box activities – rhyming words, poems, and songs

4	**Teacher-led guided practice with new concept (WE Do):** 10–15 minutes 1. Find the picture that matches the sound. Start with the sound /ă/ and the letter "a." Repeat the activity with "s" and "t." Display several objects or pictures of things that start with the sound /ă/ and things that do not. Together, find the objects or pictures that start with the sound /ă/ and circle/identify them. Ask for volunteers to come up and identify the correct pictures/items. 2. Once all three letters have been introduced, begin the blending process. "When we put sounds together, they make words." Put a VC word on the board (see word list below — real and nonsense words). Demonstrate saying and blending sounds to read the word, modeling additive blending. Blend and read several more VC and CVC words. Decide together if each word is a real word or a nonsense word.

5	**Extended independent practice activities to apply new concept (YOU Do):** 15–20 minutes
	Sound/picture sort:
	Students are given a sorting sheet with the letters "a," "s," and "t" written at the top, in three separate columns, along with a separate sheet of pictures for students to cut out. Students cut and sort the pictures by their initial sound (e.g., "alligator" starts with /ă/, "snake" starts with /s/, "turtle" starts with /t/) — but do not ask students to glue the pictures down **yet**. Students may work in pairs or as individuals. After students have independently attempted the sort, review the correct way to sort the sounds/pictures and have students glue them down in the correct column.
	    If students are still learning to use scissors, you can either precut the shapes or provide them with cards or small items to sort.
	
	Possible follow-up activities for practice and reinforcement:
	  – flash card sorts
	  – paper/pencil activities
	  – alphabet arcs. Sing the alphabet song and have students place the letters "a," "s," and "t" in the correct place along the arc.

6	**Decoding with text (YOU Do):** 10–15 minutes
	The teacher projects a list of words onto the whiteboard (or one word at a time using a PowerPoint). Focusing on one word at a time, the teacher highlights a sound in each word. If the word is "sat," the teacher may ask "Where is the /ă/?" Students respond that it is in the middle of the word. Continue to practice identifying target sounds in each of the words and then blending the sounds to read each word.
	    Once students become proficient with the activity, they can take turns coming up to the board and circling or underlining the target sound.
	Ask for volunteers to use additive or continuous blending to read the word.
	
	Possible additional activities for practice and reinforcement:
	  – word cards with the new words
	  – shared reading using blending boards with "a" in the first ring and "s" and "t" in the second
	  – shared reading of decodable books that have one word and the corresponding picture (e.g., "mat," "sat").

7	**Encoding**: 15–20 minutes
	Teach students the correct letter formation of "a," "s," "t." Start with sky writing so students become familiar with the correct formation of the letter. Once students have had sufficient practice, move to dry erase pens (using paper templates in plastic sheet protectors) and then progress to pencil and paper.
	
	    Later in the week, when students have a solid grasp of these sounds, phoneme-to-grapheme mapping may be introduced (I Do — We Do — You Do) to practice breaking VC and CVC words into their individual sounds to write the words.
	
	Additional activities for practice and reinforcement:
	  – additional sky writing
	  – finger tracing on uppercase and lowercase letters (on paper or felt/ textured letters)
	  – tracing laminated letters with a dry erase pen
	  – creating letters in sand with a tool or your finger
	  – table writing — this can be done with either fingers or a dry erase pen on the desk or tabletop
	  – using modeling clay, sensory bags (gel with glitter), small objects (pebbles, sticks, counters), pipe cleaners, Wikki Stix, etc., to create letter shapes
	  – letter tiles to build words

8	**Intervention**: Extra individual or small-group review and practice may be required for some students who are struggling to retain the letter names and sounds. Sound production using mirrors, flash cards, more picture-sound matching, and word lists can be practiced in a small group with the teacher or a support adult, and/or be sent home for parents to practice with their children.
9	**Extending**: Students who are already readers should have access to decodable books in the classroom to practice blending sounds to decode and read for meaning.

Week 4 Word Lists: a, s, t

Word List for Decoding Practice	
Real Words	**Nonsense Words**
at ta sat tat	sa tas
Word Chain a, at, ta, sa, sat, tat, tas	

Kindergarten Week 5 Target Concept: "p," "n"

(see blueprint, page 71)

Description of Concept
Letter names: **p, n**
Letter sounds: /**p**/, /**n**/

All activities should focus on the target concepts while including and referring to previously taught concepts. For example, word lists include only words with letters and sounds that students have been explicitly taught. When introducing more than one sound in a week, you may introduce them both at the same time, or introduce them and practice them separately to begin with.

Including a kinesthetic movement and key word to go with each sound helps children to retain the sounds and commit them to memory. Explicit teaching and practice of letter formation is an important part of introducing new letter names and sounds.

Keep in mind that the lesson plan below is intended to be taught over a 5-day span.

Lesson Plan

	Target Concepts: previously taught skills + p, n
1	**Warm-up:** 1–5 minutes Review: letter names and sounds for /ă/, /s/, and /t/, showing the letters and asking for the letter sound and the letter name. Have students do the kinesthetic movement to go with each sound. Review how to blend sounds to read VC and CVC words.
2	**Introduce new concepts (I Do):** 5 minutes "This week we will learn two new letters and sounds." Repeat the tray and hidden items activity from week 4 with items that begin with "p" and "n." Once the new sounds and letters have been determined, show students these letters on the board/chart paper/poster or "unveil" them on a sound wall display if you have one.
3	**Phonological awareness:** 3 minutes Start with the letter "p" and sound /p/. Repeat the following quick activity with letter "n" and its sound /n/. 1. "The sound /p/ is made by the letter 'p.'" (Show a kinesthetic movement to represent this sound.) Students repeat the sound after the teacher and copy the movement to go with the sound. Repeat several times, asking for a few students to demonstrate. Ask students to notice the position of their mouth, whether it is a voiced sound, and how the air flows when they say the letter. "Our key word for the letter 'p' is 'pig.' The word pig starts with /p/." 2. "Other words that start with this sound are: 'puppy,' 'pumpkin.'" (Emphasizing the /p/ sound.) "Can you hear the sound /p/ at the beginning of these words?" (Provide more examples as needed.) 3. "I'm going to say some words that start with the sound /p/ and some that don't. Every time you hear that sound, show me the /p/ movement." (Mix words that start with /p/ with words that start with other sounds.)

4. "Can you think of any words that start with the sound /p/?"

*Later in the week, when students have a good grasp of these sounds, repeat some of these phonological awareness activities using words where the targeted sound occurs in the middle and/or end of the word.
If you have a letter song, introduce it here.

Possible additional activities for practice and reinforcement:
  – giant flash card games
  – "I spy with my little eye, something that starts with 'p' or 'n.'"
  – Elkonin box activities
  – rhyming words, poems, and songs

4	**Teacher-led guided practice with new concept (WE Do):** 10–15 minutes
	
	1. Find the picture that matches the sound.
	Start with the letter "p" and sound /p/. Repeat the activity with "n."
	Display several pictures, some that start with the sound /p/ and some that do not. Together, find the pictures that start with the sound /p/ and circle/identify them. Ask for volunteers to come up and identify pictures.
	2. "When we put sounds together, they make words."
	Put one word or a short list of VC and CVC words on the board (see word list below). Demonstrate saying and blending these sounds using additive or continuous blending. Blend and read the remaining words together.
	
	Possible additional activities for practice and reinforcement:
	  – nonsense words
	  – begin a classroom chart of things that start with the new letters this week; students share ideas of things they think of and contribute to the chart

5	**Extended independent practice activities to apply new concept (YOU Do):** 15–20 minutes
	Sound/picture sort:
	Students are given a sorting sheet with the sounds /p/ and /n/ written at the top and a separate sheet of pictures to cut out. Students cut out and sort the pictures by initial sound (e.g., "pan" starts with /p/ and "net" starts with /n/) — but do not have students glue them down **yet**. Students may work in pairs or as individuals. After students have independently sorted the pictures, review the correct way to sort the sounds, with students correcting any that need to be adjusted before gluing them down in the correct column.
	
	Possible follow-up activities for practice and reinforcement:
	  – kinesthetic and play-based activities (e.g., making letters out of modeling clay/sticks/pebbles/beads/pipe cleaners/loose parts)
	  – paper/pencil activities

6	**Decoding with text (YOU Do):** 10–15 minutes The teacher projects a list of words onto the whiteboard (or one word at a time through a PowerPoint). The teacher focuses on one word at a time, highlighting one sound in each word. If the word is "pan," the teacher may ask, "Where is the /n/?" Students respond that it is at the end of the word. Continue to practice identifying target sounds in each of the words and then blending the sounds to read.

	Once students become proficient with the activity, they can take turns coming up and circling or underlining the target sound.
	Ask for volunteers to use additive or continuous blending to read the word. (Words in word lists include only explicitly taught letter sounds.)
	Possible follow-up activities for practice and reinforcement: – fluency phrases of one or two words – shared reading of decodable one-word books
7	**Encoding**: 15–20 minutes Students are explicitly taught the correct letter formation of "p" and "n." Start with sky writing so students become familiar with the correct formation of the letter. Once students have had sufficient practice, move to dry erase pens (using paper templates in plastic sheet protectors) and then progress to pencil and paper. **Building words with letter tiles** Students can use paper or magnetic letter tiles to build words using the letters "a," "s," "t," "p," and "n" (see word list below). Start by building one word and then changing one sound to make a new word using explicitly taught sounds. Possible follow-up activities for practice and reinforcement: – additional sky writing – painting letters with brushes, finger painting, drawing in sand or outside in the dirt – letter tiles – phoneme-to-grapheme mapping – spelling word/phrase dictation
8	**Intervention**: Extra individual or small-group review and practice may be required for students who are struggling to retain letter names and sounds. Sound production using mirrors, flash cards, more picture-sound matching, and word lists could be practiced in a small group with the teacher or a support adult and/or be sent home for parents to practice with their children.
9	**Extending**: Students who are already readers should have access to decodable books in the classroom to practice blending sounds and reading for meaning.

Week 5 Word Lists: a, s, t, **p, n**

Word Lists for Decoding and Encoding Activities	
Real Words	**Nonsense Words**
an, ap nap, pat sap, pan nan, tap tan	san tas nat sas
Word Chain pan, tan, tap, nap, sap, sat, pat, nat	

Kindergarten Week 6 Target Concept: "i"
(see blueprint, page 71)

Description of Concept
Letter name: **i**
Letter sound: /ĭ/
When introducing the letter and sound for "i," teach only the short vowel /ĭ/ sound at this time. "I" says /ĭ/, as in "itch." Continue to encourage students to focus on the mouth position, air flow, and vocalization as each sound is introduced so they build a clear understanding of how each sound is made.
When introducing a new vowel, previously introduced vowels are omitted so that students can focus solely on the new vowel sound with the consonants that have been taught. The following week, previously taught vowels are added back into the progression and are practiced with previously introduced consonants.

Week 6 Word Lists: i, s, t, p, n

Word Lists for Decoding and Encoding Activities		
Real Words		**Nonsense Words**
in	sin	ip
it	tin	nin
nip	sit	nis
pit	nit	tis (not tiz)
sip	sis	
pin	pip	
tip		
Word Chain		
it, in, pin, tin, tip, nip, sip, sit, pit, pip		

Kindergarten Week 7 Target Concept: review "a," "i," "s," "t," "p," "n"
(see blueprint, page 71)

Description of Concept
Letter names: a, i, s, t, p, n
Letter sounds: /ă/, /ĭ/, /s/, /t/, /p/, /n/
Review and practice all previously introduced letter names and sounds, including short vowels /ă/ and /ĭ/.
Including kinesthetic movements to go with each sound helps children to retain the sounds and commit them to memory. Continue to practice letter formation and correct letter sounds.

Teaching Tip:
As a review of previous letters and sounds, start an alphabet book with your students, with each page dedicated to one letter (they do not need to go in sequential alphabetical order, but they can). Students write the uppercase and lowercase letter on the page and then draw or glue in pictures of items that start with that letter. Work in alphabet books as review, not when introducing letters for the first time. Students can go back and add additional pictures over the course of the school year.

Week 7 Word Lists: a, i, s, t, p, n

Word Lists for Decoding and Encoding Activities			
Real Words			**Nonsense Words**
in	an	pat	san
at	it	sip	nin
nip	nap	pin	nat
pit	tip	tan	sas
sap	sit	sin	nis
pan	sat	tap	
nan	tin	nit	
pip	sis		
Word Chain			
an, at, it, in, pin, pan, tan, tin, tip, tap, nap, nip, sip, sap, sat, sit, pit, pat			

Kindergarten Week 8 Target Concept: "c," "d"

(see blueprint, page 71)

Description of Concept

Letter names: **c, d**

Letter sounds: **/k/, /d/**

All activities should focus on the current target concepts while including and referring to those previously taught.

When introducing more than one sound in a week, you may introduce them both at the same time, or introduce them and practice them separately to begin with. Including a kinesthetic movement to go with each sound helps children to retain the sounds and commit them to memory. Explicit teaching and practice of letter formation is an important part of introducing new letter names and sounds.

Week 8 Word Lists: a, i, s, t, p, n, **c, d**

Word Lists for Decoding and Encoding Activities				
Real Words				**Nonsense Words**
cat	dad	pic	ad	cas
cap	dip	tic	pad	dat
can	din	tac	tad	das
cad	did	sac	sad	dap
			and	dit
				nid
				pid
Word Chain				
at, cat, cap, can, cad, dad, did, dip, pip, pic, pit, pat, sat, sac				

Kindergarten Week 9 Target Concept: "o"

(see blueprint, page 71)

Description of Concept

Letter name: **o**

Letter sound: /ŏ/

When introducing the letter and sound for "o," teach only the short vowel /ŏ/ sound at this time. "O" says /ŏ/, as in "off."

   When introducing a new vowel, previously introduced vowels are omitted so that students can focus solely on the new vowel sound with the consonants that have been taught. The following week, previously taught vowels are added back into the progression and are practiced with previously introduced consonants.

Week 9 Word Lists: o, s, t, p, n, c, d

Word Lists for Decoding and Encoding Activities			
Real Words			**Nonsense Words**
on	not	dot	pon
sop	non	don	pos
sod	nod	doc	poc
top	cot	dop	nos
ton	cop	opt	nop
tod	con	ops	dos
tot	cob		dod
pot	cod		
pop	com		
pod			
Word Chain			
on, non, not, pot, pop, top, cop, cod, cot, dot, tot			

Kindergarten Week 10 Target Concept: review "o," "a," "i," "s," "t," "p," "n," "c," "d"

(see blueprint, page 71)

Description of Concept

Letter names: o, a, i, s, t, p, n, c, d

Letter sounds: /ŏ/, /ă/, /ĭ/, /s/, /t/, /p/, /n/, /k/, /d/

Review and practice all introduced letter names and sounds, including short vowels /ŏ/, /ă/, and /ĭ/.

Include kinesthetic movements to go with each sound. Continue to practice letter formation.

Week 10 Word Lists: o, a, i, s, t, p, n, c, d

Word Lists for Decoding and Encoding Activities						
Real Words					**Nonsense Words**	
in	sad	tot	nap	dip	tam	nop
it	sop	pit	not	din	tas	nic
at	sod	pin	cat	did	tid	dit
an	tip	pic	cap	dad	pid	dat
on	tin	pat	can	dot	nin	dac
sit	tic	pan	cad	doc	nid	dod
sip	tac	pad	cot	dop	nat	cas
sis	tan	pot	cop		nis	
sat	tap	pop	con			
sac	tad	pod	cod			
sap	top	nip				
Word Chain						
in, an, on, non, not, pot, pit, sit, sat, pat, cat, cot, dot, tot, top, cop, pop, sop, sip, tip, dip, did, dad, tad, tan, tin						

Kindergarten Week 11 Target Concept: "g," "m"

(see blueprint, page 71)

Description of Concept
Letter names: **g, m**
Letter sounds: **/g/, /m/**
When introducing the letter and sound for "g," teach only the hard /g/ sound at this time. "G" says /g/, as in "goat."

Week 11 Word Lists: o, a, i, s, t, p, n, c, d, **g, m**

Word Lists for Decoding and Encoding Activities				
Real Words				**Nonsense Words**
gas	mop	dog	Tom	gac
gap	mod	dig	pom	gat
got	mog	nag	nom	gop
god	mom	pig	com	gos
gig	mat	tog	Sam	gog
gag	map	tag	Pam	mon
	man	sag	cam	mip
	mac	cog	dam	mig
	mad			mim
	mag			
	mam			
	min			
	mid			
Word Chain				
got, god, mod, mop, mom, mam, man, map, gap, gas, gag, mag, mat, mad, mid, did, dig, dog				

Kindergarten Week 12 Target Concept: "e"

(see blueprint, page 71)

Description of Concept

Letter name: **e**

Letter sound: /ĕ/

When introducing the letter and sound for "e," teach only the short vowel /ĕ/ sound at this time. "E" says /ĕ/, as in "elephant."

Remember: when introducing a new vowel, previously introduced vowels are omitted so that students can focus solely on the new vowel sound with the consonants that have been taught. The following week, previously taught vowels are added back into the progression and are practiced with previously introduced consonants.

Teaching Tip:

We know a teacher who introduced the letter "e" with a practical joke. The kindergarten students and their teacher visited several classrooms, arriving with a baking dish covered with a tea towel. The teacher said the kindergarten class had made brownies to share. This was exciting news for the class that was being visited. The teacher then removed the tea towel to reveal a pan full of the letter "e" made of brown paper! They presented a brown "e" to each class and left.

Week 12 Word Lists: e, s, t, p, n, c, d, g, m

Word Lists for Decoding and Encoding Activities			
Real Words		**Nonsense Words**	
set	met	sep	deg
pet	med	tem	gep
pen	Meg	neg	ged
peg	men	mep	
net	den	pem	
ten	end	des	
get			
Word Chain			
set, pet, pen, peg, Meg, men, den, ten, Ted, med, met, get, net			

Kindergarten Week 13 Target Concept: review "e," "o," "a," "i," "s," "t," "p," "n," "c," "d," "g," "m"

(see blueprint, page 72)

Description of Concept

Letter names: e, o, a, i, s, t, p, n, c, d, g, m

Letter sounds: /ĕ/, /ŏ/, /ă/, /ĭ/, /s/, /t/, /p/, /n/, /k/, /d/, /g/, /m/

Review and practice all introduced letter names and sounds, including short vowels /ĕ/, /ŏ/, /ă/, and /ĭ/.

Continue to practice letter formation.

Week 13 Word Lists: e, o, a, i, s, t, p, n, c, d, g, m

Word Lists for Decoding and Encoding Activities								
Real Words							**Nonsense Words**	
it	sin	tin	Pam	not	dip	gas	sen	mep
in	sit	tan	pad	net	din	gig	sid	mec
at	sip	ten	pod	nag	den	god	tep	cag
an	sim	tad	pig	mat	dim	cat	pim	dag
am	sad	tag	peg	met	dam	cot	poc	dac
ad	sod	tot	pic	mam	dig	cap	nos	dit
on	sag	pit	pip	mom	dog	cop	nes	gom
sit	sac	pat	pop	mid	did	con	nim	gog
sat	sec	pot	pep	mad	dad	can	neg	mag
set	sis	pet	nip	mod	got	cam		
sip	tip	pin	nap	med	get	com		
sap	tap	pan	nod	dot	gap	cod		
sop	top	pen	non		gag	cad		
						cog		

Word Chain
dog, dig, dip, dim, sim, sit, sat, set, pet, pat, pan, pin, min, mid, mad, man, men, ten, tin, tan, tag, gag, gas, gap, cap, cop, cot, pot, tot, not, net, get, got

Kindergarten Week 14 Target Concept: review/flex week
(see blueprint, page 72)

Description of Concept
With winter break approaching for most school districts, it is likely that many schools will be participating in whole school events and holiday-related activities. The week(s) before winter break are a good time to review all concepts, catch up on scheduled concepts that have not yet been taught, and/or focus on progress monitoring of target concepts that require extra instruction and practice. Continue to practice letter formation.

Week 14 Word Lists: review using previously provided word lists.

Kindergarten Week 15 Target Concept: "k," "r"
(see blueprint, page 72)

Description of Concept
Letter names: **k, r**
Letter sounds: **/k/, /r/**

Mini Lesson — when to use "c" or "k" when spelling the /k/ sound: The letter "k" makes the same sound as a hard "c"; they both say /k/. This is easy for students to remember while reading, but when it comes to spelling, students often ask, "Is it a 'c' or a 'k'?" A rule of thumb is that, generally, "c" comes before "a," "o," and "u", while "k" comes before "i" and "e." See the graphic below regarding when to use "c" or "k."

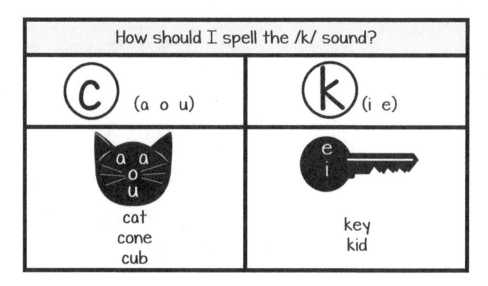

Week 15 Word Lists: e, o, a, i, s, t, p, n, c, d, g, m, **k, r**

Word Lists for Decoding and Encoding Activities					
Real Words				**Nonsense Words**	
kit	rep	rap	rid	kes	res
kin	red	ran	rig	kep	ret
kip	reg	ram		kos	rop
kim	rec	rad		kas	ras
kid	rot	rag		kad	rin
Ken	rod	rip		kig	
keg	rat	rim			
Word Chains red, reg, keg, Ken, kin, kip, rip, rap, rad rim, kim, kit, kid, rid					

Kindergarten Week 16 Target Concept: "u"

(see blueprint, page 72)

Description of Concept
Letter name: **u**
Letter sound: /ŭ/
When introducing the letter and sound for "u," teach only the short vowel /ŭ/ sound at this time. "U" says /ŭ/, as in "up."

Week 16 Word Lists: u, s, t, p, n, c, d, g, m, k, r

Word Lists for Decoding and Encoding Activities							
Real Words				**Nonsense Words**			
us	sus	dug	rut	ut	sut	mup	cun
up	tug	dud	run	ud	sug	mun	cuk
um	nun	gut	rum	ug	tup	dut	kun
pun	nut	gup	rug	uk	tud	dus	kug
pug	num	gun			pum	gud	rud
pup	mum	gum			pud	gug	ruk
sum	mud	cup			nug		
sun	mug	cut			nuk		

Word Chain
us, up, cup, pup, pug, dug, dud, mud, mug, rug, run, sun, gun, gum, gut, cut, rut

Kindergarten Week 17 Target Concept: review "a," "e," "o," "e," "u" with all consonants taught so far

(see blueprint, page 72)

Description of Concept

Letter names: a, i, o, e, u, s, t, p, n, c, d, g, m, k, r

Letter sounds: /ă/, /ĭ/, /ŏ/, /ĕ/, /ŭ/

Vowel sounds are the most challenging sounds for children to learn and remember. It is important to continually review and emphasize short vowel sounds, including focusing on how the sound is produced (mouth formation, vocalization, and air flow). Continue to practice letter formation.

Week 17 Word Lists: a, i, o, e, u, s, t, p, n, c, d, g, m, k, r

Word Lists for Decoding and Encoding Activities											

Real Words

a			i		o		u		e	
at	tad	dad	it	dip	on	cot	us	mum	Ed	get
an	tag	dam	in	dim	sop	cop	up	mud	set	Ken
am	tac	cat	sit	did	sod	con	um	mug	ten	red
ad	pat	cap	sip	din	top	cod	sun	dud	pet	rep
sat	pan	can	tip	dig	mop	cog	sum	dug	pen	
sap	pad	cam	tin	gig	mom	rot	sus	gut	peg	
sad	nap	rat	pit	kit	mod		tug	gun	net	
sag	nag	ran	pin	kin	dot		pug	gum	met	
sac	mat	ram	pig	rip	don		pun	cup	med	
tap	mam	rap	nip	rim	dog		pup	cut	men	
tan	man	rad	min	rid	got		nut	rut	den	
	mad		mid	rig			nun	run		

Nonsense Words

a	i	o	u	e						
ap	pim	op	sug	tep						
saf	nis	tos	tud	pem						
mak	dis	poc	dut	mek						
gan	gik	nop	gud	dep						
kal	rin	kom	cuk	kes						
ras		gog		dem						
		rog		reg						
				rem						

Word Chains

an, at, it, in, on, op, up, us

kit, kid, did, dad, pad, mad, med, red, rid, rod, god, got, gut, nut, net, pet, pot, pod, mod, mom, mum, mug, rug, rut, run, sun

nap, nip, tip, top, cop, cup, cap, map, mop, sop, sip, sit, set, met, mat, rat, rad, red, rod, mod, mud

Kindergarten Week 18 Target Concept: "h," "b" (+ mini lesson on "b" vs. "d")

(see blueprint, page 72)

Description of Concept

Letter names: **h, b**

Letter sounds: **/h/, /b/**

All activities should focus on the current target concept while including and referring to previously taught skills.

Mini Lesson: Avoiding Confusion with "b" and "d"

It is not uncommon for students to mix up "b" and "d" since they are reversed symbols. Some of the strategies we like to use to address this confusion are:

- The "b" hand. Place an elastic or rubber bracelet on a student's left hand and have them make a fist with their pointer finger up, forming a letter "b." This is their "b" hand. Students can refer to the elastic band when they need support with "b" and "d." Many students only require the elastic band for a few days before the concept becomes imbedded. Some educators advocate for a "b" and a "d" hand, but this is not necessary and requires more cognitive work. A simple "b" hand will support keeping these two tricky letters straight.
- Students make fists with both hands, and put up their thumbs to make the shape of a bed.

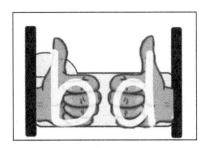

- "C" comes before "d" in the alphabet, so students must go through "c" to get to "d." When writing, they can write the "c" and add the stick for the "d."
- Little "b" fits inside of big "B" but little "d" does not fit inside of big D.

B   dD

Week 18 Word Lists: a, i, o, u, e, s, t, p, n, c, d, g, m, k, r, **h, b**

Word Lists for Decoding and Encoding Activities						
Real Words					**Nonsense Words**	
hat	hot	bat	bid	bum	han	bap
had	hop	ban	big	bus	hig	bis
ham	hog	bam	bop	bud	hom	bok
hag	hut	bad	bon	bug	hun	bup
hit	hum	bag	bod	bet	heg	bem
hip	hug	bit	bog	ben		
him	hen	bin	but	bed		
hid	hem		bun	beg		

Word Chain
hid, had, bad, bid, bud, bug, hug, hog, bog, bot, hot, hit, hut, but, bet, bed, bod, bop, hop, hip, him, hem, hen, ben, ban, bag, hag

Kindergarten Week 19 Target Concept: "f," "l"
(see blueprint, page 72)

Description of Concept
Letter names: **f, l**
Letter sounds: **/f/, /l/**

All activities should focus on the current target concept while including and referring to previously taught skills.

Week 19 Word Lists: a, i, o, u, e, s, t, p, n, c, d, g, m, k, r, h, b, **f, l**

Word Lists for Decoding and Encoding Activities						
Real Words					**Nonsense Words**	
fat	fog	lap	lop	pal	fas	lan
fan	fob	lad	log	gal	fid	lig
fad	fun	lag	lob	til	fot	lod
fab	fed	lab	lug	nil	fub	lup
fit	if	lit	let		fep	lek
fin		lip	led		fem	
fig		lid	leg			
fib		lib				
		lot				
Word Chain						
fem, fam, fad, lad, lab, lap, lip, lit, fit, fig, fog, log, lug, leg, let, led, fed, fen, fan, fun						

Kindergarten Week 20 Target Concept: "j," "v"

(see blueprint, page 72)

Description of Concept

Letter names: **j, v**

Letter sounds: **/j/, /v/**

All activities should focus on the current target concept while including and referring to previously taught skills.

Week 20 Word Lists: a, i, o, u, e, s, t, p, n, c, d, g, m, k, r, h, b, f, l, **j, v**

Word Lists for Decoding and Encoding Activities					
Real Words			**Nonsense Words**		
jam	jog	vat	von	jaf	vap
jag	job	van	vol	jip	vib
jab	jut	vac	vel	jod	vog
Jan	jug	Val	vum	jun	vun
Jim	jet	vet	vit	jes	ves
jig	Jen	vin			vid
jib		vim			
jot					
Jon					
Word Chain					
jig, jog, jug, jut, jet, vet, vat, van, Jan, jab, Jim, vim, vid, vin, von, Jon, job, jab, jam					

Heather was doing a letters and sounds progress monitoring check with a student who was struggling to remember all of her sounds. When she came to "f," she paused and put her finger on her chin. "I know it's the start of a swear," she explained. Hoping the student could retrieve the sound, Heather agreed that it did indeed come at the beginning of a swear word. Fortunately, or unfortunately, the student was not able to produce the sound.

Kindergarten Week 21 Target Concept: "w," "x"

(see blueprint, page 72)

Description of Concept
Letter names: **w, x**
Letter sounds: **/w/, /ks/**
The letter "x" is the only letter that makes two sounds, /ks/, in English, and is mapped across two boxes as shown below.
Sample phoneme-to-grapheme mapping of "x":

Week 21 Word Lists: a, i, o, u, e, s, t, p, n, c, d, g, m, k, r, h, b, f, l, j, v, **w, x**

Word Lists for Decoding and Encoding Activities							
Real Words						**Nonsense Words**	
wad	Wes	ax	fax	fix	tux	wab	rax
wag	wet	ox	lax	pox	lux	wiv	hix
wit	wed	ex	six	box	Mex	wof	mox
win	web	sax	pix	fox	Rex	wug	nux
wig		tax	nix	lox	hex	wem	pex
		max	mix		vex		tox
		Dax					vax
							vox
Word Chains							
wag, wig, win, wit, wet, wed, web							
ex, ox, ax, max, tax, fax, fix, six, mix, Mex, Rex, hex, vex, vax, sax, lax, lux, tux, lox,							
fox, box							

Kindergarten Week 22 Target Concept: "y," "z"

(see blueprint, page 72)

Description of Concept
Letter names: **y, z**
Letter sounds: **/y/, /z/**
At this time, the letter "y" is taught only as a consonant at the beginning of words, "y" says /y/ as in "yes." The "many jobs of **y**" teaches other ways to use "y" and lessons are provided in Grade 2 Weeks 21 and 22.

Week 22 Word Lists: a, i, o, u, e, s, t, p, n, c, d, g, m, k, r, h, b, f, l, j, v, w, x, **y, z**

Word Lists for Decoding and Encoding Activities							
Real Words					**Nonsense Words**		
yap	yup	zap	zen	biz	ya	zot	paz
yam	yum	zag	zed		yad	zaz	kiz
yak	yes	zig			yav	zik	roz
yip	yet	zit			yif	zof	nuz
yin	yen	zip			yog	zum	wez
					yul	zev	wiz
					yex	zin	

Word Chains
zag, zap, yap, yip, zip, zig, zit, zin, yin, yen, yep, yet, yes
yak, yam, yum, yup, yip, zip, zig, zag, zap, yap, yep, yes, yet

Kindergarten Week 23 Target Concept: review + "q," "qu"

(see blueprint, page 73)

Description of Concept
Letter name: **q**
Letter sound: **/kw/**
The letter "q" is never without "u" in English words. Tell students that "q" and "u" are best friends, and they never want to be apart from each other. The blend of "qu" says /kw/. Because /kw/ is two sounds blended together, it is mapped over two sound boxes (see sample below). Continue to teach and practice letter formation when introducing new letter names and sounds.
Sample phoneme-to-grapheme mapping of "qu":

q u	i	t	

Teacher Knowledge: In the "qu" blend, "u" is considered a consonant and two sounds are blended to say /kw/. This is revisited again in Grade 1 Week 8, when digraphs are introduced.

Week 23 Word Lists: a, i, o, u, e, s, t, p, n, c, d, g, m, k, r, h, b, f, l, j, v, w, x, y, z, **q/qu**

Word Lists for Decoding and Encoding Activities				
Real Words		**Nonsense Words**		
quit	quip	quab	quif	quet
quick	quid	quan	quat	quen
quiz	Quin	quap	quop	quem
quack		quaf	quob	quag
		quib	quok	

Word Chain
quag, quat, quit, quiz, quid, quip

Kindergarten Week 24 Target Concept: screening week

(see blueprint, page 73)

Description of Concept

This week is intentionally scheduled time to screen your students in order to inform your instruction and groupings. The following screens are recommended in midyear of kindergarten:

- recheck all fall screens *for at-risk students*
- progress monitoring

Kindergarten Week 25 Target Concept: flex/review week

(see blueprint, page 73)

Description of Concept

With spring break approaching for most school districts, it is likely that many schools will be wrapping up recent concepts. The week(s) before spring break are a good time to review all concepts, catch up on scheduled concepts that have not yet been taught, and/or focus on progress monitoring to target skills that require extra instruction and practice. Continue to practice letter formation and correct letter sounds.

Letter names taught: a, i, o, e, u, s, t, p, n, c, d, g, m, k, r, h, b, f, l, j, v, w, x, y, z, qu
Letter sounds taught: /ă/, /ĭ/, /ŏ/, /ĕ/, /ŭ/, /s/, /t/, /p/, /n/, /k/, /d/, /g/, /m/, /k/, /r/, /h/, /b/, /f/, /l/, /j/, /v/, /w/, /ks/, /y/, /z/, /kw/

Weeks 25 Word Lists: use previously provided word lists for target concepts.

Kindergarten Week 26 Target Concept: review consonants + short vowels "a," "e"

(see blueprint, page 73)

Description of Concept
Letter names: a, e
Letter sounds: /ă/, /ĕ/
Ongoing emphasis should be put on review and practicing short vowel sounds, as they can be particularly challenging for students to learn, identify, and apply when decoding and encoding. Continue to practice letter formation and correct letter sounds.

Week 26 Word Lists: a, e
See word lists for short /ă/ on page 78.
See word lists for short /ĕ/ on page 86.

Kindergarten Week 27 Target Concept: review short vowels "o," "i," "u"

(see blueprint, page 73)

Description of Concept
Letter names: o, i, u
Letter sounds: /ŏ/, /ĭ/, /ŭ/

Ongoing emphasis should be put on review and practicing short vowel sounds. Continue to practice letter formation and correct letter sounds.

Weeks 27 Word Lists: o, i, u
See word lists for short /ŏ/ on page 84.
See word lists for short /ĭ/ on page 82.
See word lists for short /ŭ/ on page 89.

Weeks 28–33 Target Concept: review all letter sounds + introduce tricky words
(see blueprint, pages 73–74)

Description of Concept
Review all letter names and sounds.
The final weeks and months of kindergarten should focus on reviewing target concepts that require additional explicit instruction, review, and practice based on progress monitoring and screens. All letter names and sounds should be reviewed while addressing lagging skills. Activities should focus on decoding words in the context of reading phrases/sentences/passages/books, as well as encoding work. Continue to practice letter formation and correct letter sounds.

Week 29
Introducing Tricky Words
Tricky words are words in which only a portion of the word can be decoded (also known as temporarily irregular) since students have a limited knowledge of phonics rules at this point. With good decoding skills, students can decode many high-frequency words, but tricky words require special attention. As you begin this work, refer to the evidence-based practices listed on pages 41–43 regarding teaching tricky words.

Introduce and practice **"the"** and **"of."**

Weeks 30–32
Teacher Knowledge: Up until this point we have taught students that "s" makes the /s/ sound, but it also makes the /z/ sound in certain situations. In short Anglo-Saxon words that end in "s," the "s" says /z/ (e.g., "as," "has"). By sharing this knowledge with students early, we enable them to decode and self-correct when working with this group of tricky words. The /z/ sound for "s" will be addressed further in Grade 1 Week 26.
Concepts introduced in kindergarten: a, i, o, e, u, s, t, p, n, m, d, g, c, k, r, h, b, f, l, j, v, w, x, y, z, q/qu

Word Lists: use previously provided word lists and word chains.
Week 29 Tricky words: set 1 — **the, of**
Week 30 Tricky words: set 1 — the, of + **as, has**
Week 31 Tricky words: set 1 — the, of, as, has + **is, his**
Week 32 Tricky words: set 1 — the, of, as, has, is, his + **was**
Week 33 Tricky words: set 1 — the, of, as, has, is, his, was + **to, do**

Kindergarten Week 34 Target Concept: screening week
(see blueprint, page 74)

Description of Concept
This week is intentionally scheduled time to screen your students in order to assess progress and plan for the next school year. The following screens are recommended in the spring of kindergarten:
- phonemic awareness screen
- uppercase & lowercase letter names
- letter sounds
- VC/CVC word decoding screen

Weeks 35–37 Target Concept: targeted review of concepts based on assessments
(see blueprint, page 74)

Description of Concept
Review all letter names and sounds and tricky words set 1.
Targeted review and instruction of concepts based on progress monitoring.
Concepts introduced in kindergarten: a, i, o, e, u, s, t, p, n, m, d, g, c, k, r, h, b, f, l, j, v, w, x, y, z, q/qu, and tricky words set 1
Tricky Words: set 1 — the, of, as, has, is, his, was, to, do

Word Lists: use previously provided word lists and word chains.

Grade 1 Blueprint

The following structure begins with 4 weeks of reviewing letter names and sounds. There are many ways to address reading instruction once foundational pieces are in place (e.g., long and short vowels, consonants, and blending). We realize that the pacing of these concepts may need to be flexed according to the needs of the students you are working with. For example, in some countries or regions, the concepts covered in this grade 1 scope and sequence are taught in kindergarten. If this is true for you, move to the grade 2 blueprint. As a professional who knows your students, you will use your expertise to adjust the pacing of introducing and reviewing concepts. This may mean speeding up or slowing down the progression of instruction. Once a concept has been taught, it should be continuously reinforced and applied through conversation, practice activities, and instruction. If your grade 1 students have not had explicit instruction in kindergarten, you may need to refer to the Kindergarten Blueprint and adjust the introduction and pacing of new concepts.

We acknowledge that there will be times throughout the year when you will be referring to concepts not yet explicitly taught (e.g., vowel teams, such as /ē/ in the word "see"). It is important to make sure that foundational concepts are taught in a logical progression, and therefore, in this progression, vowel teams come after blends and digraphs. This is cumulative work, not necessarily teaching skills in isolation.

This K–3 scope and sequence is set up so that all new concepts introduced in each grade are reviewed at the start of the following year. This allows teachers to take the time required to introduce, teach, and practice each new concept. If you do not complete all the lessons in this year, rest assured that they will be covered again for your students in the fall and next year's teacher may need to take a little more time with concepts that were not completed in the grade 1 scope and sequence.

At the end of grade 1, our hope is that students will be able to read and write initial and final digraphs and blends; VCe words; inflected endings "s," "es," and "ing"; open and closed syllables; schwa; three-letter blends; and all seventy-two tricky words.

The grade 1 phonics blueprint addresses only one of the strands of the Big 5 in classroom reading instruction and assumes parallel instruction in fluency, vocabulary, phonemic awareness, and comprehension. You will notice that we have suggested the Heggerty resource (see Resources We Recommend on page 262) for the phonemic awareness activities in the grade 1 blueprints. Any structured phonemic awareness plan can be used for teaching and strengthening these skills, always with the goal of attaching sound knowledge to letters.

Grade 1 Blueprint

SEPTEMBER

WEEK 1	WEEK 2	WEEK 3	WEEK 4
✓ review letter names & sounds, emphasize practice of short vowel sounds ✓ VC & CVC blending, building & manipulating, letter formation, spelling & reading in context ✓ tricky words — review "the," "of," and "as" from set 1 ✓ phonemic awareness activities (Heggerty, rhyming, etc.)	✓ review letter names & sounds, emphasize practice of short vowel sounds ✓ VC & CVC blending, building & manipulating, letter formation, spelling & reading in context ✓ tricky words — review "has," "is," "his" from set 1 ✓ phonemic awareness activities (Heggerty, rhyming, etc.)	✓ review letter names & sounds, emphasize practice of short vowel sounds ✓ VC & CVC blending, building & manipulating, letter formation, spelling & reading in context ✓ tricky words — review "was," "to," and "do" from set 1 ✓ phonemic awareness activities (Heggerty, rhyming, etc.)	✓ screening week: ✓ phonemic awareness screen ✓ developmental spelling ✓ letter names & sounds ✓ decoding screen (VC/CVC) ✓ tricky words — introduce **her, you, your** from set 2 ✓ phonemic awareness activities (Heggerty, rhyming, etc.)

OCTOBER

WEEK 5	WEEK 6	WEEK 7	WEEK 8
✓ introduce initial digraph **sh** ✓ CVC + digraphs (CCVC) blending, building & manipulating, letter formation, spelling & reading in context ✓ tricky words — introduce **are, you, come** from set 2 ✓ phonemic awareness activities (Heggerty, rhyming, etc.)	✓ review initial digraph sh, & add **ch** ✓ CVC + digraphs (CCVC) blending, building & manipulating, letter formation, spelling & reading in context ✓ tricky words — introduce **some, said, there** from set 2 ✓ phonemic awareness activities (Heggerty, rhyming, etc.)	✓ review initial digraphs sh, ch & add **th — 2 sounds** ✓ CVC + digraphs (CCVC) blending, building & manipulating, letter formation, spelling & reading in context ✓ tricky words — introduce **all, one, from** from set 3 ✓ phonemic awareness activities (Heggerty, rhyming, etc.)	✓ review initial digraphs sh, ch, th & add **qu, wh** ✓ CVC + digraphs (CCVC) blending, building & manipulating, letter formation, spelling & reading in context ✓ Tricky Words — introduce **have, live, give** from set 3 ✓ phonemic awareness activities (Heggerty, rhyming, etc.)

NOVEMBER

WEEK 9	WEEK 10	WEEK 11	WEEK 12
✓ introduce final digraphs **sh, ch** ✓ CVC + digraphs (CCVC/CVCC) blending, building & manipulating, letter formation, spelling & reading in context ✓ tricky words — introduce **or, what, they** from set 3 ✓ phonemic awareness activities (Heggerty, rhyming, etc.)	✓ review final digraphs sh, ch & add **th** ✓ CVC + digraphs (CCVC/CVCC) blending, building & manipulating, letter formation, spelling & reading in context ✓ tricky words — introduce **where, who, only** from set 4 ✓ phonemic awareness activities (Heggerty, rhyming, etc.)	✓ review final digraphs sh, ch, th & add **ck** ✓ mini lesson: when to use c/k/ck when spelling words ✓ C CVC + digraphs (CCVC/VCC) blending, building & manipulating, letter formation, spelling & reading in context ✓ tricky words — introduce **very, any, put** from set 4 ✓ phonemic awareness activities (Heggerty, rhyming, etc.)	✓ review final digraphs sh, ch, th, ck & add **ng** ✓ CVC + digraphs (CCVC/CVCC) blending, building & manipulating, letter formation, spelling & reading in context ✓ tricky words — introduce **many, two, old** from set 4 ✓ phonemic awareness activities (Heggerty, rhyming, etc.)

DECEMBER

WEEK 13	WEEK 14		
✓ review initial & final digraphs (sh, ch, th, qu, wh, ck, ng) ✓ CVC + digraphs (CCVC/ CVCC) blending, building & manipulating, letter formation, spelling & reading in context ✓ tricky words — introduce **were, because, want** from set 5 ✓ targeted small-group phonemic awareness *for at-risk students*	✓ flex/review	✓ winter break	

JANUARY

WEEK 15	WEEK 16	WEEK 17	WEEK 18
✓ introduce initial blends with l (**sl, cl, bl, fl, gl, pl**) ✓ CCVC blending, building & manipulating, letter formation, spelling & reading in context ✓ tricky words — introduce **other, their, love** from set 5 ✓ targeted small-group phonemic awareness *for at-risk students*	✓ introduce initial blends with r (**br, cr, dr, fr, gr, pr, tr**) ✓ CCVC blending, building & manipulating, letter formation, spelling & reading in context ✓ tricky words — introduce **would, could, should** from set 5 ✓ targeted small-group phonemic awareness *for at-risk students*	✓ introduce initial blends with s (**sc, sk, sm, sn, sp, st, sw**) ✓ CCVC blending, building & manipulating, letter formation, spelling & reading in context ✓ tricky words — introduce **mother, father, been** from set 6 ✓ targeted small-group phonemic awareness *for at-risk students*	✓ screening week: ✓ phonemic awareness & letter names & sounds *for at-risk students* ✓ progress monitoring ✓ decoding screen (blending VC & CVC words, short phrases, decodable text) ✓ tricky words screen

FEBRUARY

WEEK 19	WEEK 20	WEEK 21	WEEK 22
✓ introduce open & closed syllables ✓ blending, building & manipulating, letter formation, spelling & reading in context ✓ tricky words — introduce **every, work, again** from set 6 ✓ targeted small-group phonemic awareness *for at-risk students*	✓ introduce VCe long vowels with "magic e" (**a_e**) ✓ CVCe blending, building & manipulating, letter formation, spelling & reading in context ✓ tricky words — introduce **once, great, does** from set 6 ✓ targeted small-group phonemic awareness *for at-risk students*	✓ review VCe long vowels with "magic e" (**a_e**) & add **i_e** ✓ CVCe blending, building & manipulating, letter formation, spelling & reading in context ✓ tricky words — introduce **goes, word, school** from set 7 ✓ targeted small-group phonemic awareness *for at-risk students*	✓ review VCe long vowels with "magic e" (**a_e, i_e**) & add **o_e** ✓ CVCe blending, building & manipulating, letter formation, spelling & reading in context ✓ tricky words — introduce **open, move, eyes** from set 7 ✓ targeted small-group phonemic awareness *for at-risk students*

MARCH

WEEK 23	WEEK 24	WEEK 25	
✓ review VCe long vowels with "magic e" (a_e, i_e, o_e) & add **u_e** ✓ CVCe blending, building & manipulating, letter formation, spelling & reading in context ✓ tricky words — introduce **close, watch, idea** from set 7 ✓ targeted small-group phonemic awareness *for at-risk students*	✓ review VCe long vowels with "magic e" (a_e, i_e, o_e, u_e) & add **e_e** ✓ CVCe blending, building & manipulating, letter formation, spelling & reading in context ✓ tricky words — review & practice sets 1–7 ✓ targeted small-group phonemic awareness *for at-risk students*	✓ flex/review	✓ spring break

APRIL

WEEK 26	WEEK 27	WEEK 28	WEEK 29
✓ introduce inflected endings (**s & es**) ✓ s makes /z/ — review tricky words with s (is, as, his, has, was, goes, eyes) ✓ short discussion of irregular plurals (mouse-mice, etc.) ✓ blending, building & manipulating, spelling & reading in context ✓ targeted small-group phonemic awareness *for at-risk students*	✓ introduce final consonant blends **nt & nd** ✓ blending, building & manipulating words, spelling & reading in context ✓ tricky words — introduce **world, over, people** from set 8 ✓ phonemic awareness activities (Heggerty, rhyming, etc.)	✓ review final consonant blends nt, nd & add **mp & nk** ✓ blending, building & manipulating words, spelling & reading in context ✓ tricky words — introduce **enough, carry, answer** from set 8 ✓ phonemic awareness activities (Heggerty, rhyming, etc.)	✓ introduce **schwa** ✓ blending, building & manipulating words, spelling & reading in context ✓ tricky words — introduce **above, most, kind** from set 8 ✓ phonemic awareness activities (Heggerty, rhyming, etc.)

MAY

WEEK 30	WEEK 31	WEEK 32	WEEK 33
✓ introduce **floss rule** (**ss, ff, ll, zz**) ✓ blending, building & manipulating words, spelling & reading in context ✓ tricky words review & practice ✓ phonemic awareness activities (Heggerty, rhyming, etc.)	✓ introduce 3-letter blends with long & short vowels **str, scr, spr** ✓ blending, building & manipulating words, spelling & reading in context ✓ tricky words review & practice ✓ targeted small-group phonemic awareness *for at-risk students*	✓ introduce 3-letter blends with long & short vowels **squ, shr, thr** ✓ blending, building & manipulating words, spelling & reading in context ✓ tricky words review & practice ✓ targeted small-group phonemic awareness *for at-risk students*	✓ introduce inflected ending **ing** ✓ blending, building & manipulating words, spelling & reading in context ✓ tricky words review & practice ✓ targeted small-group phonemic awareness *for at-risk students*

	WEEK 34	WEEK 35	WEEK 36	WEEK 37
JUNE	√ screening week: √ phonemic awareness & letters & sounds *for at-risk students* √ decoding screen *for at-risk students* √ benchmark or fluency/comprehension screen √ developmental spelling screen √ tricky words screen	√ targeted review of concepts based on assessments	√ targeted review of concepts based on assessments	√ targeted review of concepts based on assessments

Weekly Concept Pages with Full Lesson Plans in Weeks 7, 19, 29, and 30

Grade 1 Weeks 1–3 Target Concept: review all letter names & sounds

Description of Concept

Letter names: all letter names

Letter sounds: all letter sounds (with an emphasis on short vowel sounds)

The first month of grade 1 should focus on review of all letter names and sounds. Specific emphasis should be put on practicing and reinforcing short vowel sounds and targeted letters and sounds based on data from kindergarten end-of-year screens. Review and practice letter formation and decoding along with the review of letter names and sounds.

Review tricky words from set 1.

Weeks 1–3 Word Lists: focus on short vowel sounds

Word Lists for Decoding and Encoding Activities									
Real Words									
a		i		o		u		e	
pan	fan	dig	fig	bog	fog	rug	mug	vet	set
van	can	big	wig	dog	log	jug	gut	pet	wet
had	dad	hip	sip	jog	cop	rut	fun	men	ten
bad	gap	lip	nip	hop	mop	sun	bun	den	pen
zap	dab	kid	lid	lop	pop	run	nub	led	red
lab	max	rim	pic	dot	lot	rub	pub	bed	wed
fax	jam	tic	tin	rot	pot	sub	mud	fed	keg
ram	rag	pin	fin	nod	rod	cup	cub	leg	peg
sag	bag	bin		god	pod	lux	mum	beg	hex
						gum	hum		
Nonsense Words									
a		i		o		u		e	
jal		riv		gom		wup		feb	
waf		kig		cov		ruk		wep	
mav		wid		lof		dus		kez	
hal		hix		wox		lun		lef	
vap		bic		rop		vug		zem	

Two-Syllable Extending Words
exact, exam, tidbit, cactus, tandem, planet, expand, tablet, basket, tennis, solid, rotten, often, pumpkin, index, upset, napkin, picnic, goblin, problem, Batman, cobweb, suntan, subset, catnip, cannot, setup, hubcap, magnet, campus, helmet, velvet, public, zigzag, pigpen

Word Chain
pan, pin, pun, pen, ten, ted, led, lad, lid, rid, rod, rad, red, bed, bud, bad, bod, cod, cob, cab, cub, sub, sun, fun, fan, fin, bin, bun, ban, bat, hat, hit, hot, hut

Tricky Words set 1: the, of, as, has, is, his, was, to, do

Grade 1 Week 4 Target Concept: screening week + introduce tricky words set 2

(see blueprint, page 99)

Description of Concept

This week is intentionally scheduled time to screen your students in order to inform instruction and grouping of students. The following screens are recommended in the fall of grade 1:

- phonemic awareness screen
- developmental spelling
- letter names & sounds
- VC/CVC word decoding screen

Tricky Words set 2: her, you, your

Grade 1 Week 5 Target Concept: initial digraph "sh"

(see blueprint, page 99)

Description of Concept

Digraph: **sh**

Digraph sound: **/sh/**

A digraph is two consonants that make one new sound.

The digraph "sh" makes the sound /sh/, as in "shop."

At this point, we are working only with words that have digraphs with short vowel sounds.

Sample phoneme-to-grapheme mapping of "sh":

s h	o	p	

Week 5 Word Lists: initial digraph sh

Word Lists for Decoding and Encoding Activities			
Real Words		**Nonsense Words**	
sham	shop	shan	
shag	shot	shig	
ship	shed	shof	
shim	shut	shud	
shin	shun	shep	
Two-Syllable Extending Words shotgun, shovel, shellfish, sheriff, shamrock, shaken, shampoo, shopping			
Word Chains shop, ship, shim, shin, shun, shen shed, shud, shut			
Tricky Words set 2: are, use, come			

Grade 1 Week 6 Target Concept: initial digraph "ch"

(see blueprint, page 99)

Description of Concept

Digraph: **ch**

Digraph sound: **/ch/**

A digraph is two consonants that make one new sound.

The digraph "ch" makes the sound /ch/, as in "chat."

At this point, we are working only with words that have digraphs with short vowel sounds.

Sample phoneme-to-grapheme mapping of "ch":

c h	i	n	

Week 6 Word Lists: initial digraph ch

Word Lists for Decoding and Encoding Activities	
Real Words	**Nonsense Words**
chat chap chip chin chug chum chop	chan chiv chot chud chep
Two-Syllable Extending Words children, channel, chicken, checkers, chopstick, chipping, choppy, chapter, chapstick	
Word Chain chop, chip, chap, chat, chan, chin, chun, chug, chum	
Tricky Words set 2: some, said, there	

Grade 1 Week 7 Target Concept: initial digraph "th" (2 sounds)

(see blueprint, page 99)

Description of Concept

Digraph: **th**

Digraph sounds: **/th/ and /TH/**

A digraph is two consonants that make one new sound (or in this case two).

The digraph /th/ can make two different sounds: a voiced hard /TH/ sound (as in "that") and an unvoiced soft /th/ sound (as in "thin"). When decoding words, tell students to try the voiced hard sound first and if that doesn't sound right, then try the unvoiced soft sound.

At this point, we are working only with words that have digraphs with short vowel sounds.

Lesson Plan

	Target Concept: th — 2 sounds
1	**Warm-up:** 2–5 minutes Review short vowel sounds and initial digraphs "sh" and "ch." Once /th/ is introduced, include it as part of the warm-up and review.
2	**Introduce new concepts (I Do):** 5 minutes "This week we will learn the digraph "th." (Write it on the board.) "A digraph is two letters that work together to make one sound. What is a digraph?" Students respond. "This digraph is unique because it can make two different sounds." "Unveil" the sounds one at a time on your sound wall if you have one, emphasizing the mouth movement used to make the sounds.
3	**Phonological awareness:** 3–5 minutes 1. "The digraph 'th' makes the unvoiced soft sound /th/ ('thin') and it also makes a voiced hard sound /TH/ ('that')." Show students that the tongue moves forward/back depending on which sound they make. Encourage students to practice making the two sounds with their hands on their voice box. Can they tell the difference between the two sounds? The teacher may show a kinesthetic movement of their choice to represent each sound. Students repeat the sounds and copy the movements that go with each sound. 2. "Some words that start with this sound are 'thin' and 'that.'" (Emphasize the /th/ and /TH/ sounds as you say the words.) "Can you hear the sound /th/ or /TH/ at the beginning of these words?" (Give more examples as needed.) 3. "I'm going to say some words that start with the sounds /th/ and /TH/; every time you hear that sound, show me the correct 'th' movement, or thumbs-up/thumbs-down." (Mix some words that start with /th/ and /TH/ and some that start with other sounds.) 4. "Can you think of any words that start with the sound /th/ or /TH/?" Possible follow-up activities for practice and reinforcement: – giant flash-card activities with "th" words – I Spy – Elkonin boxes – rhyming words, poetry, songs, and games
4	**Teacher-led guided practice with new concept (WE Do):** 10–15 minutes • Find the picture that matches the sound. Display several pictures or objects, some that start with the sound /th/ and /TH/ and some that do not. Together, find the pictures/objects that start with the sound /th/ and /TH/ and circle/identify them or sort them into two piles. Ask for volunteers to come up and identify /th/ and /TH/ words. • Put a short list of words on the board that begin with the two sounds of "th" and contain short vowels (see word list below — include real and nonsense words). Starting with the first word, demonstrate saying and blending the sounds using additive or continuous blending to read the word. Blend and read the rest of the words together. Decide if each word is a real word or a nonsense word. Ask for volunteers to try to read some words independently.

5	**Extended independent practice activities to apply new concept (YOU Do):** 15–20 minutes
	Word Sort:
	Students are given a sorting sheet that has "th" written at the top of two columns and a list of words and/or pictures with the target sounds. Students sort the words/pictures by printing words or cutting them out and placing them in the correct sound column. After students have independently attempted the sort, review the correct way to sort the sounds as a whole group and have students make corrections before gluing their words down. This activity could also be done with small items or word cards as an interactive sort.
	
	Possible follow-up activities for practice and reinforcement:
	  – flash-card activities
	  – sorting objects
	  – drawing objects that start with each sound
	  – paper/pencil activities

6	**Tricky words:** 10 minutes Introduce set 2 (**some, said, there**).

7	**Decoding with text (YOU Do):** 15–20 minutes
	1. Students are given word lists (see below) and/or blending lines to practice identifying target sounds and blend sounds to read words.
	   Go through the list together, one word at a time. Tell students to highlight (or underline or circle) the sound /th/ or /TH/ in each word. Ask for volunteers to say all the sounds in the word and blend them to read the word. *Words in word lists have only explicitly taught letter sounds.*
	2. Students are given phrases that contain "th" words to read either independently or with a partner. This could also be done with short decodable passages as well.
	
	Possible follow-up activities for practice and reinforcement:
	  – fluency phrases
	  – blending boards
	  – shared reading of decodable books/passages

8	**Encoding (YOU Do):** 15 minutes
	• Building words with letter tiles: students can use paper or magnetic letter tiles to build words using the sounds of /th/ and /TH/ (see word list below). Start by building one word and then change one sound, to make a new word using explicitly taught sounds.
	• Phoneme-to-grapheme mapping with word list below.
	
	Possible follow-up activities for practice and reinforcement:
	  – fill in the missing letter/sound practice sheets
	  – word ladders
	  – spelling word/phrase dictation
	
	Sample phoneme-to-grapheme mapping of "th":
	
	| t h
		a	t	|
				|---|---|---|---|

9	**Intervention:** Encourage students to practice making the two sounds with their hands on their voice box. Can they tell the difference between the two sounds? Activities in the classroom may include small-group work, one-on-one work with an adult, and take-home practice activities (flash cards with sounds, word lists to practice applying sounds and blending, decodable books).
10	**Extending:** Students who require additional challenge may practice target sounds with multisyllable words, words with "th" in other parts of the word (middle/end), and more advanced text.

Week 7 Word Lists: initial digraph th

Word Lists for Decoding and Encoding Activities				
Real Words		**Extending Words**	**Nonsense Words**	
them this then than that thus	thin thud thug	thick thing think	thep thas thuf thog thil	thef thad thup thox thiv
Two-Syllable Extending Words thinner, thudding, thinker, thimble, thunder, thankful, thingy, thicket				
Word Chain thud, thug, thus, this, thin, then, than, that				
Tricky Words set 3: all, one, from				

Grade 1 Week 8 Target Concept: initial digraphs "wh," "qu"

(see blueprint, page 99)

Description of Concept
Digraphs: **wh, qu**
Diagraph sounds: **/w/, /kw/**
The digraph "wh" is different from other digraphs that have been taught in that it doesn't create a new sound when the two letters are combined. In our dialect, the "h" is silent and the digraph sounds the same as the letter "w," — for example, /w/, as in "when." "Wh" may be pronounced differently for your students, depending on your region or dialect.
Although "qu" was introduced in kindergarten with the letter "q," this is an opportunity to review and practice "qu." "Qu" is commonly referred to as a digraph even though it is two sounds blended together to make the sound /kw/.
At this time in grade 1, digraph words with short vowel sounds should be the focus because the concept of long vowels has not yet been taught.
Sample phoneme-to-grapheme of "wh" and "qu":

wh	e	n	
qu		i	t

Week 8 Word Lists: initial digraphs wh, qu

Word Lists for Decoding and Encoding Activities			
Real Words		**Extending Words**	**Nonsense Words**
when whim whit whip whiz wham which	quit quiz quip quid	whack quack quick	whef whab whid whum whog quem quop quab quiv
Two-Syllable Extending Words whimper, whisker, whisper, whizzed, whether, whacky, whipping quitting, quipped, quacked, quicker, equal, liquid, banquet			
Word Chains when, whan, wham, whim, whip, whiz, whit, which quit, quiz, quid, quip			
Tricky Words set 3: have, live, give			

Grade 1 Week 9 Target Concept: final digraphs "sh," "ch"

(see blueprint, page 99)

Description of Concept
Final digraphs: **sh, ch**
Final digraph sounds: **/sh/, /ch/**
A digraph is two consonants that make one sound. The digraph sounds /sh/ and /ch/ can be the initial or final sound of a word or syllable.
The digraph /sh/, as in "mash."
The digraph /ch/, as in "much."
At this point, we are working only with words that have digraphs with short vowel sounds.
Sample phoneme-to-grapheme mapping of "sh" and "ch":

c	a	sh	
s	u	ch	

Week 9 Word Lists: final digraphs sh, ch

Word Lists for Decoding and Encoding Activities					
Real Words			**Extending Words**	**Nonsense Words**	
mash	mosh	rich	lunch	tash	gach
cash	posh	which	bunch	rish	vich
sash	gosh	such	hunch	kosh	moch
hash	Josh	much	punch	fush	puch
lash	rush		finch	pesh	wech
rash	gush		perch		
dash	lush		lurch		
gash	mush		church		
bash	hush		crunch		
wish	mesh		brunch		
fish			trench		
dish			French		
			flinch		

Two-Syllable Extending Words
catfish, codfish, selfish, polish, cherish, radish, rubbish, punish, finish, vanish, lavish, sluggish, British, blemish, banish, relish, ambush
spinach, sandwich, ostrich, unclench, detach, attach, enrich, reteach, entrench

Word Chains
which, rich, rach, rash, mash, mush, much, such
fish, wish, dish, dash, cash, gash, gosh, mosh, mesh, mush, rush, rash

Tricky Words set 3: or, what, they

Grade 1 Week 10 Target Concept: final digraph "th"

(see blueprint, page 99)

Description of Concept
Final digraph: **th**
Final digraph sound: /**th**/
A digraph is two consonants that make one new sound. The digraph "th" can make two sounds, the voiced hard sound /TH/, as in "that," and the unvoiced soft sound /th/, as in "thin." As a final digraph, "th" will generally make the unvoiced soft sound /th/, as in "math." However, the voiced hard sound /TH/ can be found at the end of a syllable, as in "feather," or after a long vowel sound, as in "bathe."

At this point, we are working only with words that have digraphs with short vowel sounds.
Sample phoneme-to-grapheme mapping of "th":

m	a	th	

Week 10 Word Lists: final digraph th

Word Lists for Decoding and Encoding Activities		
Real Words	**Extending Words**	**Nonsense Words**
math	wealth	wath
path	health	rith
bath	fourth, fifth,	voth
with	sixth, seventh,	juth
goth	eighth, ninth, tenth, etc.	feth
moth	death	
Beth	length	
	myth	

Two-Syllable Extending Words
seventh, sunbath, mammoth, blacksmith, footpath, midmonth, locksmith, unhealth, zenith, beneath

Word Chain
goth, moth, math, path, bath, wath, with

Tricky Words set 4: where, who, only

Grade 1 Week 11 Target Concept: final digraph "ck"

(see blueprint, page 99)

Description of Concept
Final digraph: **ck**
Final digraph sound: **/k/**
The digraph "ck" can only be found at the end of a word or syllable ("back"). This digraph doesn't create a new sound when the two letters are combined because the "c" in "ck" is silent. The digraph "ck" will be reviewed and practiced again in Grade 3 Week 15, when the soldier rule is introduced.
At this point, we are working only with words that have digraphs with short vowel sounds.
Sample phoneme-to-grapheme mapping of "ck":

s	o	ck	

Mini Lesson — When to use "c," "k", or "ck" when spelling words with the /k/ sound:
Hard "c," "k," and "ck" all make the sound /k/. This is easy for students to remember while reading, but when it comes to spelling, students often ask, "Is it a 'c,' a 'k,' or a 'ck'?"
Review the rule of thumb that generally "c" comes before "a," "o," and "u" at the beginning of a word, while "k" comes before "i" and "e."
"K" will also generally come after a consonant or a long vowel sound. "Ck" is generally used after a short vowel sound at the end of a word or syllable. See the graphic below for spelling rules regarding when to use "c" or "k" or "ck."

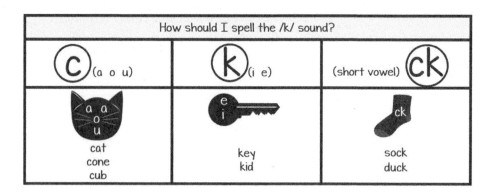

How should I spell the /k/ sound?		
(C) (a o u)	(k) (i e)	(short vowel) (ck)
cat cone cub	key kid	sock duck

Week 11 Word Lists: final digraph ck

Word Lists for Decoding and Encoding Activities

Real Words					Nonsense Words	
whack	wick	rock	puck	peck	ruck	whuck
tack	Rick	pock	suck	deck	tock	thack
yack	tick	sock	duck	heck	gack	shick
pack	pick	jock	huck	beck	bick	chack
sack	sick	dock	guck	neck	vock	queck
hack	hick	hock	luck	check	juck	
Jack	kick	lock	buck		leck	
lack	lick	mock	muck			
back	thick	shock	yuck			
shack	chick		shuck			
			chuck			
			tuck			

Two-Syllable Extending Words
backpack, packsack, pinprick, sunblock, dipstick, unpack, amuck, untuck, attack, uptick, unlock, upchuck, padlock, haddock, bannock, gimmick, bedrock, setback, hammock, unstuck, nitpick, redneck, blackjack, kickback, gridlock, lipstick, paycheck, homesick

Word Chain
neck, deck, peck, pack, tack, tuck, muck, mock, sock, rock, rack, back, lack, lick, pick, puck, huck, hack, heck

Tricky Words set 4: very, any, put

Grade 1 Week 12 Target Concept: final digraph "ng"

(see blueprint, page 99)

Description of Concept

Final digraph: **ng**

Final digraph sound: /**ng**/

The digraph "ng" will always be a final sound in words and syllables ("wing"). It is important to emphasize that this is not the suffix "ing"; the digraph "ng" is voiced using the back of the mouth/throat and it can be combined with the vowels "i," "o," "a," and "u." Encourage students to practice making the sound, paying attention to mouth position, air flow, and voicing.

There are many other words ending with the digraph "ng" that have initial consonant blends, but since those blends have not yet been taught, they will be introduced and practiced with initial blends in weeks 15, 16, and 17.

At this point, we are working only with words that have digraphs with short vowel sounds.

Sample phoneme-to-grapheme mapping of "ng":

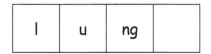

Week 12 Word Lists: final digraph "ng"

Word Lists for Decoding and Encoding Activities					
Real Words				**Nonsense Words**	
rang tang yang pang sang dang fang gang hang bang	wing ring ping sing ding king thing ting ling	tong pong song dong gong long bong thong	rung sung dung hung lung bung	nang fing jong pung deng tung mung	shong ching whung quang theng
Two-Syllable Extending Words unhang, among, along, belong, mustang, oblong, prolong, unsung					
Word Chain rang, ring, wing, sing, song, sung, sang, bang, gang, gong, long, thong, thing, ding, dang, fang, hang					
Tricky Words set 4: many, two, old					

Grade 1 Week 13 Target Concept: review initial and final digraphs
(see blueprint, page 100)

Description of Concept

Review initial and final digraphs (sh, ch, th, qu, wh, ck, ng) + introduce tricky words set 5: **were, because, want**

Word Lists: use previously provided word lists.

Grade 1 Week 14 Target Concept: flex/review

Description of Concept

Flex/review week

Grade 1 Week 15 Target Concept: initial consonant blends with "l" ("sl," "cl," "bl," "fl," "gl," "pl")
(see blueprint, page 100)

Description of Concept

Initial consonant blends with l: **sl, cl, bl, fl, gl, pl**

Initial consonant blend sounds: /**sl**/, /**kl**/, /**bl**/, /**fl**/, /**gl**/, /**pl**/

Consonant blends, also known as consonant clusters, are two-letter sounds that are blended when reading words fluently. Each letter still retains its own sound and they can be heard separately, but when decoding words it is helpful to move smoothly from one to the other. One of the most common initial consonant blend "families" is blends with the letter "l."

Blends always stay together. When breaking down multisyllable words, do not divide syllables between the two consonants of a blend.

At this point, we are working only with words that have blends with short vowel sounds.

Sample phoneme-to-grapheme mapping of initial blends:

g	l	a	d	

Week 15 Word Lists: initial consonant blends with l (sl, cl, bl, fl, gl, pl)

Word Lists for Decoding and Encoding Activities								
Real Words								
slat	slick	clap	clot	flat	flock	black	glad	plan
slap	slim	clack	clop	flap	flub	blab	glam	plot
slag	sling	clan	clod	flag	flush	blip	glop	plop
slack	slot	clam	clog	flack	flung	bling	glom	plod
slab	slop	clash	clock	flan	fled	blot	glob	plug
slam	slog	clang	cloth	flash	fleck	blog	glug	plus
slash	slosh	clip	cluck	flit	flesh	block	glum	plum
slang	slug	click	club	flip		blob		pluck
sloth	slum	cling	clung	flick		blub		pled
slit	slush			fling		blush		
slip	sled			flop		bled		
slid								
Nonsense Words								
slaf	claf	flav	blach	glack	plang			
slig	clim	flig	blif	glish	plig			
slock	clof	floth	blosh	glog	plof			
slud	clum	flut	blun	glud	plub			
sleth	cleck	flen	bleng	gleng	plev			
				glit	plip			
				glim				
Two-Syllable Extending Words								
sluggish, classic, clinic, flannel, blacktop, blanket, glitzy, gladden, planet, plasma								
Word Chains								
blab, blip, slip, slap, flap, flip, clip, clap, clop, slop, glop, plop, plot, clot, slot, slat, slack, flack, clack, click, clock, flock, block, blog, blot, blob, blab, blop, blip, flip, flick, fling, flung, clung, clang, slang, slash, slush, blush, flush, flash, clash, clan								
Tricky Words set 5: other, their, love								

Grade 1 Week 16 Target Concept: initial consonant blends with "r" ("br," "cr," "dr," "fr," "gr," "pr," "tr")

(see blueprint, page 100)

Description of Concept
Initial consonant blends with r: **br, cr, dr, fr, gr, pr, tr**
Initial consonant blend sounds: **/br/, /kr/, /dr/, /fr/, /gr/, /pr/, /tr/**

Consonant blends are two-letter sounds that are blended when reading words fluently. Each letter still retains its own sound, and they can be separated, but when decoding words, it is helpful to move smoothly from one to the other. The most challenging initial consonant blend "families" are blends with the letter "r." At this point, we are working only with words that have blends with short vowel sounds.

Sample phoneme-to-grapheme mapping of initial blends:

t	r	i	m	

Week 16 Word Lists: initial consonant blends with r (br, cr, dr, fr, gr, pr, tr)

Word Lists for Decoding and Encoding Activities						
Real Words						
brat	crab	drat	frat	grad	pram	trap
brad	cram	drag	frog	grab	prim	tram
brag	crash	drab	frock	gran	prick	track
bran	crack	drip	froth	gram	prop	trash
brash	crib	drib	fret	grit	prod	trip
Brit	crick	drop	Fred	grip	prom	trim
brig	crop	drug	fresh	grid	prep	trick
brim	crock	drum		grin		trot
brick	crud			grim		trod
bring	crush			grog		truck
broth						trek
brush						
bred						
Nonsense Words						
brab	crath	draf	fraf	grack	pras	tras
brif	crin	driv	frip	grib	prip	trid
brong	crog	drong	fron	grop	prock	trock
brud	crut	druck	frud	grush	prug	trung
brev	cresh	dreb	fruth	grung	prech	tresh
Two-Syllable Words						
Brazil, bracket, cricket, crafty, drifting, dragon, frosty, freshen, grandma, grandmom, grandpa, granddad, griffin, proper, pressing, travel, tractor						
Word Chain						
drug, drag, brag, brash, brush, crush, crash, crack, frack, track, truck, trick, brick, bring, brig, trig, trim, grim, gram, grad, grab, crab, drab, drat, frat, frap, trap, trash						
Tricky Words set 5: would, could, should						

Grade 1 Week 17 Target Concept: initial consonant blends with the "s" family ("sc," "sk," "sm," "sn," "sp," "st," "sw")

(see blueprint, page 100)

Description of Concept

Initial consonant blends with "s" family: **sc, sk, sm, sn, sp, st, sw**

Initial consonant blend sounds: /sk/, /sk/, /sm/, /sn/, /sp/, /st/, /sw/

The easiest initial consonant blend "families" are blends that start with the letter "s."

At this point, we are working only with words that have blends with short vowel sounds. The "sl" blend belongs to this family but was introduced in Week 16 with the "l" blends.

Sample phoneme-to-grapheme mapping with initial blends:

s	w	a	m	

Week 17 Word Lists: initial consonant blends with s (sl, sc, sk, sm, sn, sp, st, sw)

Word Lists for Decoding and Encoding Activities							
Real Words							
slat	slid	scat	smack	snap	spat	stat	sked
slap	slick	scab	smash	snag	span	stag	swag
slag	slim	scan	Smith	snack	spam	stab	swam
slack	sling	scam	smog	snit	spit	Stan	swack
slab	slot	scud	smock	snip	spin	stack	swim
slam	slop	scum	smug	snib	spot	stash	swing
slash	slog	skit		snot	spud	stim	swish
slang	slosh	skip		snog	spun	stick	swum
sloth	slug	skid		snob	sped	sting	swung
slit	slum	skin		snug	speck	stop	
slip	slush	skim		snub		stock	
	sled			snuck		stud	
				snick		stun	
						stub	
						stuck	
						stung	
						step	
						stem	
Nonsense Words							
slaf	scag	skav	smat	snaf	spang	stav	swaf
slib	scom	skig	smib	snid	spaj	stig	swib
slock	scuth	skob	smop	snod	spib	stosh	swong
slup	scup	skun	smud	snush	spong	stuth	swuch
slesh		skuth	smeng	sneth	spuch	stel	sweth
			smit		spem		
Two-Syllable Extending Words							
slacken, sleepy, scabby, scanning, skinny, skimming, smacking, smitten, snippy, spider, spandex, static, status, swelling, swimming							
Word Chain							
spot, snot, snap, snit, spit, spot, slot, slat, slam, scam, scan, scab, slab, stab, stack, swack, smack, slack, slash, smash, stash							
Tricky Words set 6: mother, father, been							

Grade 1 Week 18 Target Concept: screening week
(see blueprint, page 100)

Description:
This week is intentionally scheduled time to screen your students in order to inform your instruction and student groupings. The following screens are recommended in midyear of grade 1:

- phonemic awareness and letter names and sounds *for at-risk students*
- progress monitoring
- decoding screen (blending VC and CVC words, short phrases, decodable text)
- tricky words screen

Grade 1 Week 19 Target Concept: closed and open syllables
(see blueprint, page 100)

Description of Concept
This is the first time students will be working with long vowels. Take time to review long vowel sounds before teaching this lesson.

Closed Syllable: When a syllable or single-syllable word consists of a vowel followed by a consonant, the vowel sound is short ("cat," "slip," "crush"). The consonant "closes" the vowel, so it is called a closed syllable.

Open Syllable: When a syllable or single-syllable word ends in a vowel, the vowel sound is long ("me," "go," "she"). There is no consonant to close the vowel, so it is called an open syllable.

Six Syllable Rules: This is also the first lesson that addresses two of the Six Syllable Rules. When breaking words apart into syllables (with one vowel per syllable), it is important to know whether the vowel in each syllable is long or short. For syllables with a single vowel (rather than a vowel team or diphthong), this is determined by whether the syllable is open or closed.

Teacher Knowledge: This is an excellent opportunity to begin talking about the two sounds of "y" at the end of a word. If the word is short and there is no other vowel, the "y" says /ī/, as in "try," but if it is a multisyllable word (there are two or more other vowels present) then the "y" says /ē/, as in "fancy." These "y" sounds are explicitly taught in Grade 2 Week 21.

Lesson Plan

Target Concept: closed and open syllables	
1	**Warm-up/review:** 2–5 minutes Review initial blends with "s" family ("sl," "sc," "sk," "sm," "sn," "sp," "st," "sw") and any other concepts that need additional review.

2	**Introduce new concepts (I Do):** 5 minutes Explain to students that when syllables or single-syllable words consist of a vowel followed by a consonant, the vowel sound is short ("cat," "slip," "crush"). The consonant encloses the vowel, so it is called a **closed** syllable. When a syllable or single-syllable word ends in a vowel, the vowel sound is long ("me," "go," "she"). There is no consonant to enclose the vowel, so it is called an **open** syllable. Use flash cards or write sample words on the board to provide models of these two syllable types.
3	**Phonological awareness:** 3 minutes The teacher tells students that they are going to read a list of open- and closed-syllable words (see word lists below) and asks students to indicate what they hear by opening their arms wide for an open-syllable word and putting their hands together (palms touching) in front of themselves for a closed-syllable word. For example: "he" — open, "cut" — closed, "crunch" — closed. When students become skilled at identifying open and closed syllables, the teacher can introduce words with two syllables and have them identify Open-Open, Closed-Closed, Closed-Open, and Open-Closed, etc. The word lists below have been included for phonological activities and the more complex words are not intended for reading and spelling activities. We have even included three-syllable words for students who are proficient with two-syllable words.
4	**Teacher-led guided practice with new concept (WE Do):** 10–15 minutes Together as a class, create Open- and Closed-Syllable syllable houses. Instructions: 1. Place a 5 1/2" x 8 1/2" piece of card stock on each desktop in the landscape position. 2. Fold over one third of the card to create the door. For students without fine-motor skills, we score their card so that there is a predetermined line for them to fold on. 3. Create the top of the roof by cutting a triangle on each side of the top third of the card. Students may find it helpful to mark the roof with a pencil before cutting. 4. Write a chosen word on the card with the open syllable on the large section of card, and the last letter (to close the syllable) on the door flap. 5. Add windows and decorative touches. 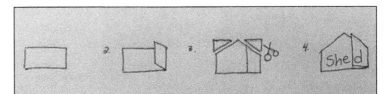 Once the house is constructed, students write as many open and closed words as they can on the back of their house. Students can look at other students' houses to get ideas for additional words.

For example: no/not, go/got, she/shed, he/help, hi/him, we/wet.

5	**Extended independent practice activities to apply new concept (YOU Do):** 15–20 minutes There are many activities that students can do to practice working with open and closed syllables. Some include: • Use blending boards with consonants in the first ring and vowels in the second ring for open-syllable words. If blending boards are set up with consonants in the first and third rings and vowels in the middle, students can switch back and forth between open- and closed-syllables by lifting the entire set of letters in the third ring for open-syllable words. • Build open- and closed-syllable words with letter tiles. • Make word chains or word ladders with open- and closed-syllable words. • Have students read blending lines (page 44) of open- and closed-syllable words. For example: hi, him, his, he, she, shed, wed, we
6	**Tricky Words:** 10 minutes Introduce set 6 (**every, work, again**).
7	**Decoding with text (YOU Do):** 15–20 minutes Using familiar texts that students have already read, have them find and highlight open- and closed-syllable words in passages or make a list of open- and closed-syllable words that they find in books they are reading.
8	**Encoding (YOU Do):** 15 minutes Practice open- and closed-syllable words with phoneme-to-grapheme spelling. Sample phoneme-to-grapheme mapping with open and closed syllables: | m	e		
---	---	---	---
m	e	t		
9	**Intervention:** This may be a challenging concept for some students as they must now decide if the vowel makes a short or long sound. Continued review and discussion of long vowels and open and closed syllables will help students learn this concept.

10	Extending:
	For students who quickly understand the open- and closed-syllable concept, have them work with the many two- and three-syllable words below, identifying if they are Open-Open-Closed, Closed-Open-Closed, etc.

Week 19 Word Lists: closed and open syllables

Word Lists for Decoding and Encoding Activities	
Open-Syllable Words	**Closed-Syllable Words**
Real Words: try, hi, no, she, dry, go, no, so, be, we, he, me, ply, why, I, sly, try **Nonsense Words:** ba, po, se, gri, vi, hu, flo, cli, spra, fe, tra, ma, pre, fro, pro, sti, mo, co, bi, de ro, bo, mu, sli, ma, si, va, po, re, ye, yo, za, ki and pu	shack, not, chip, thin, cast, now, pot, fish, got, flat, grin, pen, cat, shin, glad, thin, slip, chin, slap, fun, fin, crumb, lamb
Open-Open-Syllable Words	**Open-Closed-Syllable Words**
hobo, photo, zero, halo, silo, veto, judo, ego, hero, ago, solo, polo, tidy, baby	even, reject, prolong, edict, result, defense, bisect, hotel, robot, relax, over, human, protect, music, bacon, unit, vital
Closed-Closed-Syllable Words	**Closed-Open-Syllable Words**
bandit, invest, inflict, enchant, instruct, hardship, ransack, cartoon, metal, laptop, atom, solid, punish, contest, admit, mitten, cactus, lesson, pumpkin, pencil, helmet	tempo, tango, pinto gumbo, presto, messy, happy, echo, puppy, happy, hello, also, money, yellow
Closed-Open-Closed-Syllable Words	**Open-Open-Closed**
computer, acrobat, jellyfish	violin, ladybug, photograph, dinosaur
Open-Closed-Open-Syllable Words	**Open-Open-Open-Syllable Words**
piano	potato, tomato, radio
Closed-Closed-Closed-Syllable Words	**Closed-Open-Open-Syllable Words**
principal, president, basketball, animal, vanishing, fantastic, recommend, venison, elephant	volcano, video, broccoli
Open-Closed-Closed-Syllable Words	**Closed-Closed-Open-Syllable Words**
vitamin, gigantic	spaghetti, gravity, multiply, family, balcony, tendency, buffalo, domino
Tricky Words set 6: every, work, again	
Word Chain we, wet, bet, be, bed, shed, she, he, hi, him, hip, hop, ho, so, sod, god, go, no, nod, prod, pro, pre, prep	

Grade 1 Week 20 Target Concept: VCe ("a_e")

(see blueprint, page 100)

Description of Concept

VCe: **a_e**

VCe sound: /ā/

VCe stands for the vowel-consonant-e sequence at the end of many words. VCe is also known as "long-vowel e," "magic e," or "bossy e." These terms can help students remember the role of the silent "e" and engage with the lesson. The "e" at the end of VCe words is silent, but it has a very important role, which is to reach back and cause the vowel before it to say its long vowel sound. For example, the word "made" is a VCe word and the "a" says its long sound /ā/. Without the "e" at the end of the word, the vowel sound would be a short /ă/ sound and the word would be pronounced /măd/.

Teaching Strategy

As part of the introduction to VCe, talk about the ways that students know how to make the /ā/ sound. At this point they know the letter name "a," and they know that an open-syllable or single-syllable word that ends in "a" makes the /ā/ sound. Talk about how in closed syllables, the "a" says /ă/, as in "pan," and that the word "pan" has three phonemes or sounds. Ask students what can be done to create the word "pane." How can they make the /ā/ sound when it is a closed syllable? Be sure to count together the number of phonemes in both "pan" and "pane." Notice that they both have three sounds, so the solution is not to add another letter that has a sound, since there are only three sounds.

This foundational work reinforces the way vowels work within words. We teach open and closed syllables before VCe so that students understand the role of the silent "e." VCe or "magic e" is needed to reach back and make the short vowel long without adding any other sounds or opening the syllable. This is also reinforced when writing VCe words. In phoneme-to-grapheme spelling, the silent "e" stays in the box with the last consonant. It is silent, so it does not get its own box.

Six Syllable Rules: This is the third of the Six Syllable Rules. "VCe" always stays together when breaking multisyllable words into individual syllables.

Sample phoneme-to-grapheme mapping of VCe:

g	a	me	

Week 20 Word Lists: VCe (a_e)

Word Lists for Decoding and Encoding Activities

Real Words

bake	came	mate	fane	dale	pave
cake	dame	rate	vane	gale	rave
fake	fame	sate	wane	hale	save
lake	game	fade	safe	kale	wave
make	lame	made	babe	male	haze
rake	name	wade	cage	pale	maze
sake	same	cane	mage	sale	quake
take	tame	lane	page	tale	shade
wake	date	pane	rage	vale	shave
ware	fate	sane	sage	cave	shake
rare	gate		wage	gave	shape
dare	hate		bale		shame
fare	late				share
care					
bare					
mare					
hare					

			Nonsense Words

chase	frame		mafe
whale	grape		gake
blade	grave		vame
blame	grade		jate
blaze	trade		bape
slate	scale		nase
slave	skate		sade
flame	snake		fape
plane	spade		zabe
plate	spare		caze
brake	scare		kafe
brave	stare		lape
change	snare		jare
waste	flare		
craze	blare		
crave	glare		
drape			

Two-Syllable Extending Words
caveman, cupcake, mistake, inflate, update, translate, upgrade, classmate, insane, unsafe, makeup, aware, compare, beware, cookware

Word Chain
fake, rake, take, tale, tame, name, game, came, care, case, base, bare, bake, shake, quake, flake, brake, brave, crave, wave, wade, shade, share, scare

Tricky Words set 6: once, great, does

Grade 1 Week 21 Target Concept: VCe ("i_e")

(see blueprint, page 100)

Description of Concept

VCe: **i_e**

VCe sound: /ī/

Review a_e and introduce **i_e**.

Remind students: The "e" at the end of VCe words is silent but it has a very important role, which is to reach back and make the vowel before it say its long sound. For example, the word "pine" is a long vowel "e" word and the "i" says its long sound, /ī/. Without the "e" at the end of the word, the vowel sound would be a short /ĭ/ sound and the word would be "pin."

Teacher Knowledge: There are a select number of words where the iCe makes the /ē/ sound ("police," "prestige," "tangerine").

Sample phoneme-to-grapheme mapping of VCe:

t	i	me	

Week 21 Word Lists: VCe (i_e)

Word Lists for Decoding and Encoding Activities						
Real Words						**Nonsense Words**
bike	side	bile	pipe	quite	brine	bipe
like	ride	file	ripe	shine	bride	fibe
hike	wide	mile	wipe	shire	drive	jime
dime	fine	pile	wife	chime	grime	tife
lime	line	tile	life	while	trite	rike
time	pine	vile	five	white	spine	shile
mime	nine	fire	jive	whine	spite	chipe
bite	mine	hire	live	thine	spire	thive
kite	vine	tire	hive	slide	spike	whike
site	wine	sire	size	slime		snime
		wire	vibe	glide		flibe

Two-Syllable Extending Words

incline, decline, feline, widen, sunshine, ripen, timeline, inside, sublime, describe, define, campfire, reptile, retire, awhile, alpine

Word Chain

file, pile, mile, mine, pine, pipe, wipe, wine, vine, fine, fire, hire, hike, like, life, wife, wide, side, ride, bride

Tricky Words set 7: goes, word, school

Grade 1 Week 22 Target Concept: VCe ("o_e")

(see blueprint, page 100)

Description of Concept

VCe: **o_e**

VCe sound: /ō/

Review a_e and i_e, introduce **o_e**.

Remind students: The "e" at the end of VCe words is silent but it has a very important role, which is to reach back and make the vowel before it say its long sound. For example, the word "code" is a long vowel "e" word, and the "o" says its long sound, /ō/. Without the "e" at the end of the word, the vowel sound would be a short /ŏ/ sound and the word would be "cod."

Sample phoneme-to-grapheme mapping of VCe:

b	o	ne	

Week 22 Word Lists: VCe (o_e)

Word Lists for Decoding and Encoding Activities						
Real Words						
Coke	bode	dole	more	doze	quote	froze
poke	code	hole	sore	dose	shore	prone
woke	mode	mole	tore	dove	chose	smoke
dome	rode	pole	wore	cove	slope	snore
home	bone	role	cope	rove	drove	spoke
dote	hone	tole	dope		drone	spore
note	lone	bore	hope		grove	store
rote	tone	core	lope		clove	stone
tote	zone	fore	mope		clone	stove
vote		lore	nope		close	
			rope		clothe	
Nonsense Words						
cofe	thode					
gope	shome					
hobe	chove					
roke	whobe					
jode	quofe					
kose	froshe					
stome	glothe					
grome	boche					
clope						
drobe						
trone						
Two-Syllable Extending Words						
stovetop, pothole, explode, tadpole, suppose, expose, rehome, frozen, compose, adore, before, explore, foresee, galore, ignore, restore, therefore						
Word Chain						
woke, poke, pore, pole, role, rove, dove, dote, note, nope, slope, rope, hope, hone, stone, store, more, mole, hole, home, hone, drone, drove, grove, clove, close, chose						
Tricky Words set 7: open, move, eyes						

Grade 1 Week 23 Target Concept: VCe ("u_e")

(see blueprint, page 101)

Description of Concept

VCe: **u_e**

VCe sound: **/ū/ and /ö/**

Review a_e, i_e, and o_e, introduce **u_e.**

Remind students: The "e" at the end of VCe words is silent but it has a very important role, which is to reach back and make the vowel before it say its long sound. The concept "u_e" can be a bit tricky to learn because it can make two different sounds, /ū/, as in "cube," and /ü/, as in "tube." Without the "e" at the end of these words, the vowel sound would be a short /ŭ/ sound and the words would be "cub" and "tub."

Sample phoneme-to-grapheme mapping of VCe:

t	u	be	

Week 23 Word Lists: VCe (u_e)

Word Lists for Decoding and Encoding Activities						
Real Words				**Nonsense Words**		
rude	cute	mule	flute	vude	spute	shune
tune	mute	rule	fluke	hufe	crume	chupe
June	jute	fume	brute	lume	slupe	whule
dune	dupe		crude	duve	flube	thude
tube	huge		prune	cule	clute	kuthe
cube	duke		prude			
lube	Luke					
cure	nuke					
pure	puke					
lure						

Two-Syllable Extending Words
acute, impure, excuse, include, exclude, abuse, accuse, amuse, exude, reuse, allude, assume, defuse, dilute, immune, legume, salute, volume, commune, commute, compute, confuse, costume, dispute, tribute

Word Chain
rude, dude, duke, nuke, puke, pure, cure, cute, mute, jute, June, tune, tube, cube, lube, Luke, fluke, flute, glute, brute

Tricky Words set 7: close, watch, idea

Grade 1 Week 24 Target Concept: VCe ("e_e")

(see blueprint, page 101)

Description of Concept
VCe: **e_e**
VCe sound: /ē/
Review a_e, i_e, o_e, and u_e, introduce **e_e**.
Remind students: The "e" at the end of VCe words is silent but it has a very important role, which is to reach back and make the vowel before it say its long sound. For example, the word "Pete" is a "long-vowel e" word and the "e" in the middle says its long sound, /ē/. Without the "e" at the end of the word, the vowel sound would be a short /ĕ/ sound and the word would be "pet."

Teacher Knowledge: The VCe sequence with the letter "r" as the consonant ("ere"), can make the sound /air/, as in "where," and /er/, as in "were."

Sample phoneme-to-grapheme mapping of VCe:

h	e	re	

Week 24 Word Lists: VCe (e_e)

Word Lists for Decoding and Encoding Activities						
Real Words			**Nonsense Words**			
eve meme here mere Pete gene	Steve Swede Crete delete	theme these	fepe bese veke lete meve dete	stene spele snede greme gleve brene	prete treke crene bleme plefe fleve	shefe cheme whese queve
Two-Syllable Extending Words delete, compete, complete, athlete, extreme, concrete, sincere, recede						
Word Chains here, mere, meme, theme Pete, Crete, delete eve, Steve						
Tricky Words: review and practice sets 1–7						
Exceptions to e_e: where, there, were						

Grade 1 Week 25 Target Concept: review/flex week
(see blueprint, page 101)

Description of Concept
Review. Working with progress monitoring data, focus review on targeted concepts where students need additional instruction and/or practice.

Many school districts have a spring break at some point in March. Some schools will have a two-week break and some will have one week. The week before a break is a good time to catch up on any concepts not yet taught and use progress monitoring to determine what concepts need further review and practice.

Week 25 Word Lists: See previously provided word lists depending on your focus concepts.

Grade 1 Week 26 Target Concept: inflected endings "s," "es"

(see blueprint, page 101)

Description of Concept

Inflected endings: **"s," "es"**

Inflected ending sounds: **/s/, /z/** and **/ez/, /z/**

An inflected ending is a letter or letters added to the end of a word to change or add to its meaning. Adding "s" or "es" to the end of a word changes the word to a plural, meaning more than one, but it can also change the tense to present ("grabs"). Sometimes the "s" or "es" at the end of words makes the voiceless sound /s/ (the same as an initial "s" sound), as in "hats." Other words that end in "s" make the voiced sound /z/, the same sound heard in short Anglo-Saxon words ("as," "is," etc.). Words that end in a vowel sound and are followed by "s" or "es" make the /z/ sound ("zebras"), but so do many others.

The rule for whether to add "s" or "es" is simple: if the word ends in "ch," "sh," "s," "x," or "z" ("lunches," "wishes," "kisses," "boxes," and "fizzes"), use "es" to make it plural. All other endings simply require an "s."

One other notable change for making a plural is when a word ends in "y." Although we have not explicitly taught words that end in "y" at this point, students will be writing them and encountering them in print. If a word ends in "y," change the "y" to an "i" and add "es" ("party"/"parties").

This is also a good point to talk about words that change spelling when becoming plural ("mouse"/"mice," "man"/"men"). This is addressed further in Grade 3 Week 32 on page 219.

Sample phoneme-to-grapheme mapping of inflected ending "s" and "es":

c	a	t	s		
g	a	s	e	s	

Teachers Knowledge: For nouns and verbs that end in "s" but are not plural, a silent "e" is added to indicate a singular form. Nouns such as "house," "goose," "mouse," "horse," "purse," and "purchase" and verbs such as "tease," "please," "grease," "advise," and "amuse" all have a silent "e" added to make it clear they're not plural.

Week 26 Word Lists: inflected endings s, es

Word Lists for Decoding and Encoding Activities					
s — as in hats		**s — as in his**		**es**	
cats	trips	dogs	sings	gases	crushes
hats	flocks	dads	lines	buses	brushes
hits	camps	buds	cones	crunches	radishes
bits	socks	wins	chins	munches	fixes
lips	backs	beds	wings	bunches	mixes
cops	tents	fans	bangs	benches	boxes
reps	funds	bags	tongs	wishes	foxes
sets	sinks	pens	things	dishes	axes
tips	shops	bugs	snugs	bushes	taxes
stacks	chips	crabs	grabs	smashes	
slips	hopes				
spots					

Word Chains
hats, bats, chats, mats, pats, rats
boxes, foxes, fixes, mixes, sixes, axes, taxes
sings, wings, pings, rings, rinks, links, winks, stinks, pinks

Tricky Words: review and practice tricky words that end in "s" that make the /z/ sound (**is, as, his, has, was, goes, eyes**).

Grade 1 Week 27 Target Concepts: final consonant blends "nt," "nd"
(see blueprint, page 101)

Description of Concept
Final consonant blends: **nt, nd**
Introduce final consonant blends.
Consonant blends are two-letter sounds that are blended when reading words fluently. Each letter still says its own sound and they can be heard separately, but when decoding words, it is helpful to blend the sounds. Blends can be at the start of a word or syllable (initial) or at the end of a word or syllable (final).
Sample phoneme-to-grapheme mapping of final blends:

b	e	n	t
s	a	n	d

Teacher Knowledge: When "i" is followed by "n" it can make its long or short vowel sound. This makes words like "kind," "mind," and "blind" challenging for grade 1 students. This rule will be explicitly taught in Grade 2 Week 30.

Week 27 Word Lists: final consonant blends nt, nd

Word Lists for Decoding and Encoding Activities							
Real Words				**Nonsense Words**			
pant	slant	and	fund	fant	drant	kand	fland
hint	plant	sand	tend	hent	brint	tind	glund
lint	grant	hand	pend	bint	dront	hond	clend
mint	print	land	send	lunt	prunt	rund	quond
tint	stint	band	fend	zent	grent	slind	chind
font	flint	stand	lend	bund	shant	spond	
bent	glint	grand	vend	glant	chint	smund	
dent	grunt	brand	bend	plint	thont	grond	
lent	brunt	gland	mend	slont	whunt	brend	
rent	stunt	wind	spend	flunt	quent		
sent	blunt	pond	trend	blent			
tent	shunt	fond	blend				
vent	chant	bond					
went		blond					

Two-Syllable Extending Words
enchant, agent, absent, indent, invent, moment, patent, infant, intent, potent, mutant, extent, advent, event, content, comment
amend, upend, behind, inland, legend, offend, remind, unkind, second, expand, intend, demand, attend, defend, upwind, midland

Word Chains
pant, pent, bent, went, sent, dent, dint, hint, mint, print, flint, stint, stunt, grunt, shunt
sand, send, lend, mend, bend, band, brand, grand, gland, land, hand, stand

Tricky Words set 8: world, over, people

Grade 1 Week 28 Target Concept: final consonant blends "mp," "nk"
(see blueprint, page 101)

Description of Concept
Final consonant blends: **mp, nk**
Remind students that consonant blends are two-letter sounds that are blended when reading words fluently. Each letter still says its own sound and they can be heard separately, but when decoding words, it is helpful to blend the sounds. Blends can be at the start of a word/syllable (initial) or at the end of a word/syllable (final).
Sample phoneme-to-grapheme mapping of final blend:

l	u	m	p
s	i	n	k

Week 28 Word Lists: final consonant blends mp and nk

Word Lists for Decoding and Encoding Activities							
Real Words						**Nonsense Words**	
amp	skimp	trump	rank	wink	punk	crump	kemp
ramp	primp	frump	tank	rink	sunk	jamp	fank
tamp	crimp	grump	yank	pink	dunk	himp	tink
damp	blimp	clump	sank	sink	funk	tomp	sonk
lamp	chimp	slump	dank	fink	gunk	zump	wunk
camp	romp	plump	hank	kink	hunk	vemp	venk
stamp	pomp	stump	lank	link	junk	swump	swink
scamp	clomp	chump	bank	mink	bunk	framp	glonk
cramp	stomp	thump	stank	stink	stunk	glimp	frunk
glamp	ump	temp	spank	slink	slunk	plomp	blenk
clamp	rump	hemp	swank	brink	spunk	brump	whank
champ	pump		prank	drink	skunk	whamp	shink
imp	sump		drank	plink	plunk	thimp	quonk
wimp	dump		Frank	clink	flunk	quomp	chenk
gimp	lump		plank	blink	clunk	shump	spink
limp	bump		flank	chink	chunk	chemp	swink
			clank	think		slank	chonk
			blank	honk		brank	
			shank				
			thank				

Two-Syllable Extending Words
revamp, encamp, repump, unclamp, restamp
embank, debunk, rethink, unlink, unkink, uplink, mudbank, sandbank, kerplunk, chipmunk, cufflink

Word Chains
lamp, limp, lump, pump, dump, damp, ramp, romp, stomp, stamp, clamp, champ, chimp, crimp, cramp, gramp, grump, thump
tank, sank, sink, link, wink, rink, rank, hank, honk, hunk, sunk, stunk, skunk, chunk, plunk, plank, thank, think

Tricky Words set 8: enough, carry, answer

Grade 1 Week 29 Target Concept: schwa

(see blueprint, page 101)

Description of Concept

Schwa "ə" is an unstressed vowel sound where the vowel does not make its own long or short sound (e.g., "the," "banana," "wagon"). Schwa is the most common vowel sound in English, so it is important that it is explicitly taught. The schwa sound, /uh/, is remarkably similar to /ŭ/ but is slightly softer and weaker. Schwa can replace any vowel sound, including /y/.

Some people call schwa the "lazy vowel cousin" because you do not fully open your mouth to create the full vowel sound. Sometimes it is not even represented in spelling ("rhythm," "able") but is voiced to support the creation of a syllable, since every syllable needs a vowel (rhyth-m, a-ble). Schwa shows up in unstressed words and syllables. You will find that students love schwa and will hunt it down for themselves, bringing words to the teacher to share or check that the word does indeed include a schwa.

Teacher Knowledge:
- The use of schwa can be region-dependent. The dialect of a region may use schwa in places that other regions do not. Consider the way words are spoken in your region when adding or deleting words to the list of schwa words below.
- Schwa is a concept that is introduced here but will require ongoing discussions in grades 2 and 3.

Lesson Plan

	Target Concept: schwa
1	**Warm-up/review:** 2–5 minutes Review final consonant blends "mp" and "nk."
2	**Introduce new concepts (I Do):** 5 minutes The teacher tells students that today they will be talking about schwa. Write "schwa" and its symbol (ə) on the board and have students practice saying the word. Schwa is tricky because it can replace the sound of any vowel with the /uh/ sound. "One of the places you have already seen schwa is in the word 'the' which should say /thē/. In this word, the /ē/ is replaced with the /uh/ sound."
3	**Phonological awareness:** 3 minutes The teacher says words one at a time and students listen to hear if there is a schwa in the word. If they hear schwa, they are to make a thumbs-up gesture with both hands, and if they do not hear schwa, they are to make a thumbs-down gesture with both hands. the 👍 bridge 👎 wagon 👍 banana 👍 telephone 👍 brown 👎 balloons 👍 pinecone 👎 tomorrow 👍
4	**Teacher-led guided practice with new concept (WE Do):** 10–15 minutes Project a list of short words containing schwa on the whiteboard. Read them together as a class. Many of the words can be tricky words that students are already familiar with. Have students come up and use an erasable pen to put the schwa symbol /ə/ over the part of the word that says /uh/, or use a pre-made magnet of the schwa symbol if it's hard for students to write the upside down and backwards e. Suggested words for grade 1 can be found in the one- and two-syllable words listed below.
5	**Extended independent practice activities to apply new concept (YOU Do):** 15–20 minutes Suggested activities include: • Have student read lists of schwa words with a partner and identify the schwa. • Create a classroom list of schwa words. Students can suggest schwa words to be added to the list. These words might be discovered in conversations, through read-aloud stories, or through discussions at home. • Card sorts of tricky words. Students sort into tricky words with schwa and tricky words without schwa.

6	**Tricky Words:** 10 minutes Introduce set 8 (**above, most, kind**).
7	**Decoding with text (You Do):** 15–20 minutes It is hard to find text that is targeted to practice the schwa sound. Have students search for schwa in books they are currently reading. Create a class list of schwa words students have found (see extending words). These can be added to a sound wall if you are using one.
8	**Encoding (YOU Do):** 15 minutes Using phoneme-to-grapheme spelling, have students spell words that have a schwa. Have students indicate the schwa by putting the schwa symbol above vowels that take on the schwa sound. Sample phoneme-to-grapheme mapping of schwa:

l	ə o	ve	
wh	ə a	t	

Week 29 Word Lists: schwa

Word Lists for Decoding and Encoding Activities
One-Syllable Words the, was, love, come, some, what, does, of, from, other
Two-Syllable Extending Words other, mother, above, wagon, balloons, again, zebra, comma, sofa, data, animal, pencil, idea, area, tuna, yoga, gala, pizza, drama, extra, ribbon, carrot, item, China, quota, aroma, grandma, below, confess, police, bottom
Three- or More-Syllable Extending Words We would not expect grade 1 students to use these words but have placed them here for extending and for older grades being introduced to schwa for the first time: banana, tomorrow, important, capital, natural, manager, usually, different, movement, community, concern, person, reason, season, other, again, enemy, memory, original, oxygen, company, aroma, camera, agenda, cinema, formula, vanilla, dilemma, diploma, umbrella, orchestra, constable, alphabet, vitamin, celebrate, telephone, astronaut, elephant, gorilla, dinosaur
Tricky Words: above, most, kind

Grade 1 Week 30 Target Concept: the floss rule

(see blueprint, page 101)

Description of Concept

The floss rule is part of the closed-syllable family. Three of the letters that follow this rule are in the word "floss" ("f," "l," and "s") but if you say "zee floss rule" with an exaggerated French accent, then all four consonants are represented ("f," "l," "s," and "z").

The Rule in Writing:

If a one-syllable word ends in "f," "l," "s," or "z" and there is a short vowel before the final consonant, then double the "f," "l," "s," or "z." If the "s" says /z/ at the end of a word, don't double the final "s" ("has," "is," "was")

Do not double the consonant at the end of a word that is the shortened form of a larger word. For example, we do not double the final "s" in "bus" because it comes from the French word "l'autobus." Other examples include "gas"/"gasoline," "gel"/"gelatin," and "whiz"/"wizard."

The Rule in Reading:

Only pronounce one consonant of the doubled consonants at the end of a word. When encountering "ff," "ll," "ss," or "zz" at the end of a word, pronounce the preceding vowel as a short vowel (this follows the closed-syllable rule).

Lesson Plan

	Target Concept: the floss rule
1	**Warm-up:** 2–5 minutes Review schwa from week 29. Once you have introduced the floss rule, include a review of the floss rule.
2	**Introduce new concepts (I Do):** 5 minutes The floss rule is part of the closed-syllable family. Three of the letters that follow this rule are in the word "floss" ("f," "l," and "s") but if you say "zee floss rule" with an exaggerated French accent, then all four consonants are represented ("f," "l," "s," and "z"). **The Rule in Writing:** If a one-syllable word ends in "f," "l," "s," or "z" and there is a short vowel before the final consonant, then double the "f," "l," "s," or "z." If the "s" says /z/ at the end of a word, don't double the final "s" ("has," "is," "was"). Do not double the consonant at the end of a word that is the shortened form of a larger word. For example, we do not double the final "s" in "bus" because it comes from the French word "l'autobus." Other examples include "gas"/"gasoline," "gel"/"gelatin," and "whiz"/"wizard."

	The Rule in Reading: Only pronounce one consonant of the doubled consonants at the end of the word. When encountering "ff," "ll," "ss," or "zz" at the end of a word, pronounce the preceding vowel as a short vowel (this follows the closed-syllable rule). There are many excellent YouTube videos that explain the floss rule. Be sure to preview videos to find ones that align with this lesson.
3	**Phonological awareness:** 3 minutes Practice manipulating and substituting phonemes with the floss words. For example: Teacher: "Say 'staff.'" Students: "Staff." Teacher: "Now say 'staff' but instead of /ă/ say /ŭ/." Students: "Stuff."
4	**Teacher-led guided practice with new concept (WE Do):** 10–15 minutes • Explain the rule and then show students words that end in "ff," "ll," "ss," and "zz." Explain that with the floss rule, words that end in these four consonants require a double consonant at the end when they are one-syllable words that have a short vowel before the final consonant. • Students and teacher choral read lists of floss-rule phrases or blending lines projected onto a smartboard/whiteboard. • Students fold a piece of lined notebook paper lengthwise (hotdog fold) and open flat. At the top of the first column (created by the fold), students write "Floss rule" and then "Not the floss rule" at the top of the second column. The teacher reads a word that ends in one of the four floss consonants and students write the correctly spelled word in the appropriate column. For example, "jazz" would go into the "floss rule" column whereas "has" would go in the "Not the floss rule" column. After each word, the class decides together which is the correct column, with students explaining why they have placed it in the column they did. Students correct any errors in placement.
5	**Extended/independent practice activities to apply new concept (YOU Do):** 15–20 minutes • **"Find the Word" game:** Group students into teams of four. Give students a stack of word cards that contain floss and non-floss rule words (these can be created on your computer, written on cardstock cards, or by going to the website https://sightwords.com/sight-words/flash-cards/ to generate digital cards). Ask teams to perform a variety of tasks. Example: find three floss words that end in "ss" (or "zz," or "ff," or "ll"). Find a non-floss rule word that is part of a bigger word and therefore the floss rule does not apply (e.g., "gas," "gel," or "bus"). Choose two non-floss rule words that are exempt because the "s" at the end says /z/. • Choose a worksheet where students can practice applying the floss rule.
6	**Decoding with text (YOU Do):** Choose decodable passages to practice the floss rule in print.

7	**Encoding (YOU Do):** • **"Is It Spelled Correctly?" game:** The teacher writes two words on the board; one is spelled correctly and the other is not. Students write the word with the correct spelling in their notebooks. For example, the teacher writes "expres" and "express" on the board. Students write "express" in their notebooks. Correct as a class after each word and discuss why the floss rule was applied (or why it was not). • Use phrases to practice spelling words that contain the floss rule. Include words that do not follow the rule so that students become familiar with variations. See spelling phrase list below. Sample phoneme-to-grapheme mapping of the floss rule: | s	t	i	ff	
---	---	---	---	---
b	u	zz			
8	**Intervention:** Scaffold passages and word lists for students who are lagging.
9	**Extending:** Use multisyllable words and complex text for students who understand the concept and use it in print.
	Tricky Words: review and practice tricky words from all sets, based on ongoing progress monitoring.

Week 30 Word Lists: the floss rule

Word Lists for Decoding and Encoding Activities	
ff	**ll**
One-Syllable Words sniff, cuff, off, buff, cliff, whiff, staff, stiff, bluff, stuff, puff, huff, scoff, scuff	**One-Syllable Words** shell, drill, fall, fell, bell, cell, tell, well, yell, hill, fill, bill, mill, will, pull, grill, chill, trill, spell, swell, smell, spill, still, all, ball, call, hall tall, wall, small, stall, doll, skull, sell, skill, shall, pill, kill, shrill, quill
ss	**zz**
One-Syllable Words grass, boss, chess, mass, pass, less, mess, miss, kiss, hiss, toss, moss, loss, fuss, muss, brass, class, glass, press, dress, stress, less, bless, bliss, gloss, floss, class, pass, press, guess	**One-Syllable Words** fizz, buzz, fuzz, jazz, razz, frizz

Two-Syllable Extending Words
overstuff, distress, redress, dismiss, remiss, express, regress, befell, fulfill, basketball, foretell, surpass, abuzz, razzle, frazzle, dazzle, fizzle, jazzy, buzzes, pizzazz

Nonsense Words
juff, croff, gliff, shuff, quozz, plazz, drizz, whess, bloss, smuss, vell, brell, shull

Exceptions to the Floss Rule	**Creating Two-Syllable Words**
pal, as, was, us, if, is, thus, his, yes, this, has, of, gas (gasoline), bus (*l'autobus*), whiz (wizard), gel (gelatin)	Many two-syllable words can be created by adding a prefix or suffix to the root words above. For example, "fuzz" can become "fuzzy" and "call" can become "recall."

Spelling Phrases

ring toss	a big staff	a new class	on the bus
fire drill	get a cell	buzz says the bee	smell it
be a pal	the best jazz	a red dress	press harder
sell me some	a small bluff	off the cuff	he has a bike
fill with gas	I digress	bless this mess	sniff and smell
		dig a well	fill my glass

Word Chains
off, scoff, scuff, huff, puff, cuff, bluff, stuff, staff, stiff, cliff, whiff
bell, tell, fell, fill, fall, call, tall, till, will, wall, ball, bill, hill, chill, skill, still, swill, swell, smell, spell, shell
fuss, muss, moss, toss, boss, gloss, floss, loss, less, dress, stress, press, mess, miss, kiss, hiss, bliss
jazz, razz, frizz, fizz, fuzz, buzz

Grade 1 Week 31 Target Concept: three-letter blends "str," "scr," "spr"

(see blueprint, page 101)

Description of Concept

Three-letter blends: **str, scr, spr**

Three-letter blend sounds: **/str/, /skr/, /spr/**

Introduce three-letter blends "str," "scr," and "spr" with both short and long vowel sounds. "Str," "scr," "spr" are three-letter blends consisting of three consonants. Sample phoneme-to-grapheme mapping of three-letter blends:

s	t	r	u	t	
s	c	r	a	p	
s	p	r	i	n	t

Week 31 Word Lists: three-letter blends str, scr, spr

Word Lists for Decoding and Encoding Activities				
Real Words				
strap	strict	scrap	scrape	sprat
strip	struck	scram	scribe	sprig
strut	string	scrab	script	sprint
strum	strong	scrag		
strep	strand	scran		
strike	strength	scrim		
stripe		scrin		
stride		scrub		
strive		scrum		
stroke				
strobe				
Nonsense Words				
stram	scrat	sprad		
strit	scrid	sprin		
strod	scrob	sprom		
strug	scruk	sprug		
stren	screm	spref		
strave	scrash	sprash		
stribe	scroth	sprich		
strone	scruch	sprong		
strude	screng	spruth		
strele	scramp	spramp		
	scronk	sprink		
	scrint	spront		
	scrund	sprund		

Extending Words
spray, spree, sprain, spring, sprang, sprung, spread, stray, strain, street, streak, stream, scream, screen, screech

Two-Syllable Extending Words
strata, stranger, stricken, scramble, scrabble, scribble, scraped, scrappy, springy, sprinkle, sprinted, sprocket, describe

Word Chain
sprang, spring, string, strip, strap, scrap, scrape, scribe, scrim, scrum, strum

Tricky Words: review and practice tricky words from all sets, based on ongoing progress monitoring.

Grade 1 Week 32 Target Concept: three-letter blends with digraphs "squ," "shr," "thr"

(see blueprint, page 101)

Description of Concept
Three-letter blends: **squ, shr, thr**
Three-letter blend sounds: **/skw/, /shr/, /thr/**

Introduce three-letter blends "squ," "shr," and "thr" with both short and long vowel sounds.

"Squ," "shr," and "thr" are three-letter blends that are made up of one digraph and one consonant.

When breaking words into syllables, trigraphs stay together.

Sample phoneme-to-grapheme mapping of three-letter blends:

s	q	u	i	d	
sh	r	u	g		
th	r	o	b		

Week 32 Word Lists: three-letter blends squ, shr, thr

Word Lists for Decoding and Encoding Activities					
Real Words			**Nonsense Words**		
squid	shrub	throb	squam	shraf	thrab
squib	shrug	thrash	squip	shrin	thrim
squint	shred	thrush	squol	shrom	throp
squish	shrink	throne	squed	shrup	thrut
squinch	shrank	thrive	squath	shret	thref
squire	shrunk	thrift	squich	shrash	thrach
	shrimp	throw	squong	shrich	thrish
	shrine	thrown	squesh	shroth	thrung
			squote	shrung	thrate
			squape	shrabe	thribe
			squive	shride	throke
				shrove	thrule

Extending Words
squeeze, squeak, squeal, three, throat, thread, threat

Two-Syllable Extending Words
squinty, squishy, squadron, squirrel, shrinking, shrimpy, shrivel, shrunken, thrifty, thrasher, threaten, thriller, thriving

Word Chain
squid, squire, shire, shine, shrine

Tricky Words: review and practice tricky words from all sets, based on ongoing progress monitoring.

Grade 1 Week 33 Target Concept: inflected ending "ing"
(see blueprint, page 102)

Description of Concept

Inflected ending: **-ing**

The inflected ending "ing" plays six roles in English. In this lesson we will look at the three most common uses.

- It can be a noun (called a gerund), as in "Swimming is a healthy sport."
- It can be an adjective, as in "She is taking swimming lessons."
- It can be a present participle of a verb, as in "She is swimming."

Sample phoneme-to-grapheme mapping of inflected ending "ing":

w	a	v	i	ng	

Teaching Strategy

Have students read a short phrase or sentence and state whether the "ing" word is a noun, adjective, or verb.

Week 33 Word Lists: inflected ending -ing

Word Lists for Decoding and Encoding Activities						
"ing" Words with Single Final Consonant				"ing" Words with Doubled Final Consonant		
waving	timing	singing	quacking	hitting	betting	spinning
raving	lining	dinging	whacking	fitting	getting	grinning
saving	dining	rocking	cracking	quitting	setting	running
shaving	pining	mocking	sitting	dotting	telling	nipping
skating	whining	locking	packing	rotting	spelling	tipping
riding	hiking	licking	backing	potting	patting	whipping
hiding	liking	kicking	tucking	butting	batting	shipping
biting	biking	picking	sucking	putting	dimming	hugging
firing	finding	ticking	shocking	cutting	swimming	
hiring	jumping	hacking	shacking	shutting	pinning	
tiring	standing	tacking	shucking	rubbing	thinning	

Three-Syllable Words
amazing, disgusting, traveling, admitting, upsetting, finishing, boiling, enjoying

Four-Syllable Words
developing, astonishing, contemplating, hibernating, renovating

Extension Words
lying, dying, flying, drying, peeling, meaning, failing, staying, loaning, showing

Word Chain
waving, raving, saving, sacking, racking, cracking, whacking, shacking, shocking, shucking, tucking, ticking, picking, kicking, licking, locking

Tricky Words: review and practice tricky words from all sets, based on ongoing progress monitoring.

Grade 1 Week 34 Target Concept: screening week

(see blueprint, page 102)

Description of Concept

This week is intentionally scheduled time to screen your students in order to assess progress and plan for the next school year. The following screens are recommended in spring of grade 1:

- phonemic awareness and letters & sounds *for at-risk students*
- decoding screen *for at-risk students*
- benchmark or fluency/comprehension screen
- developmental spelling screen
- tricky words screen

Grade 1 Weeks 35, 36, & 37 Target Concept: targeted review of concepts based on assessments

(see blueprint, page 102)

Description of Concept

Targeted review of skills taught in grade 1 based on assessment.

Concepts introduced in grade 1: initial and final digraphs ("sh," "ch," "th," "qu," "wh," "ck"); initial blends with "l," "r," and "s family;" inflected endings ("s," "es," and "ing"); VCe (a_e, i_e, o_e, u_e, e_e); final blends ("s," "es," and "ing"); schwa; three-letter blends ("s," "es," and "ing"); and tricky words sets 1–8.

Word Lists: use previously provided word lists.
Tricky Words: review and practice tricky words from all sets, based on ongoing progress monitoring.

Grade 2 Blueprint

The following structure begins with eight weeks of review of concepts introduced in grade 1. If your students have not had explicit instruction in grade 1, follow this grade 2 blueprint but adjust the introduction and pacing of new concepts. In some regions/countries, the concepts covered in this grade 2 scope and sequence are taught in grade 1. If this is true for you, move to the grade 3 blueprint.

There are many ways to address reading instruction once foundational pieces are in place (e.g., long and short vowels, consonants, and blending). As a professional who knows your students, you will use your expertise to adjust the pacing of introducing and reviewing concepts. This may mean speeding up or slowing down the progression of instruction. Once a concept has been taught it should be continuously reinforced and applied through conversation, practice activities, and instruction. If you do not complete all the lessons in this year, rest assured that they will be covered again for your students in the fall and next year's teacher may need to take a little more time with concepts that were not completed in the grade 2 scope and sequence.

We acknowledge that there will be times throughout the year when you will be referring to concepts not yet explicitly taught (e.g., vowel teams and r-controlled vowels). It is important to make sure that the foundational pieces are taught in a logical progression, and therefore, in this progression, vowel teams come after blends and digraphs. This is cumulative work, not necessarily teaching skills in isolation.

By the end of grade 2, our hope is that students will be able to read and write using vowel teams, diphthongs, the many jobs of "y," r-controlled vowels, trigraph "igh," silent letters, inflected ending "ed," common contractions, and past-tense verbs.

Grade 2 Blueprint

	WEEK 1	WEEK 2	WEEK 3	WEEK 4
SEPTEMBER	✓ review open & closed syllables & schwa ✓ blending, building & manipulating words, spelling & reading in context ✓ tricky words review & practice	✓ review initial & final digraphs (qu, sh, ch, wh, th, ck, ng) ✓ mini lesson to introduce **ph** ✓ blending, building & manipulating words, spelling & reading in context ✓ tricky words review & practice	✓ review initial blends with "l," "r" & "s" families ✓ blending, building & manipulating words, spelling & reading in context ✓ tricky words review & practice	✓ review final consonant blends (nt, nd, mp, nk) ✓ blending, building & manipulating words, spelling & reading in context ✓ tricky words review & practice

	WEEK 5	WEEK 6	WEEK 7	WEEK 8
OCTOBER	✓ review floss rule (ff, ll, ss, zz) ✓ blending, building & manipulating words, spelling & reading in context ✓ tricky words review & practice	✓ review initial 3-letter blends (str, scr, spr, squ, shr, thr) ✓ blending, building & manipulating words, spelling & reading in context ✓ tricky words review & practice	✓ review inflected endings (s, es, ing) ✓ blending, building & manipulating words, spelling & reading in context ✓ tricky words review & practice	✓ review "magic e" (a_e, i_e, o_e, u_e, e_e) ✓ CVCe blending, building & manipulating words, spelling & reading in context ✓ tricky words review & practice

	WEEK 9	WEEK 10	WEEK 11	WEEK 12
NOVEMBER	✓ screening week: ✓ letters & sounds *for at-risk students* ✓ tricky words screen *for at-risk students* ✓ phonics word reading screen ✓ spelling screen ✓ benchmark or fluency/comprehension screen ✓ mini lesson(s) on words with **ie, oe, & ue**	✓ introduce vowel teams **ee, ea** ✓ Mini lesson on **the other sounds of ea** ✓ blending, building & manipulating words, spelling & reading in context ✓ targeted tricky words review & practice	✓ review vowel teams ee, ea & add **oa, ow** ✓ blending, building & manipulating words, spelling & reading in context ✓ targeted tricky words review & practice	✓ review vowel teams ee, ea, oa, ow & add **ay, ai** ✓ blending, building & manipulating words, spelling & reading in context ✓ targeted tricky words review & practice

DECEMBER		
WEEK 13 ✓ introduce diphthongs **oy, oi** ✓ blending, building & manipulating words, spelling & reading in context ✓ targeted tricky words review & practice	**WEEK 14** ✓ flex/review	✓ winter break
JANUARY		
WEEK 15 ✓ introduce vowel team **oo** — both sounds ✓ blending, building & manipulating words, spelling & reading in context ✓ targeted tricky words review & practice	**WEEK 16** ✓ introduce trigraph **igh** ✓ blending, building & manipulating words, spelling & reading in context ✓ targeted tricky words review & practice	**WEEK 17** ✓ introduce sounds of inflected ending **ed** ✓ single-syllable words & multi-syllable words ✓ blending, building & manipulating words, spelling & reading in context ✓ targeted tricky words review & practice
		WEEK 18 ✓ screening week: ✓ progress monitoring ✓ spelling *for at-risk students* ✓ benchmark of fluency/comprehension *for at-risk students*
FEBRUARY		
WEEK 19 ✓ introduce **hard & soft c** ✓ single-syllable words & multi-syllable words ✓ blending, building & manipulating words, spelling & reading in context ✓ targeted tricky words review & practice	**WEEK 20** ✓ introduce **hard & soft g** ✓ single-syllable words & multi-syllable words ✓ blending, building & manipulating words, spelling & reading in context ✓ targeted tricky words review & practice	**WEEK 21** ✓ introduce the "**many jobs of y**" (jobs 1–3) ✓ blending, building & manipulating words, spelling & reading in context ✓ targeted tricky words review & practice
		WEEK 22 ✓ the "**many jobs of y**" cont. (jobs 4–6) ✓ blending, building & manipulating words, spelling & reading in context ✓ targeted tricky words review & practice

MARCH	**WEEK 23**	**WEEK 24**	**WEEK 25**
	√ introduce vowel-r **ar** √ blending, building & manipulating words, spelling & reading in context √ targeted tricky words review & practice	√ review vowel-r ar & add **or** √ mini lesson on **second sound of or** (/er/, as in "word") √ blending, building & manipulating words, spelling & reading in context √ targeted tricky words review & practice	√ flex/review √ spring break
APRIL	**WEEK 26**	**WEEK 27**	**WEEK 28** / **WEEK 29**
	√ review vowel-r ar, or & add **er, ir, ur** √ blending, building & manipulating words, spelling & reading in context √ targeted tricky words review & practice	√ introduce diphthongs **ow, ou** √ blending, building & manipulating words, spelling & reading in context √ targeted tricky words review & practice	**WEEK 28:** √ introduce the other sounds of **ou** √ blending, building & manipulating words, spelling & reading in context √ targeted tricky words review & practice **WEEK 29:** √ introduce initial silent letters (**kn, gn, wr, mb, gh**) √ blending, building & manipulating words, spelling & reading in context
MAY	**WEEK 30**	**WEEK 31**	**WEEK 32** / **WEEK 33**
	√ flex/review week √ mini lesson on **long & short o & i** (when followed by two consonants)	√ introduce diphthong/vowel team **ew** √ mini lesson(s) on vowel teams (**eu, ui**) √ blending, building & manipulating words, spelling & reading in context	**WEEK 32:** √ introduce vowel teams **aw, au** √ mini lesson on **wa, al** √ blending, building & manipulating words, spelling & reading in context **WEEK 33:** √ introduce **past-tense verbs** √ blending, building & manipulating words, spelling & reading in context

	WEEK 34	WEEK 35	WEEK 36	WEEK 37
JUNE	√ screening week √ phonics word reading screen √ spelling screen √ benchmark or fluency/ comprehension screen	√ targeted review of concepts based on assessments	√ targeted review of concepts based on assessments	√ targeted review of concepts based on assessments

Weekly Concept Pages with Full Lesson Plans in Weeks 12, 19, 20, and 21

Grade 2 Weeks 1–8: Review

Week	Concept for Review (+ Introduction)	Original Lesson: Grade 1	Page
Week 1	open & closed syllables (short & long vowel sounds) & schwa	Weeks 19 & 29	118 & 132
Week 2	initial & final digraphs: sh, ch, th, qu, wh, ck, ng (+ **ph**)	Weeks 5, 6, 7, 8, 9, 10, 11 & 12	104–13
Week 3	initial blends with l, r & s family	Weeks 15, 16 & 17	114–17
Week 4	final consonant blends: nt, nd, mp, nk	Weeks 27 & 28	130–31
Week 5	floss rule (ff, ll, ss, zz)	Week 30	135
Week 6	3-letter blends: str, scr, spr, squ, shr, thr	Weeks 31 & 32	139–41
Week 7	inflected endings: s, es, & ing	Weeks 26 & 33	129 & 142
Week 8	VCe: a_e, i_e, o_e, u_e, e_e	Weeks 20, 21, 22, 23 & 24	122–28

Grade 2 Week 2 Target Concept: review initial and final digraphs + introduce "ph"

Description of Concept

Digraph: **ph**

Digraph sound: **/f/**

A digraph is two consonants that work together to make one new sound. "Ph" is a digraph that makes the /f/ sound. It is found in Greek-derived words such as "phone," "philosopher," and "Sophia." Greek words are commonly found in math and science terms.

Sample phoneme-to-grapheme mapping of digraph "ph":

ph	o	ne	

Week 2 Word Lists: digraph "ph"

Word Lists for Decoding and Encoding Activities	
One-Syllable Words phone, lymph, nymph, Ralph, morph, phase, sphere, phrase	**Two-Syllable Extending Words** photo, alpha, aphid, hyphen, Joseph, phenom, phoneme, phobic, phonics, orphan, gopher, dolphin, graphic, digraph
Three-Syllable Extending Words photograph, paragraph, phobia, spherical, alphabet, telephone	

Grade 2 Week 9 Target Concept: screening week + introduce "ie," "oe," "ue"

(see blueprint, page 145)

Screening Week

This week is intentionally scheduled time to screen your students in order to inform your instruction and groupings. The following screens are recommended in the fall of grade 2:

- letters & sounds *for at-risk students*
- tricky words screen *for at-risk students*
- phonics word reading screen
- spelling screen
- benchmark or fluency/comprehension screen

Mini Lesson for "ie," "oe," "ue"

Vowel teams: **ie, oe, ue**

Vowel team sounds: **/ī/ and /ē/, /ō/ and /ö/, /ū/ and /ö/**

Description of Concept

There are very few words that are spelled using "ie," "oe," or "ue," which is a pattern that contains a long vowel sound, and a silent "e" ("pie," "toe," "cue"). This week may be an appropriate spot to tuck in a mini lesson of explicit instruction for these rare spellings. If students are struggling to master VCe, this mini lesson can be put aside for a more appropriate time.

When "ie" is found in the middle of a word, it makes the /ē/ sound, as in "piece."

"Oe" has one more sound, which is /ö/, as in "shoe."

"Ue" can also make the /ö/ sound, as in "sue."

Sample phoneme-to-grapheme mapping of vowel teams:

t	oe	
p	ie	
c	ue	

Teacher Knowledge: In the Latin-originating word "subpoena," the "oe" vowel team makes the /ē/ sound as well.

Week 9 Word Lists: ie, oe, ue

Word Lists for Decoding and Encoding Activities					
ie /ī/	ie /ē/	oe /ō/	oe /ö/	ue /ū/	ue /ö/
tie	tier	toe	shoe	cue	sue
lie	pier	doe	canoe	hue	due
pie	field	foe	horseshoe	fuel	blue
vie	yield	hoe		value	clue
die	grief	woe		argue	glue
	thief	roe		venue	flue
	chief	Joe		rescue	true
	priest	Joel			duel
	shriek	aloe			cruel
	shield	oboe			gruel
		pekoe			fondue
		mistletoe			avenue

Two-Syllable Extending Words
untie, necktie, relief, believe, movie, retrieve

Grade 2 Week 10 Target Concept: vowel teams "ee," "ea" + mini lesson on the other sounds of "ea"

(see blueprint, page 145)

Description of Concept

Vowel teams: **ee, ea**

Vowel team sounds: /ē/, and /ē/, /ĕ/, /ā/

Vowel teams are two vowels that work together to make one sound. Vowel teams usually (but not always) make a long vowel sound. The vowel teams "ee" and "ea" make the /ē/ sound, as in "meet" and "meat." The vowel team "ea" can also make the /ĕ/ sound ("head") and the long /ā/ sound ("steak"). This week will focus on the /ē /sound of "ea," with a mini lesson on the other "ea" sounds.

Six Syllable Rules: This is the fourth of the Six Syllable Rules. When breaking large words into syllables, vowel teams always stay together. A vowel team will represent the vowel that is present in a syllable.

Teaching Strategy:

Every time a new long vowel sound is added, review previous knowledge regarding long vowels. For example, as part of the introduction to these vowel teams, talk about the ways that students know how to make the /ē/ sound. At this point they know the letter name "e," they know that an open syllable or word that ends in "e" can make the /ē/ sound, and they know that VCe with an "e" in the place of the vowel — "eCe" — makes the /ē/ sound. Continually reviewing previous long vowel knowledge helps students make connections and builds a strong phonics foundation.

Sample phoneme-to-grapheme mapping of vowel teams "ee" and "ea":

f	ee	t	
b	ea	n	

Teacher Knowledge: "Ea" followed by "r" makes either the /ē/ sound ("fear") or the /ĕ/ sound ("pear").

Week 10 Word Lists: vowel teams ee, ea

Word Lists for Decoding and Encoding Activities

ee					ea			
see	reed	keen	sweep	sheep	eat	read	leak	treat
eel	teed	been	sweet	sheet	seat	lead	beak	shear
reel	seed	reef	steep	sheen	heat	bead	weak	cheap
peel	feed	beef	steel	sheer	peat	mead	steal	cheat
feel	heed	teem	steer	cheer	mean	real	steam	wheat
heel	need	seem	sleep	cheek	bean	teal	spear	
keel	peer	deem	sleet	thee	neat	seal	speak	
feet	deer	week	creep	wheel	tear	deal	cream	
beet	seer	reek	creek	queen	sear	heal	creak	
meet	jeer	peek	greet		dear	veal	cleat	
weep	leer	leek	green		fear	meal	flea	
seep	veer	meek	greed		gear	ream	plea	
deep	beer	seek	breed		hear	team	pleat	
jeep	teen		freed		near	seam	plead	
beep	seen		preen		reap	beam	bleak	
weed			fleet		heap	teak	gleam	
			tree		leap	peak	dream	
			flee					

Nonsense Words

teef	sheem	dreap
heem	cheel	freat
meeb	theek	sheam
fleen	queep	cheal
gleed	queem	thean
dreet	veap	quead
treek	keaf	
	deat	
	fleam	
	glead	

"ea" short /ĕ/	"ea" long /ā/
head, lead, dead, deaf, read, bread, dread, thread, wealth, health, meant, sweat, breath, spread, threaten, breakfast	steak, break, great

Two-Syllable Extending Words for long /ē/ "ee" & "ea"
agree, agreed, redeem, coffee, asleep, between, beetle, beehive, beeswax, bungee, beefcake
eaten, easel, beacon, beagle, appeal, appear, beaten, unclean, beatbox, beanbag, backseat

Word Chain
been, bean, lean, mean, meal, meat, beat, beet, sheet, sheep, sheer, cheer, cheek, creek, creak, speak, spear, tear, team, teal, steal, steel

Grade 2 Week 11 Target Concept: vowel teams "oa," "ow"

(see blueprint, page 145)

Description of Concept

Vowel teams: **oa, ow**

Vowel team sounds: /ō/

Remind students that vowel teams are two vowels that work together to make one sound. Vowel teams usually (but not always) make a long vowel sound. The vowel teams "oa" and "ow" make the /ō/ sound, as in "goat" and "row." The vowel team "ow" also makes the /ow/ sound, as in "cow," which is introduced in Grade 2 Week 25.

Sample phoneme-to-grapheme mapping of vowel teams:

g	oa	t	
sh	ow		

Week 11 Word Lists: vowel teams oa, ow

Word Lists for Decoding and Encoding Activities						
oa		**ow**		**Nonsense Words**		
oak	roam	tow	blow	joap	droat	kow
oat	coax	row	grown	doan	groaf	jow
oaf	hoax	bow	shown	goam	gloap	zow
goat	groan	mow	thrown	stoad	ploaf	dow
boat	bloat	sow		sloam	shoam	trow
moat	float	low		swoap	choat	spow
loan	gloat	flow		snoat	thoap	smow
moan	cloak	grow		smoab	quoad	cown
road	coach	stow		scoal	whoal	plown
toad	roach	slow		broag		
load	poach	crow				
foal	broach	throw				
goal	coast	show				
coal	toast	blow				
soak	roast	glow				
soap	boast	snow				
soar	throat	bowl				
boar	loaf					

Two-Syllable Extending Words
approach, oatmeal, railroad, unload, sailboat, soapbox, coastline, afloat, cocoa, aboard, upload, goatee, boatmen, coastal
below, arrow, bellow, yellow, fellow, narrow, shadow, meadow, pillow, willow, hollow, mellow, borrow, swallow, window

Word Chains
oak, soak, soap, soar, boar, boat, oat, goat, moat, moan, loan, load, road, toad, toast, roast, roach, coach, coal, goal
tow, bow, mow, sow, stow, slow, low, glow, flow, blow, snow, show, throw, grow, crow

Grade 2 Week 12 Target Concept: vowel teams "ai," "ay"
(see blueprint, page 145)

Description of Concept

Vowel teams: **ai, ay**

Vowel teams sounds: /ā/

The vowel teams "ai" and "ay" make the /ā/ sound. The vowel team "ai" can be found at the beginning or in the middle of a word ("braid") but never at the end of a word. The vowel team "ay" is usually found at the end of a word but may appear in the middle of a word at the end of a syllable ("mayor").

Lesson Plan

	Target Concepts: ai, ay
1	**Warm-up:** 2–5 minutes Review "ea," "ee," "oa," and "ow." Review the long "a" patterns that students know up until this point: the letter "a" makes /ā/ at the end of an open syllable, /ā/ when there is "aCe" or "magic e," and "ea" in a small number of words such as "steak." Once "ai" and "ay" are introduced, include them as part of the warm-up and review.
2	**Introduce new concepts (I Do):** 5 minutes This week we will be learning the predictable vowel teams "ai" and "ay." Both "ai" and "ay" are read as /ā/. "Ai" is found at the beginning or in the middle of a word and "ay" is found at the end of a word or syllable. "Unveil" the sounds one at a time on your sound wall display if you have one, emphasizing the mouth movement, vocalization, and air flow used to make the long /ā/ sound.
3	**Phonological awareness:** 3 minutes **Part 1: Start with this activity if students do not have strong PA skills and then move on to Part 2.** Choose to work with "ai" first and do the activity below. The next day, do the same activity with "ay." Using the word list below, work with students to say "ai" words while using a roller coaster hand sign to show that "ai" makes the long /ā/ sound and is found in the middle of a word. On the following day, using the word list below, work with students to say "ay" words, while using a slide and punching hand sign (students make a fist with their right hand, touch it to their left arm, slide their right hand across their body while saying the word, and punch upward at the final /ā/ sound) to indicate that "ay" also makes the long /ā/ sound and is found at the end of a word. You can check the Heggerty videos for a demonstration. **Part 2: Start with this activity if students have strong PA skills.** Give each student a 2" x 3" "ai" card copied onto pink paper and an "ay" card copied onto green paper. Students hold the card with the text facing themselves. The teacher will know which card students are holding up because of the color.

	Using the word list below, the teacher says a word that contains "ai" or "ay" and the students hold up the cards they believe to be correct. Use words where "ai" is found in the middle of the word and "ay" is found at the end. Support students who are struggling by saying the words slowly and emphasizing the /ā/ sound or by using hand motions if necessary.
4	**Teacher-led guided practice with new concept (WE Do):** 10–15 minutes **(I Do):** Put a list of mixed "ai" and "ay" words on a whiteboard/screen. Point out and read aloud the words that contain "ai" and its placement in the word. Repeat with words that contain "ay." **(WE Do):** Read the list together as a class. Once students are familiar with the words, read the list in random order as you point to each word. **Giant Flash Cards:** Give one student the "ai" card and a second student the "ay" card. Other students in the class have consonant cards. The teacher says a word and the students with the correct consonants come to the front of the room to create the word. The class must decide if they need student "ai" or student "ay" to finish building the word. Once the correct vowel team is chosen, students finish building the word and read it together as a class. See giant flash card activity on page 63 for preparation strategies for this lesson. Possible follow-up activities for practice and reinforcement: – blending lines with "ai" and "ay" – nonsense words – repeat class reading of the word list/blending lines with a student pointing to the words – repeat class reading of the word list and include words that break the pattern
5	**Extended/independent practice activities to apply new concept (YOU Do):** 15–20 minutes Choose two or more of the following activities to provide additional practice with the vowel teams "ai" and "ay." – provide students with "ai" and "ay" word cards on rings to read through individually or with a partner – practice paper/pencil activities – word sorts using "ai" and "ay" words. Use the flash-card-creating website https://sightwords.com/sight-words/flash-cards/ to create your own cards. This is an opportunity for progress monitoring. The teacher can walk around with a clipboard and a class list, check individuals' understanding and application of the concept while they engage in independent activities, and determine who still has unfinished learning.
6	**Tricky words:** Review and practice tricky words as needed, based on progress monitoring.

7	**Decoding with text (YOU Do):** 15–20 minutes – fluency phrases containing "ai" and "ay" words – shared reading of decodable books/passages* *See recommended decodable text resources on pages 262–63.
8	**Encoding (YOU Do):** 15 minutes • **Whiteboards/letter boards:** The teacher says an "ai" or "ay" word and together the class counts the number of sounds in the word. Students draw a corresponding number of lines on their whiteboards and write the word (one sound for each line). An alternative activity is for the teacher to direct students to write either "ai" or "ay" on their whiteboards and then to give them a word using that vowel team. Students build the word around the vowel team on their board. • **Word ladders:** Put "ai" on the bottom rung of a word ladder, placing it in the middle of the rung. Have students build "ai" words, changing either the beginning of the word or the end of the previous word to move up the ladder. This can also be done with "ay" words, placing "ay" at the end of the bottom rung. Students will then change the beginning of the word as they move up the ladder (see word ladder template on page 230). • Practice phoneme-to-grapheme spelling using the word list below. • Practice spelling word/phrase dictation. Sample phoneme-to-grapheme mapping of vowel teams: <table><tr><td>r</td><td>ai</td><td>n</td><td></td></tr><tr><td>s</td><td>ay</td><td></td><td></td></tr></table>
9	**Intervention:** Scaffold word sorts (see page 45) with decodable "ai" and "ay" words. Sort cards can look the same but contain words with different reading levels. For emergent readers use pictures rather than words. For small groups of students who may need additional practice, put the "ai" and "ay" word cards in their reading bags or send home for home reading and word play.
10	**Extending:** Use multisyllable, complex words for the word sorts. Sort cards can look the same as the cards for classmates but contain words that are more complex. Vocabulary building: Choose a few "ai" and "ay" words and talk about homonyms. For example: "grain," "aim," and "sway" are all "ai/ay" words that have multiple meanings. "Aim" can be a goal or it can mean a focused direction as in archery.

Week 12 Word Lists: vowel teams ai, ay

Word Lists for Decoding and Encoding Activities					
ai		**ay**			
One-Syllable Words			**Nonsense Words**		
wait	paid	hay	waip	slaim	kay
saint	nail	tray	laif	flaip	zay
quaint	raid	play	caib	traiv	vay
rain	grain	spray	dain	graim	dray
brain	chain	gray	nain	fraid	kray
snail	faith	clay	kaid	shaib	glay
trait	jail	stray	paiz	chait	blay
aim	waist	sway		quaid	shay
train	wail	slay			chay
fail	waif	may			whay
stain	plain	pay			
braid	drain	fray			
flail	brail	ray			
swain	quail	say			
		way			

Two-Syllable Extending Words
ailment, complain, dainty, entertain, maintain, reclaim, airplane, complaint, detain, explain, mislaid, sustain, domain, repair, tailgate, contain, mailman, raisin, decay, repay, portray, inlay, today, mayor, railway, stairway

Word Chains
raid, paid, pail, jail, nail, tail, rail, sail, bail, fail, frail, trail, grail, grain, train, drain
may, day, say, sway, stay, stray, spray, pray, tray, gray, fray, flay, play, clay

Grade 2 Week 13 Target Concept: diphthongs "oi," "oy"
(see blueprint, page 146)

Description of Concept
Diphthongs: **oi, oy**
Diphthong sounds: /**oi**/
A diphthong is made up of two distinct sounds, where the pronunciation glides from one sound to the other. The diphthongs "oi" and "oy" make the same sound, /oi/, as in "oil" and "toy." Usually, although there are exceptions, the diphthong "oi" is found at the beginning and middle of words. "Oy" is most commonly found at the end of a word but can also be found at the beginning or the middle of a word as the end of a syllable ("oyster").
Sample phoneme-to-grapheme mapping of diphthongs:

b	oi	l	
j	oy		

158

Teacher Knowledge: "Diphthong" comes to us from the Greek language, meaning two ("di") sounds ("*phthongos*").

Week 13 Word Lists: diphthongs oi, oy

Word Lists for Decoding and Encoding Activities				
oi			**oy**	
oil	coin	point	boy	ploy
koi	join	joint	joy	Troy
soil	void	spoil	toy	Floyd
foil	oink	broil	coy	
coil	moist	droid	soy	
boil	hoist	noise	Roy	
toil				
Nonsense Words				
roin	sloib	gloi	poy	froy
doil	swoin	shoim	doy	kroy
foit	spoik	choip	foy	shoy
voim	smoil	quoil	swoy	choy
koib	broik	thoit	spoy	thoy
woid	proif	whoib	sloy	quoy
			groy	
Two-Syllable Extending Words				
toilet, pinpoint, poison, rejoin, ahoy, enjoy, loyal, royal, destroy, employ, deploy, annoy, decoy, oyster, loyal, gargoyle, voyeur, avoid				
Three-Syllable Extending Words				
employee				
Word Chains				
oil, soil, boil, foil, coil, coin, join, joint, point toy, joy, soy, boy, roy, troy, ploy				

Grade 2 Week 14 Target Concept: flex/review week

(see blueprint, page 146)

Description of Concept

Review and/or catchup.

Reviewing previously taught concepts is important, as is embedding those concepts into new lessons throughout the school year.

Week 14 Word Lists: review using word lists from Weeks 2–13 on pages 150–59.

Grade 2 Week 15 Target Concept: vowel team "oo"

(see blueprint, page 146)

Description of Concept

Vowel team: **oo**

Vowel team sounds: /ŏ/, /ü/, /ō/, /ŭ/

Vowel teams are two vowels that work together to make one sound. The vowel team "oo" makes four different sounds: /ü/, as in "book" and /ŏ/, as in "pool," /ō/, as in "floor," which is the vowel controlled "or" sound, and /ŭ/, as in flood. The two most common sounds are /ü/, as in "book" and /ŏ/, as in "pool." Focus on these two sounds in this lesson and with reading and activities.

Sample phoneme-to-grapheme mapping of vowel teams:

p	oo	l	
b	oo	k	

Week 15 Word Lists: vowel team oo

Word Lists for Decoding and Encoding Activities				
/ŏ/, as in pool			**/ü/, as in book**	
too	room	stool	book	hood
goo	zoom	scoop	took	good
boo	root	scoot	rook	wood
moo	hoot	spoon	cook	wool
zoo	loot	spook	look	shook
tool	boot	bloom	hook	brook
pool	poof	gloom	foot	crook
fool	roof	groom	soot	stood
cool	goof	broom		
toon	hoop	proof		
goon	loop	drool		
moon	food	tooth		
soon	mood	smooth		
doom	shoot			
/ō/, as in floor	**/ŭ/, as in flood**	**Nonsense Words**		
moor	flood	roo	choop	chood
poor	blood	mool	thoom	thook
door		bloof	zook	goor
floor		shoon	drook	slood
Two-Syllable Extending Words				
saloon, baboon, balloon, bamboo, cartoon, carpool, harpoon, monsoon, bedroom, bookshelf, footprint, woodshed, fishhook				
Word Chain				
too, tool, cool, fool, food, mood, moon, boon, boom, doom, zoom, zoo, moo, moon, spoon, spook, shook, hook, look, rook, crook, brook				

Grade 2 Week 16 Target Concepts: trigraph "igh"

(see blueprint, page 146)

Description of Concept

Trigraph: **igh**

Trigraph sound: /ī/

Trigraphs are three letters that combine to make one sound. The trigraph "igh" makes the long /ī/ sound. It is often followed by the letter "t." There are only four "igh" words that are not followed by a "t" ("high," "nigh," "sigh," and "thigh"). Sample phoneme-to-grapheme mapping of trigraph "igh":

h	igh		
s	igh	t	

Week 16 Word Lists: trigraph igh

Word Lists for Decoding and Encoding Activities		
Real Words		**Nonsense Words**
sigh	slight	bigh
high	plight	kighn
nigh	flight	smight
thigh	blight	snigh
right	bright	pright
sight	fright	gright
fight		chigh
light		quigh
night		
might		
Two-Syllable Extending Words uptight, nighttime, tonight, midnight, daylight, frighten, tighten, highlight, flashlight, highway, sightsee		
Word Chain high, thigh, sigh, sight, right, might, fight, flight, slight, plight, bright, fright, frighten, lighten, tighten, uptight		

Grade 2 Week 17 Target Concept: inflected ending "ed"

(see blueprint, page 146)

Description of Concept

Inflected ending: **ed**

Inflected ending ed sounds: /ĕd/, /d/, /t/

The inflected ending "ed" changes the verb tense from present to past (unless it is an irregular past-tense verb like "swim"/"swam" or the verb does not change in present and past tense, as in "quit").

There are three pronunciations for "ed" (/ĕd/, /d/, and /t/), but some regions and dialects will flex the "ed" sound to /ĭd/.

For students to read and spell these pronunciations correctly, they must understand that these are past-tense verbs. The final sound of "ed" varies depending on the final sound heard in the base word and the "ed" may or may not add another syllable to the word.

- /ĕd/ is used when a word ends in "d" so that there isn't a double /d/ at the end of the word ("handed," "avoided").
- /ĕd/ is used when a word ends in "t" for ease of pronunciation ("seated," "panted").
- /d/ is used when the end of a word is voiced ("played," "plowed").
- /t/ is used when a word ends with an unvoiced sound ("jumped," "cooked").

Sample phoneme-to-grapheme mapping of inflected ending "ed":

t	i	n	t	e	d
l	i	n	k	ed	
m	ow	ed			

Teaching Strategies
- Sort word lists into groups where the "ed" says /ĕd/, /t/, and /d/. This can be a card sort or a paper/pencil activity.
- Include all three pronunciations of "ed" in the phoneme-to-grapheme spelling portion of the lesson.

Week 17 Word Lists: inflected ending ed

Word Lists for Decoding and Encoding Activities			
ed /ĕd/	**ed /t/**	**ed /d/**	**Nonsense Words**
hinted	linked	mowed	lanted
tinted	helped	rowed	chinted
landed	jumped	showed	quided
handed	dumped	flowed	flimped
banded	camped	glowed	colped
planted	locked	bored	powed
quieted	rocked	scored	hoiled
rented	shocked	snored	kaibed
fated	ticked	rained	
rated	licked	stained	
gated	kicked	steamed	
waited	soaked	leaned	
braided	hoped	peeled	
chanted	honked	oiled	
supported	stamped	coiled	
digested	thanked	foiled	
		spoiled	
		coined	
		loaned	
		roamed	
		groaned	
		played	
		stormed	
		excused	
		owed	
		owned	
Irregular Past-Tense Verbs swim/swam, lead/led, come/came		**Present- and Past-Tense Verbs That Do Not Change** quit, bet, cast, cost, put, burst	
Word Chain rated, hated, handed, landed, lacked, locked, socked, soaked, sowed, showed, shored, bored			

Grade 2 Week 18 Target Concept: screening week

(see blueprint, page 146)

Description of Concept

This week is intentionally scheduled time to screen your students in order to inform your instruction and groupings. The following screens are recommended in midyear of grade 2:

- progress monitoring
- spelling *for at-risk & bubble students*
- benchmark or fluency/comprehension *for at-risk & bubble students*

Grade 2 Week 19 Target Concept: hard and soft "c"
(see blueprint, page 146)

Description of the Concept
Hard "c" says /**k**/. Soft "c" says /**s**/.

When "c" is followed by "e," "i," or "y," it makes the soft /s/ sound. When "c" is followed by any other letter (or no letter, as in "picnic"), it makes the hard /k/ sound. Since this is a consistent rule, it must be applied to words ending in "c," such as "picnic," since the "c" is not followed by "e," "i," or "y."

Spelling: When the sound /k/ occurs in words ending in "c," and "ing" or "ed" are added (which start with "e" and "i"), students must add a "k" to protect the /k/ sound ("picnicking," "mimicking"). This rule does not apply when the pronunciation of the /k/ sound changes when a suffix is added (e.g., "toxic" to "toxicity").

Lesson Plan

	Target Concept: hard & soft "c"
1	**Warm-up/review:** 2–5 minutes Review inflected ending "ed" from week 18. After day one, review hard and soft "c" concepts covered in the previous day/s.
2	**Introduce new concepts (I Do):** 5 minutes Hard "c" says /k/. Soft "c" says /s/. When "c" is followed by "e," "i," or "y," it makes the soft /s/ sound. When "c" is followed by any other letter (or no letter), it makes the hard /k/ sound. This is a predictable phonics rule. **Spelling**: When the sound /k/ occurs in words ending in "c," and "ing" or "ed" are added (which start with "e" and "i"), students must add a "k" to protect the /k/ sound ("picnicking," "mimicking"). This rule does not apply when the pronunciation of the /k/ sound changes when a suffix is added (e.g., "toxic" to "toxicity").
3	**Phonological awareness:** 3 minutes Teacher says a list of words that contain the hard and soft sound of "c." Students indicate whether they are hearing a hard or soft "c" sound. This can be done with hand signs (scratching like a cat for hard "c" or making a snake motion for soft "c") and/or verbally by saying "hard" or "soft."
4	**Teacher-led guided practice with new concept (WE Do):** 10–15 minutes As a class, read word lists with hard and soft "c" that have been projected on the whiteboard or are on chart paper. Have students identify whether "c" in each word is hard or soft. Students might verbally identify the words that include hard or soft "c," or the teacher could have students come up to the board and circle them or point to them with a pointer. This can be done over several days. Add exceptions and some nonsense words to support a solid identification of the concept.

5	**Extended independent practice activities to apply new concept (YOU Do):** 15–20 minutes • Word sorts work well here. • **"Find the Word" game:** Group students into teams of three or four. Give students a stack of word cards that contain hard and soft words (these can be created using the word lists below). Ask teams to perform a variety of tasks. Example: Find two words with a hard "c" at the end of the word. Find three soft "c" words in which "c" is followed by the letter "i," etc.
6	**Decoding with text (YOU Do):** 15–20 minutes There are many decodable texts that focus on this concept. Practice identifying the concept in print by providing students with decodable passages and having them either underline the hard "c" and circle the soft "c" or highlight all hard and soft "c" sounds in the passage. Students can also create word lists from hard and soft "c" decodable books they are using for this lesson.
7	**Encoding (YOU Do):** 15 minutes Phoneme to grapheme spelling and spelling phrases with hard and soft "c" words. Sample phoneme-to-grapheme mapping of soft "c": | c	e	n	t
---	---	---	---
8	**Intervention:** Work with words (reading, encoding, word sorts, etc.) that use CVC, four-letter words with blends, and words that are decodable. Choose words where the "c" is consistently at the beginning of the word. If students are not able to decode these words, use pictures and have students identify which items contain a hard "c" and which contain a soft "c" (e.g., "rice," "palace," "cat," "corn," etc.).
9	**Extending:** Scaffold word sorts in a way that meets the needs of all students. For students with advanced skills, add nonsense words and exceptions to the rule to the word sort deck. Choose complex text for working with the concept in print. Use multisyllable words, words where the "c" is at different places or used twice with hard and soft "c" within the word ("Pacific").

Word Lists for Decoding and Encoding Activities	
hard c	**soft c**
One-Syllable Words	**One-Syllable Words**

corn	climb	cent	face	pounce
cake	cape	city	mice	place
crab	cave	ice	peace	lice
clove	clove	price	juice	flounce
cord		race	wince	space
		acid	race	cyst
		cell	voice	mice
		fence	trace	

Two-Syllable Extending Words		**Two-Syllable Extending Words**	
cobble	combine	center	entrance
carry	object	cinder	cider
music	complete	pencil	decide
caustic	cracker	excite	science
cursive	cotton	fancy	distance
panic	uncle	citrus	lettuce
drastic	cabin	cyclops	certain
hectic	candle	process	recess
country	project		sincere

Three- or More-Syllable Extending Words		**Three- or More-Syllable Extending Words**	
conductor	cabinet	incident	circumstance
carousel	carnival	reference	citizen
electric	cardinal	extravagance	cigarette
gigantic	calculate	cylinder	centipede
Atlantic		cemetery	celery
		innocent	prophecy

Exceptions to the Rule	**Exceptions to the Rule**
Caesar	soccer
indict	cello
facade	arcing

Words That Include Hard & Soft c	**Spelling Phrases**
Pacific, circus, condolence, bicycle, concert, vaccine, acceptable, Celtic, accent	an ear of corn, I like to climb, three pink mice, in the center, white cotton, a small cardinal, sweet cider, you can decide, meet me at recess, a good citizen, a sharp pencil, I have lice, a star in space

Nonsense Words	**Nonsense Words**
calt, coss, camb, cang, cust, coch, culsh, cose, cupe, cank, cashe	cill, cimp, cint, cerp, celd, cezz, ciss, ceff, cile, ceke, cyph

Grade 2 Week 20 Target Concept: hard and soft "g"
(see blueprint, page 146)

Description of the Concept
Hard "g" says /g/. Soft "g" says /j/.
When "g" is followed by "e," "i," or "y," the "g" makes the soft /j/ sound. When "g" is followed by any other letter (or no letter), it makes the hard /g/ sound.
This is less predictable than the hard and soft "c" phonics rule. There are times when "g" retains its hard sound even when followed by "e," "i," or "y" ("get," "girl," "baggy").

Spelling: There are many spellings that seem unusual but make sense because of the hard and soft "g" rule. For example, when adding the ending "able" to a word that ends in "ge," the "e" is retained in order to keep the soft /j/ sound ("judge-able," "cagey").

Teacher Knowledge: When a language "borrows" words from other languages, as English often does, there are times when a silent letter is inserted to protect the hard "g" sound because it is followed by "e," "i," or "y." In Italian words, an "h" is inserted to separate the "g" and the "e" ("ghetto," "spaghetti"). In French and Spanish words, a silent "u" is inserted to separate the "g" from "e" and "i" and retain the hard "g" sound ("guide," "plague," "guerilla," "guitar").

Lesson Plan

	Target Concept: hard and soft "g"
1	**Warm-up/review:** 2–5 minutes Review of hard and soft "c" from Week 19. After day one, review hard and soft "g" concepts covered in the previous day/s.
2	**Introduce new concepts (I Do):** 5 minutes Hard "g" says /g/. Soft "g" says /j/. When "g" is followed by "e," "i," or "y," it makes the soft /j/ sound. When "g" is followed by any other letter (or no letter), it makes the hard /g/ sound. This is less predictable than the hard and soft "c" phonics rule. There are times when "g" retains its hard sound even when followed by "e," "i," or "y" ("get," "girl," "baggy").
3	**Phonological awareness:** 3 minutes The teacher says a list of words that contain the hard and soft sound of "g." Students indicate whether they are hearing a hard or soft "g" sound. This can be done with hand signs and/or verbally by saying "hard" or "soft." Once hard and soft "g" sounds are in place, mix the list with hard and soft "c" and "g."

4	**Teacher-led guided practice with new concept (WE Do):** 10–15 minutes As a class, read word lists and/or blending lines with hard and soft "g" that have been projected onto the whiteboard. Have students identify whether a word contains a hard or soft "g." Students might verbally identify the words that include hard or soft "g" or the teacher could have students come up to the board and circle them or point to them with a pointer. This can be done over several days. Add exceptions and some nonsense words to support a solid identification of the concept. Once hard and soft "g" sounds are in place, mix the list with hard and soft "c" and "g."
5	**Extended independent practice activities to apply new concept (YOU Do):** 15–20 minutes Word sorts, paper/pencil activities, and games where students must identify hard and soft "g."
6	**Decoding with text (YOU Do):** 15–20 minutes There are many decodable texts that focus on this concept. Practice identifying the concept in print by providing students with decodable passages and have them either underline the hard "g" and circle the soft "g" or highlight all hard and soft "g" words in the passage. Near the end of the week, work with texts that include both hard and soft "c" and "g."
7	**Encoding (YOU Do):** 15 minutes Spell phrases with hard and soft "g" words. Mix hard and soft "c" and "g" words once hard and soft "g" has been explicitly taught and practiced. Sample phoneme-to-grapheme mapping of soft "g": | s | t | a | ge | |
8	**Intervention:** Choose one-syllable, decodable words for extra practice activities.
9	**Extending:** The word bank for hard and soft "g" includes many complex, multisyllable words. Use more challenging words for students with strong reading and spelling skills. Incorporate complex text.

Week 20 Word Lists for Encoding and Decoding Activities: hard & soft g

Word Lists for Decoding and Encoding Activities	
hard g	**soft g**

One-Syllable Words / One-Syllable Words

hard g			soft g	
got	gap	golf	gem	verge
game	glint	gulf	gin	germ
get	great	gasp	judge	gym
gone	goose	smog	page	lunge
good	goat	drag	rage	change
grand	ghost	graft	large	badge
grin	gull	green	fudge	cage
grime	rug	glow	hinge	ledge
grip	glass	leg	huge	fridge
egg	globe		stage	
crag				

Two-Syllable Words / Two-Syllable Words

hard g		soft g	
grandma	gopher	giraffe	gesture
grandpa	dragon	giant	gentle
goodness	begun	stranger	engine
glimmer	danger	gypsy	ginger
progress	dagger	tragic	divulge
gurgle	gravel	urgent	orange
gosling	glitter	gerbil	
disgust	garter		
bragging	gather		

Three- or More-Syllable Words / Three- or More-Syllable Words

hard g		soft g	
migration	catalogue	energy	margarine
graduation	cardigan	gelatin	vegetable
gradual	configure	origin	gentleman
alligator		gymnasium	geography

Exceptions to the Rule	Exceptions to the Rule
Gaol (Irish), judgment, acknowledgement, fledgling	beige, hunger, trigger, giggle, begin, get, give, longer, bigger, linger, gear, gill, gift, anger, argyle

Words That Include Hard and Soft g	Spelling Phrases
baggage, engage, gadget, garage, garbage, geography, gorge, grudge, grunge, language, pilgrimage, gauge, ginseng	go to the gym, a new judge, the large fish, white as a ghost, the egg cracked, the brown gopher, lack of energy, do not giggle, soon we will begin, the gelatin is orange, I like ginger ale, do not divulge secrets, the story is tragic, let's eat some fudge.

Nonsense Words	Nonsense Words
gan, goff, gump, gant, goch, gult, goash, gount, garn, gorp, gafe, gome	gick, gish, gint, gilsh, gife, gealt, geel, geach, gele, gyll, gyde, gych

Grade 2 Week 21 Target Concept: the many jobs of "y" (Jobs 1–3)
(see blueprint, page 146)

Description of Concept

The letter "y" plays more than six different roles in words. "Y" as a consonant was introduced in kindergarten and "ay" was introduced in Grade 2 Week 11. Four other jobs of "y" will be introduced over the next two weeks. The following are the six jobs of "y" we will be focusing on.

Job 1: If "y" is the first letter of a word or syllable, it will work as a consonant /y/ ("yellow," "yank," "canyon"). If "y" is found anywhere other than at the beginning of a word or syllable, it will work as a vowel /ĭ/ or /ī/ ("gym," "myth," "rhyme").

Job 2: If "y" is the **only** working vowel in a word or syllable, it will work the same as the letter "i," saying /ĭ/ or /ī/ ("sky," "type," "crypt"). This may have been taught with open and closed syllables in grade 1.

Job 3: "Y" acts as a long "e," /ē/, when found at the end of a word that has more than one syllable ("fancy," "pony").

Job 4: When "y" follows the vowel "a," the "a" will be long (/ā/) and the "y" will be silent ("play," "maybe").

Job 5: When "y" comes at the end of a word with more than one syllable and is preceded by "n," "f," or "l," and the word is a verb, it will make the long "i" sound, /ī/ ("deny," "apply").

Job 6: When "y" comes at the end of a syllable it can say the short or long sound of "i," /ĭ/ or /ī/ ("by," "python," "rhythm").

Lesson Plan

	Target Concepts: the many jobs of "y"
1	**Warm-up:** 2–5 minutes Review hard and soft "c" and "g." There are 6 jobs of "y" that will be covered this week and next, so it is important to continue reviewing all of the jobs of "y" once they have been introduced and taught.
2	**Introduce new concepts (I Do):** 5 minutes The many jobs of "y" cannot be taught in one lesson because there are too many! "Y" at the beginning of a word (Job 1) has already been taught but not at the beginning of a syllable (canyon). "Ay" has been taught as a vowel team in Grade 2 Week 12 (Job 4). In the two weeks of introducing the "many jobs of y" in grade 2, you could cover all 6 rules in the following way: Week 21: Review Job 1 and teach Jobs 2 and 3. Week 22: Review Job 4 and teach Jobs 5 and 6. **Days 1 & 2 of Week 21** **Review Job 1:** If "y" is the first letter of a word, it will work as a consonant ("yellow," "yank"). Introduce the concept that "y" at the beginning of a syllable also says /y/ ("canyon"). **Job 2:** If "y" is the only working vowel in a word or syllable, it will work the same as the letter "i" ("sky," "type," "crypt"). **Days 3 & 4 of Week 21** **Job 3:** "Y" acts as a long "e" when at the end of a word that has more than one syllable ("fancy," "pony").
3	**Phonological awareness:** 3 minutes Teacher says a variety of words that contain "y" and students decide if it is a consonant or vowel (e.g., "yard" — consonant; "fry" — vowel).
4	**Teacher-led guided practice with new concept (WE Do):** 10–15 minutes Each time a new job is taught, as a class read and discuss lists of words that use "y" in the place that job teaches, as well as lists where "y" is used in a variety of roles previously taught. Word ladders, whiteboards, and other high-impact activities can be used to practice each new concept. Include vocabulary activities to connect words with meanings. There are many excellent YouTube videos that explain the many jobs of "y." Be sure to preview videos to find ones that align with this lesson.

5	**Extended independent practice activities to apply new concept (YOU Do):** 15–20 minutes • Use word sorts that incorporate the "y" concepts that have been covered. Have students sort the words according to the job that "y" plays within that word. • Use games and worksheets to reinforce the jobs of "y" being covered. This is an opportunity for progress monitoring. The teacher can walk around with a clipboard and a class list during independent activities and check each individual's understanding and application of the concept and determine who still has unfinished learning.
6	**Decoding with text (YOU Do):** 15–20 minutes Read and identify the many jobs of "y" within print. *See recommended decodable text resources on pages 262–63.
7	**Encoding (YOU Do):** 15 minutes • spelling using phrases • spelling lists that incorporate the many jobs of "y" Sample phoneme-to-grapheme mapping of jobs of "y":

s	k	y		
m	y	th		
c	a	n	d	y

|
| 8 | **Extending:**
Use multisyllable words and complex text for students who understand the concept and use it in print. |

Week 21 & 22 Word Lists: the many jobs of y
(Words with the suffix "ly" can be found in Grade 3 Week 24.)

Word Lists for Decoding and Encoding Activities					
Job 1 "y" as a consonant /y/		**Job 2** If "y" is the only working vowel, it takes on the role of the letter "i" /ĭ/ or /ī/		**Job 3** "Y" acts as a long "e" /ē/ at the end of a word with more than 1 syllable	
At the beginning of a word: yellow yes you yummy yak yank yield year young yourself yesterday yeast yard yacht yogurt	**At the beginning of a syllable:** canyon yoyo kayak mayor brayer	sky cry type dry pry gym myth crypt style		pretty happy jumpy comedy family sticky lucky candy probably jelly kidney monkey honey donkey parsley easy	hockey journey money lady alley chimney valley deny reply berry baby charity ability archeology party
Job 4 "y" following the letter "a" makes the /ā/ sound		**Job 5** "Y" preceded by "n," "f," and "l" makes the /ī/ sound		**Job 6** When "y" comes at the end of a syllable it can say /ĭ/ or /ī/	
play stay fray clay sway hallway runway crayon birthday paycheck yesterday holiday subway Sunday maybe today essay		**ny:** deny **ly:** apply rely reply fly supply sly analyze paralyze **fy:** glorify intensify nullify pacify fortify terrify classify justify personify gratify exemplify		/ī/: tyrant typhoon dynamic hyphen hyena pylon hygiene psychology cycle /ĭ/: rhythm	

173

Grade 2 Week 22 Target Concept: the many jobs of "y" (Jobs 4–6)

(see blueprint, page 146)

Description of Concept

Job 4: When "y" follows the vowel "a," the "a" will be long /ā/ and the "y" will be silent ("play," "maybe").

Job 5: When "y" comes at the end of a word with more than one syllable and is preceded by "n," "f," or "l" and the word is a verb, it will make the /ī/ sound ("deny," "apply").

Job 6: When "y" comes at the end of a syllable it can say /ĭ/ or /ī/ ("dynamic," "rhythm").

Sample phoneme-to-grapheme mapping of jobs of "y":

d	e	n	y	
p	y	l	o	n

Teaching Strategy

Jobs 1–3 were taught in Week 21 and Jobs 4–6 will be taught this week. Job 4 (when "y" follows the vowel "a," the "a" will be long /ā/ and the "y" will be silent — "play," "maybe") has been previously taught, so it is a quick review to start the week.

Word lists for all six jobs of "y" lessons are found in Week 21 above.

Grade 2 Week 23 Target Concept: vowel-r "ar"

(see blueprint, page 147)

Description of Concept

Vowel-r: **ar**

Vowel-r sound: /är/

Vowel-r (also known as vowel-controlled "r" or "bossy r") is called vowel-controlled because the "r" impacts the vowel before it. Rather than make its long or short sound, the vowel makes a new sound. Although there are five vowel-controlled spellings ("ar," "er," "ir," "or," and "ur"), there are only three pronunciations: /är/, as in "barn," /ōr/, as in "corn," and /er/, as in "bird," "fern," and "curl." "Ar" is a good team to start with because students like the fact that it makes the sound of a pirate — *argh!* "Ar" can occur at the beginning ("article"), middle ("dart"), or end of a word ("far").

Six Syllable Rules: Vowel-r is considered one of the six syllable rules because it stays as a team when dividing words into syllables.

Sample phoneme-to-grapheme mapping of vowel-r "ar":

f	ar	m	

Week 23 Word Lists: vowel-r "ar"

Word Lists for Decoding and Encoding Activities			
ar			
One-Syllable Words			
star	harm	large	cart
art	charm	barge	Mark
farm	harp	scarf	Carl
car	sharp	tarp	barn
far	part	ark	tar
jar	start	arm	dart
scar	carve	shark	tart
hard	starve	yard	chart
yard	arch	smart	spar
bark	march	yarn	
dark			
Two-Syllable Extending Words			
army	tarnish	nectar	lizard
artist	party	arcade	mustard
carpet	alarm	scarlet	orchard
darken	sparkle	bombard	Richard
carton	pardon	darling	standard
farmer	margin	discard	wizard
garden	marble	lunar	forward
garlic	gargle	vicar	backward
harvest	depart	burglar	inward
market	solar	pedlar	upward
partner	polar	custard	
scarlet		drunkard	
Three- or More-Syllable Extending Words			
apartment, carpenter, calendar, afterward, preparation, paragraph, apparel, apparently, transparency, stepparent			

Exceptions		**Nonsense Words**	
marry, dollar		lar, gar, dar, sar, bart, jart, jarm, larm, sart, arg, arp, marp, parp, larp	

Word Chain
arm, art, cart, car, card, yard, hard, harm, charm, farm, fart, part, chart, smart, start, tart, tarp, sharp, shark, mark, bark, spark

Grade 2 Week 24 Target Concept: vowel-r "or"

(see blueprint, page 147)

Description of Concept

Vowel-r: **or**

Vowel-r sound: /ōr/

Vowel-r (also known as vowel-controlled "r" or "bossy r") is called vowel-controlled because the "r" impacts the vowel before it. Rather than make its long or short sound, the vowel makes a new sound. "Or" makes the sound /ō/, as in "corn."

When "e" is added to the end of the "or" team, it is a VCe pattern but the sound does not change ("pore," "snore," "forewarn").

Six Syllable Rules: Vowel-r is considered one of the six syllable rules because it stays as a team when dividing words into syllables.

Mini Lesson: The vowel-r "or" makes the /er/ sound in words with "wor" /wer/ ("work," "worm," "worst," "world," "worth," "word").

Sample phoneme-to-grapheme mapping of vowel-r "or":

b	or	n	

Teacher Knowledge: A word describing a working person that has a Latin root uses "or" instead of "er" ("tutor," "doctor," "actor").

Week 24 Word Lists: vowel-r "or"

Word Lists for Decoding and Encoding Activities					
or					
One-Syllable Words					
fork	cord	fort	horse	short	ford
sort	corn	form	north	snort	lord
north	cork	floor	or	storm	norm
born	chord	forth	port	stork	sport
storm	dorm	hornet	pork	thorn	torch
torn	for		porch	worn	
Two-Syllable Extending Words					
acorn	factor	labor	splendor	rumor	tenor
razor	forgot	odor	tutor	valor	vigor
major	forty	organ	armor	horror	favor
armor	glamor	orbit	favor	minor	flavor
doctor	gory	rigor	harbor	pastor	savor
actor	glory	resort	parlor	sailor	story
Three- or More-Syllable Extending Words memory, emperor					
Exceptions work, tractor, word, worm Latin roots: tailor, professor, tutor, actor			**Nonsense Words** ort, lort, jort, bort, orm, torm, glorm, flort, slort, jort, morsh, smorn, storn, florm, skorm, scorg, borg, florg, vorg, worg		
Word Chain or, for, fork, pork, port, short, fort, wort, worn, horn, corn, cork, stork, storm, storn, thorn, torn, torch					

Grade 2 Week 25 Target Concept: review/flex week

(see blueprint, page 147)

Description of Concept

Review and/or catchup.

Reviewing previously taught concepts is important, as is embedding those concepts into new lessons throughout the school year.

Week 25 Word Lists: review using previously provided word lists.

Grade 2 Week 26 Target Concept: vowel-r "er," "ur," "ir"
(see blueprint, page 147)

Description of Concept

Vowel-r: **er, ur, ir**

Vowel-r sound: /**er**/

These three vowel-r teams make the sound /er/. Once students understand this, "er," "ur," and "ir" words are easy to read but can be quite difficult to spell because there is no rule to guide students when they are spelling a word with the /er/ sound. One helpful hint is that "er" is the most common, followed by "ur" and finally "ir." If students are unsure of the correct spelling, this knowledge can help them make a knowledgeable choice, rather than guessing.

Six Syllable Rules: Vowel-r is considered one of the six syllable rules because it stays as a team when dividing words into syllables.

Sample phoneme-to-grapheme mapping of vowel-r "er," "ur," "ir":

h	er	d	
g	ir	l	
f	ur		

Week 26 Word Lists: vowel-r er, ur, ir

Word Lists for Encoding and Decoding Activities					
er		ur		ir	
One-Syllable Words		One-Syllable Words		One-Syllable Words	
her	germ	cur	lurk	irk	swirl
herd	stern	fur	slur	fir	first
nerd	nerve	turn	spur	sir	thirst
jerk	serve	burn	church	stir	chirp
verb	swerve	yurt	churn	girl	shirt
fern	verse	hurt	curse	bird	birth
berg	perch	curt	purse	dirt	girth
		curl	nurse	firm	quirk
		curb	burst	third	smirk
		surf	slurp	skirt	squirm
		turf	curve	flirt	squirt
		turd	spurt	whirl	birch
		burp		twirl	
Two-Syllable Extending Words		Two-Syllable Extending Words		Two-Syllable Extending Words	
ever	pattern	return	surprise	twirling	birthday
never	sister	Thursday	turtle	confirm	blackbird
over	enter	further	sunburn	thirteen	
after	western	burning	disturb		
finger	eastern	surfing	nurture		
flower	southern	burger	burlap		
tower	northern	purple	murky		
river	person				
mixer	expert				
whisper	perfume				
faster	perfect				
slower	kernel				
lantern					
Nonsense Words ner, verm, dersh, sterch, gur, durl, murnk, churt, nir, lirp, flirch, whirt					
Word Chain her, herd, nerd, bird, birch, birth, burn, turn, turf, surf, sir, stir, slur, slurp, burp, burg, burger					

Grade 2 Week 27 Target Concept: diphthongs "ow," "ou"

(see blueprint, page 147)

Description of Concept
Diphthongs: **ow, ou**
Diphthongs sound: **/ow/**
A diphthong is made up of two distinct sounds: the pronunciation glides from one sound to the other.

The letters "ow" can make two different sounds, the vowel team /ō/ sound, as in "row" (which was taught in Grade 2 Week 10) and the dipthong /ow/, as in "cow." This week will focus on the sound /ow/, as in "cow."

The diphthong "ou" as in "ouch" is the most common use of "ou," but it can also make four other sounds: /ō/, as in "soul," /ö/, as in "group," /ŭ/, as in "country," and /ü/, as in "could." These four other sounds will be taught in week 24, following this lesson.

"Ou" can be used at the beginning and in the middle of a word, but never at the end of a word.

Sample phoneme-to-grapheme mapping of diphthongs "ow" and "ou":

t	ow	n		
c	ou	ch		

Week 27 Word Lists: diphthongs ow, ou

Word Lists for Decoding and Encoding Activities								
ow **One-Syllable Words**			**ou** **One-Syllable Words**			**Nonsense Words**		
pow	chow	frown	our	count	grout	gow	scrowd	fouch
sow	town	clown	sour	mount	grouch	powk	sprowl	houth
how	down	crown	out	proud	spout	slowt	throwl	strout
cow	owl	drown	rout	sound	snout	spowl	kout	scrout
bow	howl	growl	pout	round	scout	stown	boud	sproun
now	dowl	scowl	gout	hound	sprout	drowd	spour	shrout
wow	jowl	prowl	lout	bound	shroud	glowt	slout	squoud
vow	cowl	crowd	bout	wound	mouth	frowl	swout	throud
brow	fowl	browse	foul	pound	south	showd	stoud	
plow	brown		loud	found	shout	lowch	plout	
			noun	mound	ouch	thowt	gloud	
			house	ground	couch	shrown	droud	
			mouse	stout	pouch	strowp	frout	
			flour	clout	crouch			
			cloud	trout				
Two- or More-Syllable Extending Words power, flower, shower, tower, towel, vowel, allow, browser, chowder, empower			**Two- or More-Syllable Extending Words** about, aloud, around, abound, astound, amount, compound, outside, outfit, counselor					
Word Chains our, out, pout, lout, loud, cloud, clout, snout, spout, sprout, trout, grout, ground, found, sound, pound, compound, astound, around now, wow, cow, cowl, howl, hown, town, crown, clown, drown, down, dow, vow, vowel, towel								

Grade 2 Week 28 Target Concept: the other sounds of "ou"

(see blueprint, page 147)

Description of Concept

The other sounds of: **ou**

The "ou" sound heard in "ouch" is a diphthong, and it is the most common use of "ou" (taught in Week 23). "Ou" can also make four other sounds. With these sounds, "ou" is no longer a diphthong but works as a vowel team, because the two vowels make a single sound:

- /ō/, as in "soul"
- /ö/, as in "group"
- /ü/, as in "could"
- /ŭ/, as in "country"

"Ou" can be used at the beginning and in the middle of a word, but never at the end.

Sample phoneme-to-grapheme mapping of vowel team "ou":

s	ou	l		
y	ou			
t	ou	ch		

Word Lists for Decoding and Encoding Activities			
/ō/, as in soul	/ö/, as in group	/ü/, as in could	/ŭ/, as in country
soul your pour four fourth court mourn gourd	you soup group coup croup tour route youth couth ghoul wound mousse	could would should	touch young
Two-Syllable Extending Words /ō/ shoulder boulder poultry gourmet amour	**Two-Syllable Extending Words /ö/** doula recoup detour contour tourist coupon velour		**Two-Syllable Extending Words /ŭ/** country trouble double doubly couple cousin
Word Chains pour, your, four, fourth, court soup, croup, group, coup, couth, youth, you could, should, would			

Grade 2 Week 29 Target Concept: silent letters "kn," "gn," "wr," "gh," "mb"

(see blueprint, page 147)

Description of Concept

Silent letters: **kn, gn, wr, gh, mb**

Silent letter sounds: **/n/, /n/, /r/, /g/, /m/**

The digraphs "kn," "gn," and "wr" can be thought of as having initial silent letters, with the second letter in the digraph being the one that makes the sound. For example, "kn" makes the consonant sound /n/, "gn" makes the sound /n/, and "wr" makes the sound /r/. The digraphs "gh" and "mb" are a little bit different in that the first letter makes the sound, and the second letter is silent.

Sample phoneme-to-grapheme mapping of silent letters "kn," "gn," "wr," "gh," "mb":

gn	a	t		
kn	o	t		
wr	a	p		
l	i	mb		
gh	o	s	t	

Teacher Knowledge: When "gh" is found in Italian words like "ghetto" and "spaghetti," the "h" is inserted to retain the hard /g/ sound (as per the rule that when "g" is followed by "e," "i," or "y" it makes a hard /g/ sound).

Week 29 Word Lists: silent letters kn, gn, wr, gh, mb

Word Lists for Decoding and Encoding Activities					
kn	**gn**	**wr**	**gh**	**mb**	**Nonsense Words**
know	gnu	wry	ghetto	comb	knuck
known	gnaw	wrap	ghost	dumb	knuf
knew	gnat	writ	ghast	numb	kneep
knit	gnome	wren	ghoul	bomb	gnup
knot	gnarl	wreck		lamb	gnook
knob	gnash	wrist		limb	gnout
knock	sign	wrath		climb	wrilt
knack		wrong		crumb	wroan
knick		wrung		thumb	wruke
knee		wrench		plumb	ghop
kneel		write		womb	ghair
knead		wrote		tomb	ghooch
knight		wreak			tamb
knife		wreath			slomb
knoll					whumb

Two- or More-Syllable Extending Words
kneecap, knitting, knowing, knotty, design, signing, written, writer, wrapping, unwrap, shipwreck, spaghetti, gherkin, yogurt, plumber, bomber, dumber, combed, climber, succumb

Grade 2 Week 30 Target Concepts: flex week + "o," "i" when followed by two consonants

(see blueprint, page 147)

Description of the Concept
Review and catch up on unfinished concepts.

Mini Lesson: When "o" and "i" are followed by two consonants, they can say either their short or long sound ("fold"/"follow," "print"/"pint"). This rule will support students in reading, as they will now know to check both sounds if one does not make sense, rather than following the open- and closed-syllable rule. Sample phoneme-to-grapheme mapping of "o" and "i" when followed by two consonants:

k	i	n	d
o	l	d	

Week 30 Word Lists: o, i when followed by two consonants

Word Lists for Decoding and Encoding Activities							
/ō/		/ŏ/		/ī/		/ĭ/	
old	colt	pond	cost	kind	grind	print	lift
cold	molt	bond	posh	mind	pint	hint	silk
fold	volt	off	lost	rind	mild	lint	milk
gold	roll	fond	frost	hind	wild	mint	wilt
hold	toll	font	soft	find	child	tint	sift
sold	poll	gong	loft	bind	climb	stint	shift
mold	troll	long	moss	wind		flint	drift
bold	stroll	wrong	toss	blind		glint	mist
told	post	song	loss			ink	fist
scold	host		gloss			stink	list
bolt	most					wink	limp
jolt	comb					link	blimp
						pink	imp
						brink	gift
						drink	lift
						rink	drift
						wind	rift

Two- or More-Syllable Extending Words
octopus, behind, remind, unkind, simple, dimple, pimple

Word Chains
old, cold, fold, gold, hold, sold, bold, bolt, jolt, volt
kind, mind, rind, hind, find, bind, blind, grind
mild, wild, child

Grade 2 Week 31 Target Concept: vowel team/diphthong "ew" + vowel teams "eu," "ui"

(see blueprint, page 147)

Description of Concept

Vowel team/diphthong: **ew,** and vowel teams: **eu, ui**

Vowel teams/diphthongs sounds: /ö/ and /ū/, /ö/

A vowel team is two vowels working together to make one sound. A diphthong is made up of two distinct sounds and the pronunciation glides from one sound to the other.

"Ew" can work as a vowel team and a diphthong. The diphthong "ew" makes the /ö/ sound, as in "flew," and the vowel team "ew" makes the /ū/ sound, as in "few." Other vowel teams that make the /ö/ sound, as in "flew" are "eu", as in "neutral" and "ui," as in "fruit."

Sample phoneme-to-grapheme mapping of vowel teams and diphthongs "ew," "eu," "ui":

n	ew			
n	eu	t	r	a	l
f	r	ui	t	

Week 31 Word Lists: vowel team/diphthong ew and vowel teams eu, ui

Word Lists for Decoding and Encoding Activities				
ew /ö/	ew /ū/	eu /ö/	ui /ö/	**Nonsense Words**
new	few	neutral	suit	vew
dew	pew	pneumonia	fruit	frew
flew	yew		juice	unshewl
blew			recruit	ew
slew	**Exception**			trewn
grew	sew			sprew
drew				peut
brew				cheup
crew				abeud
stew				kuit
chew				cruit
screw				muish
shrew				
threw				

Two- or More-Syllable Extending Words

cashew, mildew, dewdrop, curfew

Word Chain

new, dew, stew, flew, blew, brew, grew, drew, crew, chew, screw, shrew, threw

Grade 2 Week 32 Target Concept: vowel teams "aw," "au" + "wa," "al"

(see blueprint, page 147)

Description of Concept

Vowel teams: **aw, au** and **wa, al**

Vowel teams sounds: /ä/

Remind students that a vowel team is two or more letters working together to make one vowel sound. The vowel teams "aw" and "au" make the sound /ä/, as in "saw" and "pause." "Au" can be found at the beginning and middle of words, but never at the end. "Aw" can be found at the beginning, middle, and end of words ("awful," "drawl," "law").

Mini Lesson: The /ä/ sound is also created when the letter "a" follows "w" or comes before the letter "l" ("water," "fall").

Sample phoneme-to-grapheme mapping of vowel teams "aw," "au," "wa," and "al":

l	aw	n	
s	au	n	a
w	a	n	t
a	l	s	o

Word Lists for Decoding and Encoding Activities							
aw		**au**		**wa, al**		**Nonsense Words**	
paw	bawl	haul	cause	wad	all	faw	vaun
jaw	hawk	Paul	pause	water	tall	gawn	jaul
law	Shawn	maul	clause	watt	call	trawd	flaum
saw	spawn	laud		wand	alto	blawt	graud
caw	prawn	vault		want	bald	shawd	shaub
raw	drawn	fault		wasp	also	rawth	mauch
claw	crawl	fraud		waft	always	kawch	bauth
flaw	drawl	haunt		wash	salsa	thrawt	quault
slaw	shawl	jaunt		walk	halt		whaut
draw	scrawl	launch		wall	malt		
thaw	straw	haunch		waffle	calm		
yawn	squawk			swab	palm		
pawn				swap	balm		
lawn				swat			
fawn				swan			
dawn				swamp			

Two- or More-Syllable Extending Words

awning, crawfish, rawhide, sawdust, scrawny, jigsaw, withdraw, outlaw, awesome, awful, audit, sauna, August, author, applaud, because, exhaust, laundry, trauma, gauntlet, cauldron, astronaut, nautical, narwal, appal, alder, albeit

Word Chains

jaw, saw, draw, claw, lawn, prawn, drawn, drawl, crawl, scrawl, shawl
haul, Paul, pault, fault, vault, jault, jaunt, haunt, haunch, launch

Grade 2 Week 33 Target Concept: past-tense verbs

(see blueprint, page 147)

Description of Concept

There are two forms of past verbs in English: **simple past** and **past participle**. Simple past-tense verbs communicate that a completed action took place at a specific point in time (e.g., "it broke"). Past participle verbs are used as an adjective (e.g., "a broken wheel") or to form a verb tense (e.g., "they have broken"). Past-tense verbs often end in "ed," "d," "t," "en," or "n." Inflected ending "ed" was covered in Grade 2 Week 17.

Most of the irregular past-tense verbs in English follow a **general** pattern. While there are definite spelling rules associated with past-tense verbs, correct spoken language will cue students to the proper past-tense word choice. Working with irregular verbs will continue in grades 4 and beyond, but six patterns are introduced here.

Some past-tense verbs do not change whether they are past or present tense (e.g., "cut," "shut").

- If a verb contains a vowel team (except "ee"), simple past changes the vowel team to "oCe" (e.g., "break"—"broke"). For past participle, an "n" is added to the end of the word ("steal"—"stole"—"stolen").

- If a verb contains "ee," for simple past and past participle, one "e" is used ("bleed"—"bled," "meet"—"met").
- If a verb ends in "p," for both simple past and past participle, a "t" is added ("sleep"—"slept").
- If a verb ends in the vowel team "ay," for both simple past and past participle, the "ay" is changed to "ai" and a "d" is added ("lay"—"laid").
- A small number of verbs change "i" to "a" in the past tense and then "a" to "u" in past participle ("begin"— "began"—"begun").

Teaching Strategies

- Create activities where students find and match present verbs with simple past and past participle verbs. These can be card sorts or paper/pencil activities.
- **Extending:** Have students generate a list of words where the verb has only two variations (present and past) with different spellings ("do"—"did," "go"—"went").
- Create cloze sentences where students must insert the correct irregular past verb.
  For example: ("sing"— "sang"— "sung").
  After the choir had _____, they got back on the bus.
  The students will _____ first, followed by the adults.
  Amy _____ with the choir for the first time.

Week 33 Word Lists: past-tense verbs

Word Lists for Decoding and Encoding Activities		
Pattern 1: no change	**Pattern 2: C to Ce to Cen**	**Pattern 3: ee to e**
bet, bid, bust, cast, cost, cut, hit, hurt, let, quit, put, set, shut, spit, spread, wed	break-broke-broken choose-chose-chosen steal-stole-stolen **Variations that adds "n"** blow-blew-blown bite-bit-bitten fly-flew-flown **Exception** freeze-froze-frozen	bleed-bled meet-met feed-fed breed-bred flee-fled **Variation** lead-led
Pattern 4: p to pt	**Pattern 5: ay to aid**	**Pattern 6: i to a to u**
sleep-slept creep-crept weep-wept keep-kept sweep-swept leap-leapt **Variations** burn-burnt dream-dreamt spill-spilled-spilt bend-bent	pay-paid lay-laid say-said **Variations** slay-slain	cling-clang-clung shrink-shrank-shrunk drink-drank-drunk sing-sang-sung wring-wrang-wrung spring-sprang-sprung **Variations** begin-began-begun hang-hung fling-flung swing-swung sting-stung swim-swam

Grade 2 Week 34 Target Concept: screening week

(see blueprint, page 148)

Description of Concept

This week is intentionally scheduled time to screen your students in order to assess progress and plan for the next school year. The following screens are recommended in spring of grade 2:

- phonics word reading screen
- spelling screen
- benchmark or fluency/comprehension screen

Grade 2 Weeks 35–37 Target Concept: targeted review of concepts based on assessments

(see blueprint, page 148)

Description of Concept

Targeted review of skills taught in grade 2 based on assessment.

Concepts introduced in grade 2: vowel teams ("ee," "ea," "oa," "ow," "oo," "ou," "ew," "eu," "ui," "aw," "au"), diphthongs ("ow," "ou," "oi," "oy"), the many jobs of "y," r-controlled vowels ("ar," "or," "er," "ur," "ir"), trigraph "igh," silent letters, inflected ending "ed," common contractions, and past-tense verbs.

Word Lists: use previously provided word lists.

Tricky Words: targeted review and practice of tricky words based on ongoing progress monitoring.

Grade 3 Blueprint

The following blueprint begins with 12 weeks of review of concepts introduced in grade 2. There are many ways to address reading instruction once foundational pieces are in place (e.g., long and short vowels, consonants, and blending). As a professional who knows your students, you will use your expertise to adjust the pacing of introducing and reviewing concepts. This may mean speeding up or slowing down the progression of instruction. Once a concept has been taught, it should be continuously reinforced and applied through conversation, practice activities, and instruction.

By the end of grade 3, our hope is that students will be prepared for further work with multisyllable words, morphology (the meaning of word parts), etymology (where words come from), and grammar.

Grade 3 Blueprint

	WEEK 1	WEEK 2	WEEK 3	WEEK 4
SEPTEMBER	✓ review vowel teams (ee, ea) ✓ single-syllable words & multi-syllable words ✓ building & manipulating words, spelling & reading in context	✓ review vowel teams (oa/ow — long o) ✓ single-syllable words & multi-syllable words ✓ building & manipulating words, spelling & reading in context	✓ review vowel teams/diphthongs (ay, ai, oy, oi) ✓ single-syllable words & multi-syllable words ✓ building & manipulating words, spelling & reading in context	✓ screening week: ✓ spelling screen ✓ phonics word reading screen ✓ benchmark or fluency/comprehension screen ✓ review trigraph (igh) & digraph (ph)

	WEEK 5	WEEK 6	WEEK 7	WEEK 8
OCTOBER	✓ review inflected endings (ed) ✓ single-syllable words & multi-syllable words ✓ building & manipulating words, spelling & reading in context	✓ review hard & soft c/g ✓ single-syllable words & multi-syllable words ✓ building & manipulating words, spelling & reading in context	✓ review the "many jobs of y" ✓ single-syllable words & multi-syllable words ✓ building & manipulating words, spelling & reading in context	✓ review vowel–r (ar, or, er, ur, ir) ✓ single-syllable words & multi-syllable words ✓ building & manipulating words, spelling & reading in context

	WEEK 9	WEEK 10	WEEK 11	WEEK 12
NOVEMBER	✓ review initial & final silent letters (kn, wr, gn, gh, mb) ✓ single-syllable words & multi-syllable words ✓ building & manipulating words, spelling & reading in context	✓ review vowel teams/diphthongs (oo — both sounds, ew, ui, eu) ✓ single-syllable words & multi-syllable words ✓ building & manipulating words, spelling & reading in context	✓ review vowel teams/diphthongs (ou, ow, au, aw + wa/al) ✓ single-syllable words & multi-syllable words ✓ building & manipulating words, spelling & reading in context	✓ review past-tense verbs ✓ review long/short i & o followed by 2 consonants ✓ single-syllable words & multi-syllable words ✓ building & manipulating words, spelling & reading in context

DECEMBER	WEEK 13	✓ introduce **possessive plurals** ✓ single-syllable & multisyllable words ✓ building & manipulating words, spelling & reading in context
DECEMBER	WEEK 14	✓ flex/review
DECEMBER		✓ winter break
JANUARY	WEEK 15	✓ introduce common contractions (**am, are, is, has, not**) ✓ blending, building & manipulating words, spelling & reading in context
JANUARY	WEEK 16	✓ introduce common contractions (**have, would, had, will, shall**) ✓ blending, building & manipulating words, spelling & reading in context
JANUARY	WEEK 17	✓ review digraphs ck & ch, introduce **soldier rule (trigraph tch)** ✓ single-syllable words & multi-syllable words ✓ building & manipulating words, spelling & reading in context
JANUARY	WEEK 18	✓ introduce **soldier rule (trigraph dge)** ✓ single-syllable words & multi-syllable words ✓ building & manipulating words, spelling & reading in context
FEBRUARY	WEEK 19	✓ introduce **consonant –le** ✓ single-syllable words & multi-syllable words ✓ building & manipulating words, spelling & reading in context
FEBRUARY	WEEK 20	✓ introduce vowel teams (**ei, eigh, ey**) ✓ single-syllable words & multi-syllable words ✓ building & manipulating words, spelling & reading in context
FEBRUARY	WEEK 21	✓ introduce **doubling rules + adding suffixes to words that end in silent e** examples: clap to clapping, clapped, etc. ✓ single-syllable words & multi-syllable words ✓ building & manipulating words, spelling & reading in context
FEBRUARY	WEEK 22	✓ introduce common suffixes (**est, er**) ✓ single-syllable words & multi-syllable words ✓ building & manipulating words, spelling & reading in context

MARCH

WEEK 23	WEEK 24	WEEK 25	
✓ introduce common suffixes (**ish, ness, less**) ✓ single-syllable words & multi-syllable words ✓ building & manipulating words, spelling & reading in context	✓ introduce common suffixes (**y, ly, en**) ✓ single-syllable words & multi-syllable words ✓ building & manipulating words, spelling & reading in context	✓ screening week: ✓ progress monitoring ✓ spelling *for at-risk students* ✓ benchmark or fluency/ comprehension *for at-risk students*	✓ spring break

APRIL

WEEK 26	WEEK 27	WEEK 28	WEEK 29
✓ introduce common suffixes (**ful, ment, ive**) ✓ single-syllable words & multi-syllable words ✓ building & manipulating words, spelling & reading in context	✓ introduce (**ough, augh**) ✓ single-syllable words & multi-syllable words ✓ building & manipulating words, spelling & reading in context	✓ introduce common prefixes (**re, un, in, ex**) ✓ single-syllable words & multi-syllable words ✓ building & manipulating words, spelling & reading in context	✓ introduce common prefixes (**pre, dis, non, mis**) ✓ single-syllable words & multi-syllable words ✓ building & manipulating words, spelling & reading in context

MAY

WEEK 30	WEEK 31	WEEK 32	WEEK 33
✓ introduce **homonyms** (same pronunciation & sound, different meaning) ✓ single-syllable words & multi-syllable words ✓ building & manipulating words, spelling & reading in context	✓ introduce **homophones** (same sound, different spelling & meaning) ✓ single-syllable words & multi-syllable words ✓ building & manipulating words, spelling & reading in context	✓ introduce **irregular plurals** ✓ begin year-end screens ✓ single-syllable words & multi-syllable words ✓ building & manipulating words, spelling & reading in context	✓ introduce Latin spellings for /sh/ (**ti, si, ci**) ✓ single-syllable words & multi-syllable words ✓ building & manipulating words, spelling & reading in context

JUNE

WEEK 34	WEEK 35	WEEK 36	WEEK 37
✓ introduce endings (**ture & sure**) ✓ single-syllable words & multi-syllable words ✓ building & manipulating words, spelling & reading in context	✓ introduce additional sounds of **ch** ✓ single-syllable words & multi-syllable words ✓ building & manipulating words, spelling & reading in context	✓ screening week: complete year-end screens ✓ spelling ✓ phonics word reading screen ✓ benchmark or fluency/ comprehension screen	✓ targeted review of concepts based on assessments

Weekly Concept Pages with Full Lesson Plan in Week 18

Grade 3 Weeks 1–12: Review

Week	Concept for Review	Original Lesson: Grade 2	Page
Week 1	vowel teams: ee, ea	Week 10	152
Week 2	vowel teams: oa, ow (/ō/)	Week 11	154
Week 3	vowel teams/diphthongs: ay, ai, oy, oi	Weeks 12 & 13	155 & 158
Week 4	trigraph: igh & digraph: ph	Weeks 16 & 2	161 & 150
Week 5	inflected ending: ed	Week 17	161
Week 6	hard & soft c & g	Weeks 19 & 20	164 & 167
Week 7	the many jobs of y	Weeks 21 & 22	170 & 174
Week 8	vowel-r: ar, or, er, ur, ir	Weeks 23, 24 & 26	174, 176 & 178
Week 9	silent letters: kn, wr, gn, mb, gh	Week 29	182
Week 10	vowel teams/diphthongs: oo, ew, eu, ui	Weeks 15 & 31	160 & 185
Week 11	vowel teams/diphthongs: ou, ow, au, aw + wa/al	Weeks 27, 28 & 32	179, 181 & 186
Week 12	past-tense verbs + long/short i & o when followed by 2 consonants	Weeks 33 & 30	187 & 184

Grade 3 Week 4 Target Concept: screening week

(see blueprint, page 192)

Description of Concept

This week is intentionally scheduled time to screen your students in order to inform instruction and groupings. The following screens are recommended in fall of grade 3:

- spelling screen
- phonics word reading screen
- benchmark or fluency/comprehension screen

Review trigraph "igh" and digraph "ph" from grade 2.

Grade 3 Week 13 Target Concept: *possessive plurals*

(see blueprint, page 193)

Description of Concept

Possessive plurals are nouns that show ownership. With a possessive plural, a person, place, or thing changes to a person, place, or thing that owns something.

- If the noun does not end in "s," add an apostrophe and the letter "s" ("Mom's," "David's").
- If a singular noun ends in "s," it is correct to add an apostrophe and the letter "s" or just an apostrophe ("Willms'" or "Willms's").
- If the noun is plural, add an apostrophe but no "s" ("boys'," "scissors'"). Knowing this rule can aid comprehension when encountering words that could be singular or plural. For example, if it is the "student's books," they belong to one student, but if it is the "students' books," they belong to more than one student.
- If something is owned by more than one person, only the name of the last person mentioned receives the apostrophe and the letter "s" ("Cinta and Heather's book").

If the owner is an object, rather than a person/people, no apostrophe is required in singular or plural (rather than "Shut the cabin's door," it is correct to say, "Shut the cabin door").

Week 13 Word Lists: possessive plurals

Word Lists for Decoding and Encoding Activities	
Nouns That Do Not End in s	**Nouns That End in s**
dog's, cow's, boy's, student's, teacher's, doctor's	Willms' or Willms's, James' or James's Kas' or Kas's, Phyllis' or Phyllis's
Plural Nouns	**More Than One Person**
students', dogs', cats', teachers', doctors', farmers', cows', janitors', workers', elephants', helpers'	Joe and Katie's Tom and Jerry's ice cream Mutt and Jeff's

Grade 3 Week 14 Target Concept: *flex/review week*

(see blueprint, page 193)

Description of Concept

Review of targeted concepts based on rescreening data. The week before winter break is a good time to rescreen and assess student progress with skills.

Week 14 Word Lists: review using previously provided word lists for target concepts.

Grade 3 Week 15 Target Concept: common contractions "am," "are," "is," "has," "not"

(see blueprint, page 193)

Description of Concept

Common contractions are two words combined into a shortened form. With most contractions, an apostrophe is put in place of the letter(s) that has been removed. For example, "I am" is shortened to "I'm" and the apostrophe takes the place of the "a" in the word "am." When "has" is part of a past-tense verb it can be contracted with its preceding subject ("he's gone") and the apostrophe takes the place of the "ha."

Sample phoneme-to-grapheme mapping of a common contraction:

h	e	' s	

Week 15 Word Lists: common contractions am, are, is, has, not

Word Lists for Decoding and Encoding Activities				
am	**are**	**is/has**	**not**	
I am = I'm	we are = we're you are = you're they are = they're what are = what're who are = who're	it is/has = it's he is/has = he's she is/has = she's here is/has = here's that is/has = that's what is/has = what's where is/has = where's there is/has = there's who is/has = who's	is not = isn't are not = aren't cannot = can't do not = don't did not = didn't does not = doesn't had not = hadn't has not = hasn't have not = haven't	were not = weren't could not = couldn't would not = wouldn't should not = shouldn't must not = mustn't shall not = shan't will not = won't

Grade 3 Week 16 Target Concept: common contractions "have," "would," "had," "will," "shall"

(see blueprint, page 193)

Description of Concept

Common contractions are two words combined into one short form. With most contractions, an apostrophe is put in place of the letter(s) that has been removed. For example, "you have" is shortened to "you've" and the apostrophe takes the place of the "ha" in the word "have."

Sample phoneme-to-grapheme mapping of a common contraction:

th	ey	' ll	

Week 16 Word Lists: common contractions have, would, had, will, shall

Word Lists for Decoding and Encoding Activities		
have	**would/had**	**will**
I have = I've you have = you've we have = we've they have = they've	I would/had = I'd you would /had= you'd we would/had = we'd he would/had = he'd she would/had = she'd they would/had = they'd who would/had = who'd where would = where'd	I will = I'll you will = you'll we will = we'll he will = he'll she will = she'll they will = they'll who will = who'll what will = what'll

Grade 3 Week 17 Target Concept: soldier rule (review "ck" and "ch"), + introduce trigraph "tch"

(see blueprint, page 193)

Description of Concept
Trigraph: **tch**
Trigraph sound: /**ch**/
When a short vowel is followed by the digraph "ch," a silent letter "t" is inserted between the short vowel and the digraph to protect the short vowel.
This rule is often called the soldier rule because the silent letter "t" acts as a soldier on duty. Engage students in a conversation on why soldiers do not talk when they are on duty (to not be distracted and to stay focused on the job) and explain that this is the case with soldier "t." Soldier "t" is not needed if the short vowel has a friend (another letter between the short vowel and "ch," like "hunch") or if the vowel sound is long (vowel team like speech).
"Tch" is a trigraph — three letters that make one sound.
Review digraph "ck": Although "ck" was introduced in Grade 1 Week 11, the soldier rule explains why the "c" is silent. The "c" protects the short vowel from the "k" (e.g., "snack," "luck," "pick"). If there is another letter (a friend) between the short vowel and the "k," the "c" is not required (e.g., "chunk," "blank," "chalk").

Teacher Knowledge: There are a small number of exceptions to the soldier rule with "tch" where the "t" is not added after the short vowel (such, much, rich, which, sandwich).
Sample phoneme-to-grapheme mapping of "ck" and "tch":

p	i	tch	
t	r	u	ck

Week 17: soldier rule, -tch

Word Lists for Decoding and Encoding Activities			
itch	hitch	scotch	snatch
fetch	catch	thatch	twitch
pitch	batch	swatch	glitch
watch	witch	sketch	gotcha
match	ditch	stitch	snitch
patch	latch	crutch	etch
hatch	hutch	blotch	scratch
notch	retch	clutch	stretch
	switch		

Two-Syllable Extending Words
itchy, catchy, kitchen, catcher, ratchet, butcher, hatchet, bewitch, matchup, pitcher, sketchy, ketchup, satchel, unlatch, catching, watchdog, mismatch, matchbox, britches, chitchat, dispatch, wretched, fetching, scratchy, latchkey, watchful, potlatch, stretchy, catchall, catchment, hatchback, sketchpad, topstitch, patchwork, stopwatch, hopscotch, hitchhike, stretcher, pitchfork, matchbook, hatchling, witchcraft, matchstick, backstitch, wristwatch, crosshatch, sketchbook, switchback, switchboard

Three- or More-Syllable Extending Words
hatchery, stitchery, dispatcher, dogcatcher, watchtower, switcheroo, outstretched, butterscotch, birdwatching, oystercatcher, whatchamacallit

Nonsense Words
atch, gatch, hetch, lutch, satch, metch, gritch, brotch, snutch, swutch, platch, flitch, prutch

Word Chain
itch, pitch, witch, hitch, hutch, hatch, match, catch, batch, botch, blotch, notch, natch, snatch, latch, letch, fetch, sketch, stretch

Grade 3 Week 18 Target Concept: review soldier rule + introduce trigraph "dge"

(see blueprint, page 193)

Description of the Concept
Trigraph: **dge**
Trigraph sound: /j/

When the /j/ sound is heard at the end of a word, "ge" is used (see hard and soft "g" lesson, Grade 2 Week 20). When a short vowel is followed by "ge," the short vowel must be protected by the silent letter "d" ("fudge," "ledge," "grudge"). This rule is often called the soldier rule because the "d" silently protects the short vowel. The "d" is not necessary if there is another consonant between the short vowel and "ge" ("lunge," "fringe," "flange") or if there is a long vowel sound ("page"). "Dge" is a trigraph — three letters that make one sound.

Lesson Plan

	Target Concept: soldier -dge
1	**Warm-up/review:** 2–5 minutes Review soldier rule "ck" and "tch." When a short vowel is followed by "k" or "ch," a silent letter "c" or "t," respectively, is inserted after the short vowel to protect it. This rule is often called the soldier rule because the silent letter "t" acts as a soldier on duty.
2	**Introduce new concepts:** 5 minutes "The lesson today is another soldier rule. The /j/ sound at the end of a word is always spelled with a "ge" (see hard and soft "g," Grade 2 Week 20). Like "ck" and "tch," when "g" and "e" are together, a silent letter is needed to protect the short vowel that comes before it. In words ending in "ge," the short vowel is protected by soldier "d" ("fudge," "ledge," "grudge"). Soldier "d" is not necessary if the short vowel has a friend (there is another letter between the short vowel and "ge") — for example, in words like "lunge" and "fringe." Soldier "d" is also not needed if the vowel sound is long ("page").
3	**Teacher-led guided practice with new concept (WE Do):** 10–15 minutes **Choral reading** • Put a list of "dge" and "ck" and "tch" words or blending lines on the whiteboard and read them together as a class. • Have students come up and underline words that contain soldier "dge" or circle all the "dge" trigraphs and underline all the "ck" and "tch" trigraphs. **Applying the concept and sorting together** • Each student has a sheet of lined paper folded lengthwise (hotdog fold) and opened again. At the top of one column, students write "Soldier" and at the top of the other column "No Soldier." • The teacher writes a word on the board and reads it with the class. The teacher asks students if the word needs a soldier "d." For example, if the teacher writes the word "juge" on the board, students indicate it requires a soldier "d" because there is a short "u" and no other consonant between the "u" and the "ge." Students write "judge" under the column heading "Soldier" on their lined paper. Some students will say it needs a "d" because it does not "look right." Discourage this type of spelling and remind students that they do not have to decide on whether something "looks right" because they can know whether it is correct or not by following the phonics patterns. • Continue with several examples together and then move to the teacher writing the word on the board, the students and teacher reading the word together, and students writing it in the column they believe is correct, before discussing it as a class. Once everyone has independently decided, discuss together, correct if necessary, and move on to the next word. • When students become confident with this new pattern, incorporate "tch" and "ck" into the activity.
4	**Extended independent practice activities to apply new concept (YOU Do):** 15–20 minutes Word sorts with words that use the soldiers "ck," "tch," and "dge."

5	**Decoding with text (YOU Do):** 15–20 minutes Use short passages that include multiple examples of "tch" and "dge" words.
6	**Encoding (YOU Do):** 15 minutes Phoneme-to-grapheme spelling, whiteboard word building, practicing spelling in short phrases. Sample phoneme-to-grapheme mapping of "dge": | j	u	dge		
7	**Intervention:** If you have students who are emergent readers and not ready to read words using this concept, use pictures to teach the soldier rules. Use letter tiles and phoneme-to-grapheme spelling to practice encoding.
8	**Extending:** Use multisyllable words like "curmudgeon" and "acknowledge." Have students find their meaning and include them in writing a meaningful paragraph.

Week 18 Word Lists: soldier rule, -dge

Word Lists for Decoding and Encoding Activities

judge	lodge	smidge	trudge
fudge	ridge	drudge	fledge
grudge	dodge	dredge	pledge
edge	ledge	bridge	
wedge	budge	fridge	
nudge	badge	sludge	

Two-Syllable Extending Words
codger, hedgehog, smidgen, budget, ledger, badger, widget, gadget, midget, fidget, lodger, abridge, partridge, bludgeon, porridge, dislodge, selvedge, hedgerow, misjudge, knowledge, judgment, cartridge, ridgeline, dodgeball, ridgepole, hodgepodge, bridgework, drawbridge, straightedge

Three- or More-Syllable Extending Words
unabridged, curmudgeon, acknowledge, sledgehammer, drudgery

Nonsense Words
pedge, kadge, hudge, rodge, bidge, flidge, pradge, glodge, smedge, crudge, shradge, thridge, squodge, whudge, quedge

Word Chain
ridge, fridge, bridge, badge, budge, judge, fudge, nudge, drudge, grudge, sludge, sledge, wedge, fledge, ledge, lodge

Grade 3 Week 19 Target Concept: "consonant-le"
(see blueprint, page 193)

Six Syllable Rules: "Consonant-le" ("C-le") is the last of the Six Syllable Rules because the consonant, "l," and silent "e" must be kept together when breaking multisyllable words into individual syllables for decoding.

Description of Concept

Spelling: This syllable type is an accented final syllable that contains a consonant followed by "le" ("turtle," "bubble"). It always occurs at the end of a word and produces a schwa sound before the "l" /əl/. The silent "e" is added to support the consonant and "l" in creating a syllable, since every syllable contains a vowel.

Reading: This becomes an important reading rule as it impacts whether the syllable before it is read as open or closed. If students count back three letters ("C-le"), they will see the syllable that is before it. ("Ck" is never separated from "le" so in the case of a "ckle" the "c" stays with the "k.") Students often say /bŭg-le/ for /bū-gle/ because they do not understand this reading rule.

Sample phoneme-to-grapheme mapping of "consonant-le":

c	a	b	le
r	a	ff	le

Teaching Strategies

When working with this rule, it is important to address both the spelling and reading component.

Use numerous multisyllable words and have students break them into syllables, identifying which are open and closed. This is the perfect lesson for using syllable boards.

When practicing spelling "C-le," address the schwa /ə/ sound that is voiced/heard between the consonant and the "le" but not indicated in the spelling ("bubble," "table").

Teacher Knowledge: When "s" precedes "tle," the "t" becomes silent ("castle").

Week 19 Word Lists: "consonant-le"

Word Lists for Decoding and Encoding Activities	
cle	**dle**
circle, cycle, bicycle, uncle, article, vehicle, icicle, miracle, tentacle, obstacle, Popsicle, cubicle	handle, paddle, idle, puddle, muddle, candle, poodle, toddle, waddle, saddle, cradle, ladle, middle, cuddle, riddle, handle, bundle
ble	**kle**
table, jumble, humble, bubble, fumble, able, mumble, nimble, rumble, crumble, tremble, stumble, bobble, cable, stable, tumble, marble, pebble, double, noble, nibble, dabble, cobble, kibble, feeble, enable	ankle, sprinkle, buckle, pickle, fickle, heckle, tickle, twinkle, wrinkle, freckle, crinkle, knuckle, sparkle, shackle, speckle ***When breaking words into syllables, "ck" always stays together.**
gle	**tle**
eagle, bugle, angle, beagle, giggle, goggle, bungle, jangle, wiggle, jiggle, tingle, struggle, jingle, jungle, single, triangle, toggle, tangle, gargle, google	turtle, little, beetle, cattle, gentle, startle, battle, rattle, kettle, brittle, settle, throttle, mantle, title
stle	**ple**
castle, bustle, wrestle, whistle, hustle	purple, trample, apple, maple, simple, staple, ripple, topple, sample, ample, example, temple, crumple, people, pimple, dimple, couple
fle	**zle**
waffle, shuffle, raffle, sniffle, baffle, stifle, rifle, trifle	puzzle, muzzle, drizzle, sizzle, fizzle, dazzle, nozzle, guzzle, frazzle
Nonsense Words rackle, bacle, grodle, stiple, hugle, tiggle, chutle, hample, zottle, distle, chustle, shortle, huzzle, vizzle, boffle, nuffle, kifle	

Grade 3 Week 20 Target Concepts: vowel teams "ei," "eigh," "ey"

(see blueprint, page 193)

Description of Concept
Vowel teams: **ei, eigh, ey**
Vowel teams sounds: /ā/, /ē/, /ī/ and /ā/, /ī/ and /ā/, /ē/
The most common sounds of the "ei" vowel team are /ā/, as in "vein," and /ē/, as in "ceiling." There are a small number of words where "ei" says other sound: /ā/, as in "their," /ī/, as in "stein," "feisty," and "apartheid," /ĕ/, as in "heifer," and /ĭ/, as in "foreign," "forfeit," and "sovereign." It's a troublesome team!

The "eigh" vowel team makes two sounds: /ā/, as in "weigh," and /ī/, as in "height." "Ey" at the end of a word says either /ē/, as in "honey," or /ā/, as in "obey." There are only eleven common words ending in "ey" that make the /ā/ sound, so once students know these words, they can spell all other words that end in /ā/ with "ay" (Grade 2 Week 12).

There are a small number of words where "ey" can be found at the beginning or in the middle of the word and can say /ī/ or /ē/ (e.g., "eye," "geyser").

Sample phoneme-to-grapheme mapping of "eigh," "ei," and "ey":

eigh	t			
ei	th	er		
c	o	n	v	ey

Week 20 Word Lists: vowel teams ei, eigh, ey

Word Lists for Decoding and Encoding Activities			
ei /ā/	ei /ē/	eigh /ā/	eigh /ī/
lei, vein, heir, rein, veil, reign, skein, beige, heinous, feigned, reindeer, heirloom	weir, seize, deity, weird, either, deceit, geisha, leisure, receive, protein, seizure, atheist, conceit, neither, receipt, deceive, perceive, conceive, caffeine, ceiling	weigh, sleigh, eight, weight, freight, neighbor	height, sleight

ei can also make the following sounds: /ā/ their /ī/ stein, feisty, apartheid /ĕ/ heifer /ĭ/ foreign, forfeit, sovereign

ey /ā/	ey /ē/
they, convey, obey, hey, prey, purvey, survey, whey, osprey **Middle of the word:** abeyance	key, money, alley, honey, abbey, valley, turkey, hockey, monkey, donkey, pulley, kidney, barley, storey, volley, jersey, jockey, galley, medley, parsley, journey, trolley, chutney, chimney, attorney

Grade 3 Week 21 Target Concept: doubling rules + adding suffixes to words that end in silent "e"

(see blueprint, page 193)

Description of Concept

When adding suffixes, there are specific rules that guide whether you should double the final consonant of a word before adding the suffix.

No, do not double:

- if the suffix begins with a consonant ("flatness")
- if the base word ends in two consonants ("renting")
- if the base word has a vowel team ("swooped")

Yes, double:

- if the base word is one syllable ("clipping")
- if the word ends in only one consonant that is preceded by one vowel ("nutty").

Suffixes and Silent "e"

Words that end in silent "e" require special attention when adding suffixes because sometimes the "e" is dropped and at other times it is retained. There is no final consonant to double since these words end in silent "e."

General rule for working with silent "e" and suffixes:

1. If the suffix begins with a consonant, retain the silent "e" ("likely," "extremely").
2. If the suffix begins with a vowel, drop the silent "e" ("liking," "perceiving").

   However, the silent "e" is retained if it is needed to fulfill another rule:

   - It is retained if the "e" is required to maintain a soft "c" or "g" ("arrangeable," "noticeable"). If a suffix is added that starts with an "i," the "e" can be dropped because the "i" will keep the "c" or "g" soft ("sufficing," "ranged"). Hard and soft "c" and "g" were introduced in Grade 2 Weeks 19 and 20.
   - It is retained if the "e" is needed to make the vowel long ("mileage").

Sample phoneme-to-grapheme mapping of doubling rules and adding suffixes where there is a silent "e":

c	l	a	pp	i	ng
m	i	le	a	ge	
h	o	p	ed		

Week 21 Word Lists: doubling rule

Word Lists for Decoding and Encoding Activities	
No, do not double.	**Yes, double.**
Words that contain a vowel team/diphthong: swooped, swooping, boiling, boiled, boiler, aiming, aimed, cheated, cheating, cheater, needed, needing, needy, toaster, toasted, toasting, cloudy, clouded, draining, drained, steamy, steamer, spoiler, spoiled, spoiling, roofer, roofing, roofed, groaner, groaning, groaned, counter, counting	**Base words that are one syllable:** nutty, funny, runny, chippy, flippy, grippy, fatty, witty, whammy, batty, catty, clammy, strappy, foggy, baggy, sunny, muggy, muddy, piggy, peppy, clipped, flipped, flapped, chatted, fitted, pitted, lapped, dropped, strapped, trapped, bugged, hopped, banned, napped, padded, rapped, tagged, wagged, begged, dimmed, jogged, mopped, nodded, rubbed, hitting, sitting, batting, hopping, shopping, shipping, tapping, chipping, slapping, flapping, chatting, running, fitting, flipping, lapping, dropping, shredding, strapping, trapping, clipping, napping, padding, rapping, wagging, begging, letting, petting, wedding, bidding, dimming, jogging, mopping, nodding, cutting, rubbing
Words where the suffix begins with a consonant: flatness, flatly, hotly, hotness, handful, spoonful, glassful, roomful, sinful, helpful, gladly, slowly, childless, fondness, sleepless, painless, painful, wishful, blissful, coldness, pleasantness, madness, kindness, wetness, fitness, sadness, dimness, bluntness, crispness, stillness, quietness, steepness, brightness, strictness, bitterness	**Words that end in a consonant preceded by a vowel:** clipping, beginning, compelling, forbidding, unwilling, dropping, dripping, trimming, gripping, humming, clapping, slapping, whipping, plugging, willing
Words that end in two consonants: faster, fastest, renter, renting, brushing, brushed, farmer, farmed, farming, perched, perching, charming, charmed, charmer, sorter, sorting, sorted	

Adding suffixes to words that end in silent e						
If the suffix begins with a consonant, retain the silent "e."		If the suffix begins with a vowel, drop the silent "e."		Retain the silent "e" if it is needed to make the vowel long.		Retain the silent "e" if it is needed to keep the "c" or "g" soft.
gamely	senseless	troubling	driving	wavey	dyeing	danceable
rudely	noiseless	liking	doubling	dicey	ageing	noticeable
movement	shapeless	hoping	smiling	pokey	eyeing	traceable
likely	blameless	sizing	rattling	pricey	hoeing	replaceable
extremely	careful	siding	hustling	smiley	blueing	changeable
safely	hopeful	edging	stifling	spacey	puréeing	manageable
timely	wakeful	piping	fumbling	homey	freeing	serviceable
widely	prideful	fading	edgy		tiptoeing	packageable
lovely	graceful	paving	simply		mileage	
rarely	houseful	casing	doubly			
rudeness	plateful	tubing	gently			
blueness	casement	raging	stably			
soleless	movement	tiding	marbly			
boneless	statement	boring	tangly			
homeless	placement	gaming	jumbly			
faceless	entitlement	daring	crumbly			
toneless	management	waking	audibly			
treeless	wholesome	biting	sparkly			
wasteless		caring	twinkly			
voiceless		coming	perceiving			
		losing	drizzly			
		taking	bubbly			
		timing	giggly			
		writing				

Grade 3 Week 22 Target Concepts: common suffixes "er," "est"
(see blueprint, page 193)

Description of Concept

An affix (from the verb "fasten") is a word portion attached to a base. Over the next few months, there are several lessons that explore common prefixes and suffixes and their meanings. A prefix is attached to the beginning of a word, and a suffix is attached to the end of a word — their role is to provide further meaning to the base word. There are many prefixes and suffixes in English. We start exploring them in grade 3 with some of the most common ones, but more work should be done with prefixes and suffixes as students move into morphology work in grade 4.

Decoding Words with Prefixes and Suffixes

When breaking down multisyllable words, suffixes and prefixes should be identified as individual word parts. They are the first thing students should look for when decoding large words. They also provide important information about a word's meaning.

The suffix "er" has five meanings but for grade 3, the focus will be on meanings 1–3:

1. It is added to a verb to describe the person doing a task or role ("teacher," "swimmer").
2. It can be used with short adjectives and adverbs for comparison ("faster," "higher," "easier").
3. It can indicate someone is from a certain place ("Londoner," "northerner").
4. A person who is knowledgeable in a certain field ("philosopher").
5. Someone connected to or involved with an activity or group ("3rd grader").

For some words the American and British spellings of /er/ differ. The American spelling of the suffix is "er" but the British spelling of "er" is "r" followed by a silent "e" ("re") ("center"-American and "centre"-British or "fiber"-American and "fibre"-British). Like C-le (Week 19) every syllable must have a vowel; therefore, the silent "e" is added after the "r" to fulfill this rule.

The suffix "est" means "the most."
If a word ends in "e," drop the "e" and add "er" or "est" ("late," "later," "latest," "tame," "tamer," "tamest").

Week 22 Word Lists: common suffixes er, est

Word Lists for Decoding and Encoding Activities	
er	**est**
helper, teacher, fighter, speaker, renter, sticker, baker, hater, safer, cuter, ruder, rider, loner, higher, lower, voyager, counter, farmer, faster, slower	oldest, loudest, quietest, proudest, happiest, biggest, fastest, shortest, brightest, deepest, softest, longest, strongest, weakest, smartest, greatest, sharpest
British "re" centre, lustre, spectre, fibre, litre, theatre, metre	

Grade 3 Week 23 Target Concept: common suffixes "ish," "less," "ness"
(see blueprint, page 194)

Description of Concept
The suffix "ish" is an Old English suffix that means "less in intensity" ("greenish") or acts to liken to an attribute ("selfish"). Words with "ish" are adjectives, but when derived from Old French present participle words, they can also take on the form of a verb ("establish").
The Old English suffix "less" is the opposite of the suffix "ful" and means "without" ("heartless").
"Ness" is an Old English suffix that means "the state, condition, or degree" ("happiness").

Week 23 Word Lists: common suffixes ish, less, ness

Word Lists for Decoding and Encoding Activities	
ish (adjective)	**ish (verb)**
selfish, blackish, blueish, bookish, Finnish, babyish, amateurish, bearish, brownish, childish, feverish, clownish, foolish, freakish, garish, lavish, littlish, longish, lumpish, mulish, newish, oafish, owlish, peckish, pinkish, Polish, reddish, rubbish, Scottish, sheepish, sickish, sluggish, lowish, smallish, snobbish, Spanish, squeamish, stylish, Turkish, wolfish	abolish, admonish, anguish, astonish, banish, burnish, blemish, cherish, demolish, diminish, embellish, establish, extinguish, punish, famish, finish, flourish, furnish, garnish, impoverish, nourish, perish, polish, publish, skirmish, tarnish, vanish, varnish
less	**ness**
nameless, harmless, painless, spotless, countless, mindless, backless, breathless, homeless, thankless, endless, helpless, jobless, careless, gutless, useless, hopeless, meaningless, sleepless, fearless, restless, powerless	brightness, sadness, illness, weakness, blackness, carelessness, coldness, boldness, goodness, darkness, sickness, awareness, closeness, boldness, greatness, highness, rudeness, dampness, madness, fitness, freshness

Grade 3 Week 24 Target Concept: suffixes "y," "ly," "en"

(see blueprint, page 194)

Description of Concept

The suffix "y" has four possible uses.

1. The Old English suffix "y" creates an adjective ("healthy").
2. It can be a noun suffix ("army," "country").
3. "Y" can be added to a noun to create a "pet" name or term of endearment ("Johnny," "puppy," "kitty").
4. It can indicate a state, condition, or subject ("victory," "misery," "history").

When the suffix "ly" is added to the end of a word, it means "having the qualities of" or "in the manner of."

1. When added to a noun it changes the noun to an adjective ("manly," "friendly").
2. When added to an adjective, it changes the adjective to an adverb ("quickly," "sadly").

If a word ends in "y," change the "y" to an "i" and add "ly" ("lazy"—"lazily").
If a word ends in "le," drop the "le" ("terrible"—"terribly," "wobble"—"wobbly").

"En" can be added to the beginning or the end of a word to add meaning. The addition of the suffix "en" can create nouns, verbs, and adjectives. When added to the end of a word, the Latin/Greek source means "to be made of," and it creates a noun or adjective ("linen," "woolen"). When the Old English suffix "en" is added to the end of a word to mean "to become," the word becomes a verb ("lengthen," "darken").

The Relationship between "i" and "y": This is a good time to draw students' attention to the deeply connected relationship between the letters "y" and "i."

- In Grade 1 Week 26, students were introduced to the concept that when a word ends in "y," we change the "y" to an "i" and add "es."
- The many jobs of "y" lessons (Grade 2 Weeks 21 and 22) taught that the letter "y" can say /ĭ/ or /ī/ when it is the only working vowel in a word, when it is comes after "n," "f," or "l," or when it comes at the end of a syllable.
- This lesson introduces the concept that when words end in "y," we change the "y" to an "i" before adding "ly."

While all these lessons have "y" changing to "i" or saying the sound of "i," it is not commonly known that the letter "i" sometimes says /y/ — for example, in words like "onion," "union," "opinion," and "brilliant."

Week 24 Word Lists: suffixes y, ly, en

Word Lists for Decoding and Encoding Activities

y as an adjective	y as a noun	y as a pet name	y as a state/condition
grumpy, healthy, salty, dirty, crispy, grisly, achy, airy, angry, artsy, baggy, balmy, batty, beefy, beady, blurry, blotchy, bony, bossy, breathy, brainy, boxy, breezy, bulky, bumpy, bushy, buttery, catchy, chalky, chatty, cheeky, cheery, cheesy, chilly, choosy, choppy, chubby, classy, corny, crabby, cranky, crazy, creamy, creaky, crummy, crunchy, curly, curvy, dippy, dodgy, dreamy, dressy, drippy, dusty, edgy, fatty, faulty, fiery, filthy, fishy, flaky, flashy, floppy, fluffy, foggy, freaky, frilly, frosty, funny, furry, gassy, goofy, gory, grassy, greasy, grimy, groovy, gutsy, hairy, handy, happy, hungry, icy, itchy, juicy, jumpy, lacy, leaky, lengthy, lofty, lousy, lucky, lumpy, messy, misty, moldy, moody, mouthy, muddy, naughty, noisy, nosy, nutty, oily, perky, picky, pricey, puffy, pushy, rainy, rocky, roomy, runny, rusty, saggy, sandy, saucy, scary, shaky, shiny, skinny, sleepy, slopy, smelly, smoky, snowy, soggy, speedy, sporty, squeaky, steady, sticky, stinky, sunny, sweaty, tasty, thirsty, tidy, tiny, tricky, wavy, windy, witty, worthy, **and so many more!**	army, city, country, history, discovery, jewelry, stationery, embroidery, registry, upholstery	puppy, Johnny, Susy, Betty, kitty, baby, daddy, mommy, hubby, kiddy, piggy, sonny, Teddy	victory, history, discovery, expiry, leprosy, matriarchy, mutiny

ly (adjective)	ly (adverb)	en (suffix)
brotherly, bubbly, bully, chilly, coolly, courtly, cowardly, crumbly, daily, deadly, deeply, drizzly, elderly, fairly, fatherly, firstly, friendly, gnarly, giggly, ghostly, godly, grizzly, hardly, heavenly, hilly, homely, hotly, husbandly, impartially, impishly, justly, kindly, kingly, knightly, leisurely, likely, lively, loudly, lovely, lowly, madly, manly, monthly, motherly, neighbourly, oily, only, openly, orderly, pearly, poorly, princely, publicly, quarterly, queenly, rightly, sickly, sisterly, thinly, weakly, weekly, wizardly, woolly, worldly, wrinkly, yearly	abruptly, affectionately, actually, angrily, anxiously, arrogantly, boldly, bravely, briskly, brightly, calmly, carefully, carelessly, cheerfully, clearly, closely, continuously, correctly, curiously, darkly, delightfully, desperately, diligently, distinctly, earnestly, enormously, entirely, especially, evenly, exactly, fairly, faithfully, finally, fearlessly, foolishly, generally, greatly, gently, heavily, highly, hungerly, immediately, instantly, intensely, kindly, knowingly, likely, madly, meekly, mentally, mostly, miserably, naturally, neatly, nearly, nervously, obviously, openly, partially, patiently, perfectly, playfully, politely, peacefully, poorly, properly, proudly, quickly, quietly, readily, reluctantly, rightfully, rudely, sadly, safely, selfishly, seriously, slowly, softly, strictly, terribly, thankfully, thoroughly, thoughtfully, tightly, totally, truthfully, wearily, wildly, wisely, **and so many more**	**Adjective:** wooden, golden, woolen, earthen, olden **Noun:** linen, aspen, heathen, oxen **Verb:** blacken, brazen, brighten, broaden, cheapen, dampen, deafen, deepen, darken, weaken, lengthen, flatten, freshen, frighten, harden, heighten, lessen, lighten, loosen, moisten, neaten, ripen, sadden, sharpen, shorten, sicken, soften, stiffen, strengthen, straighten, sweeten, thicken, toughen, whiten, widen, worsen

Grade 3 Week 25 Target Concept: screening week
(see blueprint, page 194)

Description of Concept
This week is intentionally scheduled time to screen your students in order to inform your instruction and groupings. The following screens are recommended in midyear of grade 3:

- progress monitoring
- spelling *for at-risk & bubble students*
- benchmark for fluency/comprehension *for at risk & bubble students*

Grade 3 Week 26 Target Concept: common suffixes "ful," "ment," "ive"
(see blueprint, page 194)

Description of Concept
"Ful" is an Old English suffix that, when added to a noun, means a containing item ("handful"), an amount contained ("spoonful"), or an adjective describing a quality contained or possessing an attribute ("joyful").
If a word ends in "y," change the "y" to an "i" when adding "ful" ("beauty"—"beautiful").

The Latin suffix "ment" means "the result or product of" ("fulfillment," "accomplishment").

The French/Latin suffix "ive" has two meanings. The first creates an adjective that means "having a character, quality, or tendency" ("festive," "massive"), and the second use of "ive" creates a noun of adjective origin ("detective," "captive"). It is important to note that the suffix "ive" does not follow the VCe rule.

Week 26 Word Lists: suffixes ful, ment, ive

Word Lists for Decoding and Encoding Activities		
ful (noun)	**ful (adjective)**	**ment**
handful, cupful, earful, armful, bellyful, mouthful, houseful, carful, boxful	artful, restful, joyful, painful, hateful, gleeful, hurtful, playful, blissful, dreadful, fearful, peaceful, colorful, careful, hopeful, harmful, useful, helpful, faithful, eventful, graceful, shameful	ailment, payment, segment, torment, basement, shipment, pavement, movement, document, argument, judgment, placement, accomplishment, investment, abandonment
ive (noun)	**ive (adjective)**	
detective, native, votive, captive, operative, relative, executive, explosive, narrative, locomotive, alternative, conservative	festive, massive, active, captive, passive, elusive, pensive, creative, positive, cursive, invasive, expensive, sensitive, offensive, selective, inclusive, effective, addictive, decorative, repetitive, attractive, impressive, productive, supportive, competitive, cooperative, destructive, conservative, comprehensive	

Grade 3 Week 27 Target Concept: vowel teams "ough," "augh"

(see blueprint, page 194)

Description of Concept

Vowel Team: **"ough"**

When English is criticized as being too unpredictable to teach, "ough" is the perfect example! It is a tricky one, since it can make individual sounds such as the long /ō/ in "dough" as well as combined sounds like /ŭf/, as in "rough." For this lesson we encourage teaching awareness of these sounds but not testing and drilling this concept, since it is not a common vowel team. Focusing on sorting words by sound and word play with this vowel team might be the best way to expose students to the different possibilities "ough" brings to the table.

Sounds that the vowel team "ough" can make:

- /ŏ/, as in "ought"
- /ō/, as in "dough"
- /ö/, as in "through"
- /ŏf/, as in "cough"
- /ŭf/, as in "rough"
- /ow/, as in "bough"

Vowel Team: **"augh"**

"Augh" makes two sounds: /ä/, as in "caught," and /ăf/, as in "draught." These are very rare spellings and should be taught for exposure and to provide an opportunity to work with this unusual Old English vowel team.

Teaching Strategies

Tell students they will be working with "ough" this week and that it is a tricky team because "ough" makes six different sounds!

Read a list of "ough" words together and have students identify the sound that "ough" makes in each word. Approach it as a wonderment: "Can you believe one vowel team can make so many sounds?"

Sample phoneme-to-grapheme mapping of "ough" and "augh":

b	ough		
t	augh	t	

Week 27 Word Lists: ough

Word Lists for Decoding and Encoding Activities		
ough makes the /ŏ/ sound	**ough makes the /ō/ sound**	**ough makes the /ŭf/ sound**
One-Syllable Words ought, sought, fought, bought, thought, brought, wrought	**One-Syllable Words** dough, though	**One-Syllable Words** tough, rough
Two- or More-Syllable Extending Words besought, thoughtful, thoughtless, forethought, overwrought, afterthought	**Two- or More-Syllable Extending Words** although, thorough, doughnut, furlough, borough (Marlborough, Scarborough, etc.,), sourdough, thoroughbred, thoroughfare	**Two- or More-Syllable Extending Words** enough, roughneck
ough makes the /ow/ sound	**ough makes the /ö/ sound**	**ough makes the /ŏf/ sound**
bough, drought, plough	through, throughout, breakthrough	cough, trough
Exception: hiccough		
Word Chains ought, sought, fought, bought, brought, wrought, thought dough, though, although, thorough, borough rough, tough, trough, enough		

Week 27 Word Lists: augh

Word Lists for Decoding and Encoding Activities	
augh makes the /ăf/ sound	**augh makes the /ä/ sound**
One-Syllable Words laugh, draught	**One-Syllable Words** aught, caught, taught, naught, fraught
Two-Syllable Extending Word laughter	**Two-Syllable Extending Words** haughty, onslaught, slaughter, naughty, daughter, distraught, retaught, untaught, uncaught
Three-Syllable Extending Word laughingstock	**Three- or More-Syllable Extending Words** manslaughter, stepdaughter, granddaughter, slaughterhouse
Word Chain aught, caught, taught, naught, fraught, draught	

Grade 3 Week 28 Target Concept: common prefixes "re," "un," "in," "ex"

(see blueprint, page 194)

Description of Concept

"Re" is a Latin prefix meaning "again" ("retry," "readjust").

"Un" is an Old English prefix meaning "not." It can be added to many adjectives, adverbs, and verbs to reverse their meaning ("unhealthy," "unlikely").

"In" is a Latin prefix meaning "not" "or the opposite of." It has the same meaning as the prefix "un," so a good rule of thumb is to use "in" with Latin bases and "un" with all others ("incomplete," "unhappy").

"Ex" is a Latin prefix meaning "out or away" ("extend" = reach out, "exclude" = keep out).

Week 28 Word Lists: common prefixes re, un, in, ex

Word Lists for Decoding and Encoding Activities	
re	**un**
redo, remake, retake, resave, react, reappear, reuse, reread, rewrite, retry, replay, renew, rewind, repaint, rename, remix, rerun, repay, reshape, retell, repack, revise, revisit, rethink, refit, restore, remind, restart, research, refill, resell, reset, redirect, recycle, recover	undo, unlucky, unhappy, unkind, untie, untrue, unwell, untidy, unfinished, undress, unfair, unable, unstable, unfit, unlike, unfortunate, unwrap, unclean, unsafe, unafraid, unbearable, uncover, unexpected, unlock, unpack, unbelievable, unhelpful, unknown, unwilling
in	**ex**
into, inert, insert, inept, inlet, input, infer, index, inset, intro, infect, infest, inform, inject, ingest, influx, infant, indoor, indent, income, indeed, induct, infuse, inhale, injure, insane, include, incident, increase, incubate, inactive, incomer, indicate	exit, expo, exam, exec, expat, expel, exact, exist, exile, exude, exert, extra, examen, excuse, exhale, expand, expire, expose, extend, except, exceed, excite, exempt, exhume, exotic, expect, expert, export, exsert, examine, execute, exhibit, expense, extort, exclaim, example, excavate, exercise, excessive, executor, executer, exertion, exhaust

Grade 3 Week 29 Target Concept: common prefixes "pre," "dis," "non," "mis"

(see blueprint, page 194)

Description of Concept

"Pre" is a Latin prefix meaning "before" ("prepaid," "preview").

"Dis" is a Latin prefix meaning "apart" ("discontinue," "discouraged"). It is now commonly used to mean the opposite of ("dislike," "discolor"). In speech it can mean "mistaken" or "incorrect."

"Non" is a French/Latin prefix meaning "not" ("nonsense," "nonexistent").

"Mis" is an Old English prefix meaning "wrong, bad, or mistaken" ("mistrust," "mistake").

Week 29 Word Lists: common prefixes pre, dis, non, mis

Word Lists for Decoding and Encoding Activities	
pre	**dis**
precut, prefab, premix, prepay, prefix, prefer, prenup, precept, precook, predawn, preface, preheat, preload, precede, precise, prelude, premium, preclean, prepaid, preview, precure, preamble, precheck, predate, prebook, prebuilt, precursor, predict, preapprove, prebiotic, preclude	disarm, dislike, discuss, dismay, disown, disable, disband, discord, disease, disgust, dispel, disrupt, distant, disbar, discard, dismiss, dispense, dispose, disrobe, distill, distort, disjoin, disport, display, dispute, disturb, disarray, discolor, discover, disclose, disloyal, disagree, disguise, disdain, discrete, discount, discontinue, disobey, discomfort
non	**mis**
nonfat, nonstop, nondairy, nonowner, nonsense, nonissue, nonfatal, nonlegal, nonlocal, nonhuman, nonmajor, nonprint, nonethnic, nonfactor, nonfrozen, nonformal, noncolor, nonbelief, noncrisis, nonfamily	misdo, misuse, misact, mishap, miscue, misfed, mislay, misaim, miscut, misfit, misled, misfire, mishear, mistake, mistrust, misread, miscall, misdraw, mislead, miscarry, misalign, misbegun, misdeal, misfile

Grade 3 Week 30 Target Concept: *homonyms*

(see blueprint, page 194)

Description of Concept

Homonyms are words with the same spelling and pronunciation but different meanings (e.g., "fair" means "equal," "a fall festivity," and "light in color"). "Homo" means "same" and "nym" means "name." Students enjoy searching for a variety of meanings for the same word.

Week 30 Word Lists: homonyms

Word Lists for Decoding and Encoding Activities				
air	change	groom	light	spring
arm	chip	bum	man	stalk
band	close	hail	match	tank
bank	club	horn	nail	tie
bark	die	iron	pot	tire
base	down	jam	pound	trip
bat	duck	judge	ring	trunk
bear	dust	just	rock	wave
book	even	key	row	well
bow	fall	kid	scale	yard
box	fair	kind	seal	
bright	fly	left	sink	
can	grave	lie	space	

Two- or More-Syllable Extending Words
address, chicken, express, general, pitcher, remote

Grade 3 Week 31 Target Concept: homophones
(see blueprint, page 194)

Description of Concept
Homophones are words with the same pronunciation but different spellings and meanings ("peace"/"piece," "where"/"wear"). "Homo" means "same," and "phone" means "sound." Understanding homophones is important for vocabulary building and for spelling.

Teaching Strategies
Card sort: Have sixteen to twenty homophones on cards of one color, with definitions on cards of a second color. Make sure both homophones are represented. In groups of two or three, have students sort the cards into their homophone/definition pairs.

Spelling: When practicing spelling with homophones, choose phrases that clearly indicate the meaning of the word. For example, for "where"/"wear" use the phrases "I wear it" and "Where is it?"

Week 31 Word Lists: homophones

Word Lists for Decoding and Encoding Activities		
Word Pairs		**Word Triplets**
eye/I	heal/heel	two/too/to
dual/duel	here/hear	there/their/they're
peace/piece	hour/our	sight/cite/site
caret/carrot	idle/idol	
bawl/ball	knight/night	
pain/pane	not/knot	
plain/plane	pour/poor	
real/reel	write/right	
vain/vane	sea/see	
flew/flu	soul/sole	
male/mail	sun/son	
hour/our	steel/steal	
new/knew	tail/tale	
where/wear	whether/weather	
brake/break	whole/hole	
cell/sell	be/bee	
scent/sent	bear/bare	
dye/die	waste/waist	
flour/flower	weak/week	
for/four		

Grade 3 Week 32 Target Concept: irregular plurals
(see blueprint, page 194)

Description of Concept
An irregular plural is a word that changes spelling to indicate a plural. Adding "s" or "es" (Grade 1 Week 26) is not appropriate for these words. There are many ways to sort irregular plurals.

- The final letter changes before adding "s" or "es" ("calf"—"calves").
- Nouns ending in "us" change to "i" ("cactus"—"cacti," "octopus"—"octopi").
- Words ending in "is" become "es" ("axis"—"axes," "crisis"—"crises").
- Words ending in "um" become "a" ("medium"—"media").
- Words ending in "a" become "ae" ("formula"—"formulae").
- Words ending in "ix" or "ex" become "ices" ("index"—"indices").
- The plural is made by changing vowels ("man"—"men") or word parts ("child"—"children").
- Two distinct words are used ("mouse"—"mice").
- The plural word has the same spelling and pronunciation as its single form ("pants," "scissors," "deer," "sheep").
- Non—count nouns are words that have no plural form because they are assumed to be plural ("hair," "money").
- Some animals can be noted as plural by adding "s" or "es," or leaving the word intact ("shrimp"/"shrimps," "quail"/"quails").

Week 32 Word Lists: irregular plurals

Word Lists for Decoding and Encoding Activities				
"f" to "ve"	"us" to "i"	"is" to "es"	"um" to "a"	Spelling does not change.
half—halves calf—calves loaf—loaves dwarf—dwarves hoof—hooves scarf—scarves thief—thieves wharf—wharves wife—wives knife—knives life—lives wolf— wolves leaf—leaves elf—elves proof—proves roof—rooves self—selves	octopus—octopi cactus—cacti focus—foci fungus—fungi hippopotamus— hippopotami	axis—axes crisis—crises oasis—oases basis—bases thesis—theses analysis—analyses	curriculum— curricula datum—data medium—media memorandum— memoranda	pants scissors deer sheep moose aircraft fish
Changing Vowels	Adding Word Parts	"a" to "ae"	Word Change	"ix" or "ex" to "ices"
man—men woman—women goose—geese foot—feet tooth—teeth	child—children ox—oxen	formula—formulae antenna—antennae larva—larvae	mouse—mice die—dice louse—lice person—people	index—indices vertex—vertices matrix—matrices appendix— appendices

Grade 3 Week 33 Target Concept: Latin spellings for /sh/ ("ti," "si," "ci")

(see blueprint, page 194)

Description of Concept

In grade 1, students were taught that the digraph "sh" says /sh/ (Grade 1 Week 5). This is true when it is found at the beginning of a base word or at the end of a word or syllable. However, "sh" is not the only letter combination that makes this sound. At the beginning of a syllable (except for the suffix "ship"), there are three Latin spellings that make the /sh/ sound: "ti" ("promotion," "addition," "petition"), "ci" ("delicious," "appreciate"), and "si" ("confession," "passion"). These three /sh/ spellings cannot be used at the beginning of a base word and are used only at the beginning of a syllable after the first syllable. This is important for students to understand, not just for spelling, but for syllable division when reading larger words.

There are seven suffixes that can start with the /sh/ sound spelled "ti," "ci," or "si" and they are: "al," "an," "ary," "ate," "ent," "on," and "ous"). The most common suffixes are used in word lists below.

Sample phoneme-to-grapheme mapping of "ti," "si," and "ci":

f	i	c	ti	o	n
v	i	si	o	n	
f	a	ci	a	l	

Week 33 Word Lists: Latin spellings for /sh/ (ti, si, ci)

Word Lists for Decoding and Encoding Activities	
ti	**ci**
tial: torrential, partial **tian:** Egyptian **tiary:** penitentiary **tiate:** negotiate **tient:** quotient **tion:** election, exception, addiction, promotion, petition, prohibition, dietitian **tious:** cautious	**cial:** commercial, facial **cian:** clinician, physician **ciary:** judiciary **ciate:** appreciate **cient:** sufficient **cion:** coercion, suspicion **cious:** precious, luscious, vicious, delicious, spacious, gracious, conscious, ferocious, vivacious, malicious, tenacious, suspicious
si	**ion for words with Latin roots that end in "de "or "se"**
sial: controversial **sion:** vision, fusion, lesion, recession, version, pension, erosion, mission, passion, mansion, progression, tension, evasion, decision, omission, revision, aversion, invasion, division, emulsion, delusion, occasion, emission, illusion, cohesion, incision, emersion, provision, explosion, revulsion, intention, expansion, admission, exclusion, excursion, remission, extension, immersion, dimension, collision, submission, television, permission, expression, discussion, conversation, impression, concession, confession, transfusion	**de:** divide—division, explode—explosion, allude—allusion **se:** diffuse—diffusion, fuse—fusion

Grade 3 Week 34 Target Concepts: endings "ture," "sure"

(see blueprint, page 194)

Description of the Concept

The letter combinations "ture" and "sure" make three unique sounds. At the end of a word, "ture" says /chur/, as in "future," and "sure" says /zjur/, as in "closure" and /shur/, as in "pressure." Knowing these unique sounds is important in both reading and writing.

Sample phoneme-to-grapheme mapping of endings "ture" and "sure":

p	i	c	t	ure	
c	l	o	s	ure	

Week 34 Word Lists: "ture," "sure"

Word Lists for Decoding and Encoding Activities		
ture /chur/	sure /zjur/	sure /shur/
adventure, agriculture, capture, creature, culture, departure, future, feature, fixture, furniture, lecture, nature, manufacture, mature, mixture, moisture, picture, posture, torture, venture, structure, fracture, scripture, signature, sculpture, temperature, texture, venture	leisure, closure, measure, treasure, exposure, pleasure, composure, enclosure, disclosure, foreclosure	assure, insure, pressure, reassure

Grade 3 Week 35 Target Concept: additional sounds of "ch"

(see blueprint, page 194)

Description of the Concept
Digraph: **ch**
Digraph sounds: /**ch**/, /**k**/, /**sh**/
In Grade 1 Week 6, students were introduced to the digraph "ch" and its sound /ch/ ("church," "chunk"). The "ch" spelling has two other sounds: in Greek-based words, the "ch" spelling says /k/ ("orchid," "stomach") and the French spelling of the sound /sh/ is "ch" ("machine," "chef"). This is important for students to understand for both reading and spelling.

Week 35 Word Lists: additional sounds of ch

Word Lists for Decoding and Encoding Activities	
Greek words with "ch"	French words with "ch"
orchid, epoch, stomach, anchor, ache, chaos, chemist, chorus, echo, monarch, scheme, architect, chemistry, character, cholera, orchestra, mechanic, technical, school, technology	machine, chef, cliché, ricochet, mustache, chagrin, chaperone, champagne, Chicago, parachute, chenille, chandelier, chic, brochure, cache, pistachio, fuchsia, machete, niche, chauffeur, charade, château, chivalry, chute, quiche, chiffon, chalet, crochet, Charlotte, Chevrolet, Michelle

Grade 3 Week 36 Target Concept: screening week
(see blueprint, page 194)

Description of Concept
This week is intentionally scheduled time to screen your students in order to assess progress and plan for the next school year. The following screens are recommended in spring of grade 3:

- spelling
- phonics word reading screen
- benchmark or fluency/comprehension screen

Grade 3 Week 37 Target Concept: targeted review of concepts based on assessments
(see blueprint, page 194)

Description of Concept
Targeted review of concepts taught in grade 3 based on assessment.

Concepts introduced in grade 3: possessive plurals, soldier rule, consonant –le, "ei" and "eigh," doubling rules, common suffixes ("est," "er," "y," "ly," "ful," "ment"), words that end in "ey," "ough," and "augh," common prefixes ("re," "un," "in," "ex," "pre," "dis," "non"), homonyms, homophones, irregular plurals, Latin spellings for /sh/ ("ti," "si," "ci"), "ture" and "sure," and the additional sounds of "ch."

Word Lists: use previously provided word lists.

6

Concluding Thoughts

After spending a significant amount of time sharing the "how" of teaching reading, we would like to conclude with its impact on student success. When teachers screen their students and teach targeted sequential, explicit, high-interest phonics in the classroom, and when this is supported by the same evidence-based strategies with intervention, students grow as readers. Classroom teachers have been especially happy to see the rapid rate at which many students have progressed in skill development and confidence through this approach.

Student Confidence and Engagement

Heather walked into the office of a school she was working in and found a student sitting at a desk, picking at a snack. She told him to finish up what he was doing because she was going to teach a group lesson in five minutes. The supervising educational assistant (EA) started to explain that the student was there for being disruptive and he needed to finish his snack and take his meds. While the EA was explaining, the student shoved the snack in his mouth along with the meds, took a swig of water from his water bottle, and announced he was ready to go.

We both gather data in our work with students in the classroom and reading support room, but there is no screen or assessment that measures students who were discouraged or disliked reading and now are confident and excited about reading after engaging in explicit and systematic phonics instruction. Students begin to engage with confidence because they are receiving instruction at their reading level. This requires a level of trust between the reader and the teacher, but we have seen students go from rolling on the floor and refusing to engage, to sitting at a table manipulating letter tiles or coming into class and choosing to sit and look at a book rather than wander aimlessly around the room.

As teachers move to explicit instruction, addressing the specific needs of all learners, and students grow in confidence, there is a shift in engagement. Students who have given up begin to hope that they might figure out "this reading thing" after all. Once students learn that educators will not ask them to do something they are not able to do, there is a willingness to take risks and try. With fast-paced, targeted lessons, no one is bored, and students quickly learn what is expected of them through structured routines and familiar activities. It may take time to learn the structure of the classroom and the activities, but once it is learned, students are able to move to their assigned tasks and get started.

Growing Skills

When skills are taught explicitly and sequentially, students move forward, and we have seen significant growth in the students we work with in the classroom and the reading support room. Many students have not been able to finish a phonics and word reading screen when initially administered. When rescreening takes place, even if students do not score 100 percent, they are able to complete the screen because they have strategies to tackle unknown words. There is nothing more gratifying than watching students "break the code" and begin to read, or become stronger readers through the application of concepts they've been explicitly taught.

Bubble Students

When we started with this approach and began rescreening, we noticed that all of our students who were reading just below grade level jumped up to grade level reading achievement. These were students in grades 3, 4, and 5 who had been lagging behind their peers for several years, and discussions had begun as to whether they would need further testing. Teachers were wondering if these students had an underlying reading disability that was being masked by excellent work habits. We had not anticipated this improvement, and in reflecting on these students and their engagement in class, we believe that all they needed was explicit phonics instruction in order to tackle unknown words. They needed the tools to work with words.

Strong Readers Love Explicit Instruction

Teachers are often concerned about strong readers being bored with explicit instruction, but we have found the opposite to be true. These students are highly engaged in lessons because they are able to make so many connections with their own reading. While they intuitively implement phonics concepts when reading, they often do not understand why they use these reading and spelling patterns. In almost every grades 4 to 7 class that Heather has worked in, there has been one student who gets so involved in the lessons that she finally suggests they consider studying linguistics when they get to university! Phonetics is a branch of linguistics, and it is fascinating. Learning about the English language — its origins, morphology, and patterns — can be exciting.

Intervention Clientele

As explicit, sequential phonics instruction is introduced in the classroom and then reinforced and practiced in the reading support room, the number of students requiring support outside the classroom drops. We have seen this in the data of other educators and researchers, and we have seen it for ourselves. Students begin moving out of reading support programming because they now have the skills and strategies they need to move forward as readers. This is something we have not seen for a very long time! It leaves the reading support teacher with students who truly do need extra practice and instruction and allows them space in their schedules to provide the time they need for targeted intervention work.

Summary

In summary, we hope this book is the tool you need to help you work with your students where they are, as well as where you are, in the phonics journey. If you are beginning the shift to explicit phonics instruction, we recommend you start with screening. Find your students' strengths and gaps in phonics knowledge first, and then look to see where those gaps are addressed in the blueprints if they are before the grade you are teaching. Begin by addressing those gaps and then start the blueprint sequence for your grade. Using high-impact activities, work through the blueprint progression, pausing or moving ahead at a rate that works for you and your students. Continue with informal progress monitoring and midyear screens to see if what you are doing is supporting students' growth. If yes, carry on. If no, reflect on what your students may still need and make the necessary adjustments. If you are feeling pressure to finish all the lessons in your grade level blueprint, remember that these concepts will be reviewed in the following year.

When phonics (along with the other four of the Big 5 of Reading) is explicitly taught in K–3, students will be prepared for the work that is designed for grade 4 and above. You will have noticed that as we move further into the blueprints, we begin to talk about where words come from (etymology) and word part meaning (morphology) because they impact pronunciation and spelling. This lays the foundation for concepts to be addressed more thoroughly in grades 4 and above: comprehension, etymology, morphology, and multisyllable work. Teachers teaching above grade 3 have spent the last twenty years adjusting their content and practice because students have not been able to read. They cannot wait for the day when they begin to receive students who can read, so that they can return to the content that is intended for these grades.

Finally, this is a journey of three to five years, so do not feel you need to shift everything in your practice tomorrow. Choose one or two high-impact activities, work through the blueprints at a rate that works for you and your students, and give yourself permission to fail. If something does not go well, reflect on why it hasn't worked, shift, and try again. One of the great things about teaching is that tomorrow is a new day, and your students will return to try again.

Resources

Reproducible Templates

Lesson Plan Template

Lesson Plan : Kindergarten & Grade 1

	Target Concept:
1	**Warm-up/review:** 2–5 minutes
2	**Introduce new concept (I Do):** 5 minutes
3	**Phonological awareness:** 3 minutes
4	**Teacher-led guided practice with new concept (WE Do):** 10–15 minutes
5	**Extended independent practice activities to apply new concept (YOU Do):** 15–20 minutes
6	**Tricky words:** 10 minutes
7	**Decoding with text (YOU Do):** 15–20 minutes
8	**Encoding (YOU Do):** 15 minutes
9.	**Intervention:**
10.	**Extending:**

Pembroke Publishers © 2022 *This Is How We Teach Reading...And It's Working* by Heather Willms & Giacinta Alberti ISBN 978-1-55138-357-6

Lesson Plan Template

Lesson Plan: Grades 2 & 3

	Target Concept:
1	**Warm-up/review:** 2–5 minutes
2	**Introduce new concept (I Do): 5** minutes
3	**Phonological awareness:** 3 minutes
4	**Teacher-led guided practice with new concept (WE Do):** 10–15 minutes
5	**Extended independent practice activities to apply new concept (YOU Do):** 15–20 minutes
6	**Decoding with text (YOU Do):** 15–20 minutes
7	**Encoding (YOU Do):** 15 minutes
8	**Intervention:**
9	**Extending:**

Pembroke Publishers © 2022 *This Is How We Teach Reading...And It's Working* by Heather Willms & Giacinta Alberti ISBN 978-1-55138-357-6

Word Ladders

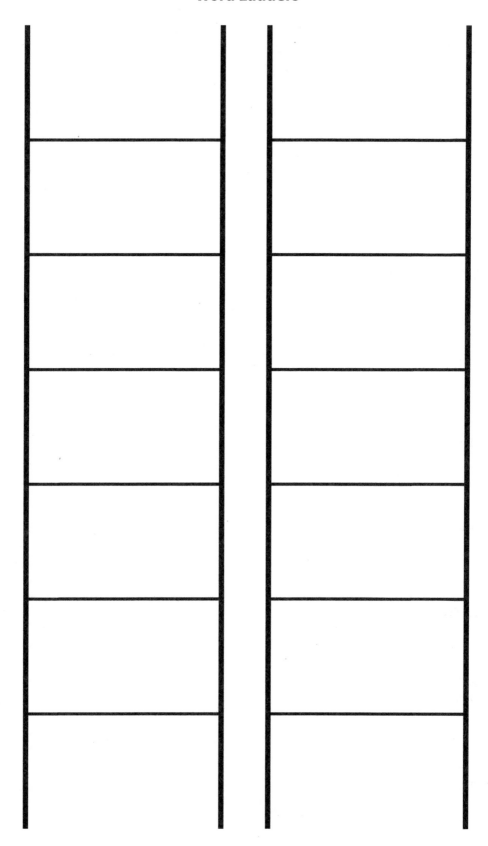

Phoneme-to-Grapheme Grid (up to 4 sounds)

Split Grid for Phoneme-to-Grapheme Mapping (up to 4 sounds)

Phoneme-to-Grapheme Grid (up to 5 sounds)

Pembroke Publishers © 2022 *This Is How We Teach Reading...And It's Working* by Heather Willms & Giacinta Alberti ISBN 978-1-55138-357-6

Split Grid for Phoneme-to-Grapheme Mapping (up to 5 sounds)

Phoneme-to-Grapheme Grid (up to 6 sounds)

Split Grid for Phoneme-to-Grapheme Mapping (up to 6 sounds)

10-Frame for Mapping with Letter Tiles (up to 5 sounds)

Elkonin Boxes

Word Sort Template (2 concepts)

Pembroke Publishers © 2022 *This Is How We Teach Reading…And It's Working* by Heather Willms & Giacinta Alberti ISBN 978-1-55138-357-6

Word Sort Template (3 concepts)

Letter Names and Sounds Screen, Teacher Page

Teacher Score Sheet	Date			
Name:	Uppecase Letter Names	____ /26	____ /26	____ /26
Teacher:	Lowercase Letter Names	____ /26	____ /26	____ /26
	Letter Sounds	____ /26	____ /26	____ /26

Letter Names		Letter Sounds	Comments/Observations
A	a	a	
S	s	s	
T	t	t	
P	p	p	
N	n	n	
I	i	i	
C	c	c	
D	d	d	
O	o	o	**Confusions/Unknown Letters**
G	g	g	
M	m	m	
E	e	e	
K	k	k	
R	r	r	
U	u	u	
H	h	h	
B	b	b	
F	f	f	**Strengths**
L	l	l	
J	j	j	
V	v	v	
W	w	w	
X	x	x	
Y	y	y	
Z	z	z	
Q	q	q	

Pembroke Publishers © 2022 *This Is How We Teach Reading...And It's Working* by Heather Willms & Giacinta Alberti ISBN 978-1-55138-357-6

Letter Names and Sounds Screen, Student Page

A	S	T	P	N	I
C	D	O	G	M	E
K	R	U	H	B	F
L	J	V	W	X	Y
Z	Q				

a	s	t	p	n	i
c	d	o	g	m	e
k	r	u	h	b	f
l	j	v	w	x	y
z	q				

Pembroke Publishers © 2022 *This Is How We Teach Reading...And It's Working* by Heather Willms & Giacinta Alberti ISBN 978-1-55138-357-6

VC/CVC and Phrases Decoding Screen Record, Teacher Page

Student:
Grade:

VC Words			
Date:			
at			
in			
up			
on			
it			

CVC Words			
Date:			
sad			
lip			
dog			
fun			
bet			

Phrases

Date:			
	on a mat	on a mat	on a mat
	up in a bed	up in a bed	up in a bed

Pembroke Publishers © 2022 *This Is How We Teach Reading...And It's Working* by Heather Willms & Giacinta Alberti ISBN 978-1-55138-357-6

VC/CVC and Phrases Decoding Screen, Student Page

at	sad
in	lip
up	dog
on	fun
it	bet

Phrases

on a mat

up in a bed

Tricky Words Screen (sets 1–4)

Name: _____   Grade: _____

Tricky Words Set 1			Tricky Words Set 2			Tricky Words Set 3			Tricky Words Set 4		
Date:			Date:			Date:			Date:		
the			her			all			where		
of			you			one			who		
as			your			from			only		
has			are			have			very		
is			use			live			any		
his			come			give			put		
was			some			or			many		
to			said			what			two		
do			there			they			old		
TOTAL			TOTAL			TOTAL			TOTAL		

Tricky Words Screen (sets 5–8)

Name: _____   Grade: _____

Tricky Words Set 5			Tricky Words Set 6			Tricky Words Set 7			Tricky Words Set 8		
Date:			Date:			Date:			Date:		
were			mother			goes			world		
because			father			word			over		
want			been			school			people		
other			every			open			enough		
their			work			move			carry		
love			again			eyes			answer		
would			once			close			above		
could			great			watch			most		
should			does			idea			kind		
TOTAL			TOTAL			TOTAL			TOTAL		

Pembroke Publishers © 2022 *This Is How We Teach Reading…And It's Working* by Heather Willms & Giacinta Alberti ISBN 978-1-55138-357-6

Kindergarten Class-Wide Screening Data Record

Student	Fall			Midyear				Spring				
	Oral Language Checklist	Concepts of Print	Phonemic Awareness	Oral Language Checklist *(for at-risk/ bubble)*	Concepts of Print *(for at-risk/ bubble)*	Phonemic Awareness *(for at-risk/ bubble)*	Phonemic Awareness	Uppercase Letter Names	Lowercase Letter Names	Letter Sounds	Decoding (VC/CVC)	

Pembroke Publishers © 2022 *This Is How We Teach Reading...And It's Working* by Heather Willms & Giacinta Alberti ISBN 978-1-55138-357-6

Grade 1 Class-Wide Screening Data Record

Student	Fall				Midyear				Spring						
	Phonemic Awareness	Developmental Spelling Test	Letter Names & Sounds	Decoding Screen (VC/CVC)	Phonemic Awareness *(for at-risk/bubble)*	Letter Names & Sounds *(for at-risk/bubble)*	Decoding Screen (VC/CVC)	Tricky Words Screen	Phonemic Awareness *(for at-risk/bubble)*	Letter Names & Sounds *(for at-risk/bubble)*	Decoding Screen *(for at-risk/bubble)*	Benchmark/ Fluency/Compre-hension Screen	Developmental Spelling Screen	Tricky Words Screen

Pembroke Publishers © 2022 *This Is How We Teach Reading...And It's Working* by Heather Willms & Giacinta Alberti ISBN 978-1-55138-357-6

Grade 2 Class-Wide Screening Data Record

Student		Fall					Midyear		Spring		
		Letter Names & Sounds (for-at-risk/ bubble)	Tricky Words Screen (for at-risk/bubble)	Phonics Word Reading Screen	Spelling Screen	Benchmark or Fluency/ Comprehension Screen	Spelling Screen (for at-risk/bubble)	Benchmark or Fluency/Compre-hension (for at-risk/ bubble)	Phonics Word Reading Screen	Spelling Screen	Benchmark or Fluency/ Comprehension Screen

Grade 3 Class-Wide Screening Data Record

Student	Fall			Midyear		Spring		
	Spelling Screen	Phonics Word Reading Screen	Benchmark or Fluency/ Comprehension Screen	Spelling Screen *(for at-risk/bubble)*	Benchmark/ Fluency/ Comprehension *(for at-risk/bubble)*	Spelling Screen	Phonics Word Reading Screen	Benchmark or Fluency/ Comprehension Screen

Pembroke Publishers © 2022 *This Is How We Teach Reading...And It's Working* by Heather Willms & Giacinta Alberti ISBN 978-1-55138-357-6

Class-Wide Progress Monitoring Record

Student																				

Pembroke Publishers © 2022 *This Is How We Teach Reading...And It's Working* by Heather Willms & Giacinta Alberti ISBN 978-1-55138-357-6

Letters-to-Sounds Correlation Charts

....

Letters-to-Sounds Correlation Chart 1
(single consonants and vowels)

Letters	Sounds & Word Examples			
a	/ă/ man	/ā/ take	/ä/ call	
b	/b/ bid			
c	/k/ cot	/s/ city		
d	/d/ dig			
e	/ĕ/ hen	/ē/ me		
f	/f/ fog			
g	/g/ gum	/j/ gem		
h	/h/ hop			
i	/ĭ/ kid	/ī/ like	/ē/ radium	/y/ union
j	/j/ jog			
k	/k/ kid			
l	/l/ lost			
m	/m/ mud			

Letters	Sounds & Word Examples			
n	/n/ not			
o	/ŏ/ off	/ō/ no		
p	/p/ pot			
qu	/kw/ quit			
r	/r/ red			
s	/s/ sand	/z/ his		
t	/t/ ten			
u	/ŭ/ sun	/ū/ cube	/ö/ tune	/ü/ put
v	/v/ vest			
w	/w/ wave			
x	/ks/ mix	/z/ xenon		
y	/y/ yam	/ĭ/ myth	/ī/ cry	/ē/ ivy
z	/z/ zebra			

Pembroke Publishers © 2022 *This Is How We Teach Reading...And It's Working* by Heather Willms & Giacinta Alberti ISBN 978-1-55138-357-6

Letters-to-Sounds Correlation Chart 2
(sounds represented by more than one letter)

Letters	Sounds & Word Examples		
ai	/ā/ r*ai*n		
ar	/är/ st*ar*		
au	/ä/ c*au*se		
augh	/ä/ c*augh*t	/ăf/ l*augh*	
aw	/ä/ p*aw*		
ay	/ā/ s*ay*		
bu	/b/ *bu*ilt		
ch	/ch/ *ch*op	/k/ *ch*aracter	/sh/ ma*ch*ine
cei	/sē/ *cei*ling		
ci	/sh/ deli*ci*ous		
ck	/k/ lu*ck*		
dge	/j/ we*dge*		
ea	/ē/ s*ea*t	/ĕ/ h*ea*d	/ā/ br*ea*k
ed	/ĕd/ fad*ed*	/d/ skill*ed*	/t/ hack*ed*

Letters	Sounds & Word Examples		
ee	/ē/ f*ee*t		
ei	/ā/ v*ei*n	/ē/ s*ei*ze	/ī/ h*ei*st
eigh	/ā/ w*eigh*	/ī/ sl*eigh*t	
er	/er/ f*er*n		
es	/ez/ rush*es*	/z/ cri*es*	
eu	/ö/ n*eu*tral		
ew	/ö/ bl*ew*	/ū/ f*ew*	
ey	/ā/ pr*ey*	/ē/ mon*ey*	
gh	/g/ *gh*ost		
gn	/n/ ali*gn*		
gu	/g/ *gu*ess	/gw/ lin*gu*ist	
ie	/ī/ t*ie*	/ē/ th*ie*f	
igh	/ī/ r*igh*t		
ir	/er/ th*ir*d		

Pembroke Publishers © 2022 *This Is How We Teach Reading…And It's Working* by Heather Willms & Giacinta Alberti ISBN 978-1-55138-357-6

Letters-to-Sounds Correlation Chart 2 cont.

(sounds represented by more than one letter)

Letters	Sounds & Word Examples				
kn	/n/ *kn*ee				
mb	/m/ la*mb*				
ng	/ng/ lo*ng*				
oa	/ō/ b*oa*t				
oe	/ō/ f*oe*	/ŏ/ can*oe*			
oi	/oi/ c*oi*n				
oo	/ö/ c*oo*l	/ü/ b*oo*k	/ō/ d*oo*r	/ŭ/ fl*oo*d	
or	/ōr/ t*or*n				
ou	/ow/ *ou*ch	/ō/ f*ou*r	/ö/ s*ou*p	/ŭ/ tr*ou*ble	/ü/ w*ou*ld
ough	/ŏ/ f*ough*t	/ō/ d*ough*	/ö/ thr*ough*		
	/ow/ dr*ough*t	/ŭf/ t*ough*	/ŏf/ tr*ough*		
ow	/ow/ c*ow*	/ō/ r*ow*			
oy	/oi/ t*oy*				

Letters	Sounds & Word Examples	
ph	/f/ *ph*onics	
schwa (ə)	/uh/	
sh	/sh/ *sh*ip	
si	/sh/ mis*si*on	/zh/ vi*si*on
tch	/ch/ ma*tch*	
th	/th/ *th*ick	/TH/ *th*em
ti	/sh/ po*ti*on	
ue	/ö/ s*ue*	/ū/ c*ue*
ui	/ö/ s*ui*t	
ur	/er/ b*ur*n	
wh	/w/ *wh*ale	
wor	/wer/ *wor*d	
wr	/r/ *wr*ap	

Pembroke Publishers © 2022 *This Is How We Teach Reading...And It's Working* by Heather Willms & Giacinta Alberti ISBN 978-1-55138-357-6

Glossary

additive blending. A strategy to support emergent readers with learning to combine letter sounds/phonemes, in order to pronounce a word in print. Readers start with the first letter sound and add sounds one at a time (always returning to the beginning of the word for each new sound) until they pronounce all the sounds in the word.

alphabet arc. A teaching graphic where the letters of the alphabet (uppercase or lowercase) are arranged, in alphabetical order, on a large piece of paper in the form of an arc. A variety of activities can be used to focus on building knowledge about the letters and sounds of the alphabet, as well as their order and orientation.

analytic phonics. A method of teaching reading that is based first on memorizing sight words and then analyzing the phonetic structure of those words. Word analysis may include looking at the shape of the word, the initial sound of the word, and its context (including picture cues).

assessment for instruction. Assessment for instruction, or assessment for learning, evaluates a student's ongoing comprehension and skill during the teaching and learning process to shape future instructional decisions. Data gathered from these evaluations helps teachers decide whether to provide additional instruction or review, or begin teaching a new concept.

at-risk reader. A student who requires additional instruction and practice of reading concepts due to lagging skills that have been determined as a result of early testing and screening.

balanced literacy. A program that strives to combine the best of whole-language and phonics strategies to build a comprehensive literacy program. Key concepts include guided reading, reading and writing workshop, and shared reading.

base. The form of a word to which prefixes and suffixes can be added to create new words that add to its meaning.

benchmark or benchmarking. In reading, benchmarking is an assessment system used to determine levels of achievement in fluency and comprehension. Benchmarks often consist of twenty-six to thirty stages of reading development, assessing a student's independent and instructional reading level.

Big 5 of reading. The National Reading Panel of 2000 identified five key areas that contribute to reading success: phonemic awareness, phonics, fluency, vocabulary, and comprehension.

biliterate. Someone who is able to read and write in two languages.

blend. Two or more consonants that occur before or after a vowel. Each consonant retains its own unique sound. Blends are not separated when breaking large words into single syllables.

blending board. A teaching tool where two or more letters are attached to a fixed surface, typically with rings. Letters can be flipped back and forth (by the reader) to create new words and provide opportunities to practice blending an assortment of letter combinations. Blending board formats can vary from binders to letter stands.

blending lines. A reading strategy where lines of text (words or sentences) are used to provide reading practice. Each line focuses on a different part of a word (beginning, medial, end).

breve. A curved diacritic marking over a vowel grapheme to indicate that it makes the short vowel sound (ă, ĕ, ĭ, ŏ, ŭ).

bubble students. A colloquial term used to describe students who, year after year, lag approximately one grade level behind their peers in reading skills.

C. A common symbol used in phonics instruction to represent one consonant.

consonant. A speech sound that is created with complete or partial closure of the vocal tract.

continuous blending. A word-reading strategy where the reader verbally sustains one sound until moving to the next sound — for example, "fffffffaaaaaat."

CVC. A common symbolic pattern used in phonics to reference a word that contains a consonant followed by a vowel and ending with a consonant (e.g., the word "cat").

decode. The ability to match printed symbols (letters) with sounds, to create meaning. It includes the ability to match letters to sounds and connect the resulting sound to knowledge of spoken words and their meaning.

decoding. The process of matching printed symbols (letters) with sounds, to create meaning.

diacritic. A mark placed over, under, or next to a letter to indicate a specific pronunciation.

digraph. Two letters that combine to create one new sound (e.g., "ch," "sh," "wh").

diphthong. A sound made up of two distinct sounds, where the pronunciation glides from one sound to the other (e.g., /oi/ and /ö/).

Elkonin boxes. Also known as sound boxes, Elkonin boxes are a research-based strategy that uses boxes or cubes to represent sounds. Activities using the boxes build and strengthen phonological skills in emergent readers.

emergent reader. A student who does not yet understand that the sounds of letters on a page align with the sounds in spoken words to create meaning.

encoding. Building or creating words through spelling, manipulatives, or keyboarding.

English language learners (ELLs). Students whose first language is not English and who are not able to communicate fluently or learn effectively in English. ELLs may speak and/or be literate in more than one language.

evidence-based strategy. A strategy that is aligned with what neuroscience, psychology, and cognitive science have found to be effective for instruction AND that shows consistent, measurable success in the classroom setting.

explicit instruction. Instruction that is unambiguous, systematic, direct, and engaging for students.

flash cards. A teaching tool consisting of squares or rectangles of heavy paper printed with letters, words, and/or pictures for reading practice.

fluency. The ability to read quickly, accurately, and with expression.

fluency passages. Several sentences of meaningful text that are used to teach students to read quickly, accurately, and with expression. The texts should contain targeted concepts that have been, or are currently being, taught.

fluency phrases. Short sentence fragments that are used to teach students to read quickly, accurately, and with expression. Sentence fragments often contain targeted concepts that have been, or are being, taught.

formative assessment (also known as progress monitoring). Assessment that is implemented during the independent practice of new concepts to check if students have mastered the target concept or require additional instruction and/or practice.

grapheme. A letter, punctuation mark, or symbol in a writing system. In this book a grapheme refers to a letter.

high-frequency words. The most common words found in print. Lists of high-frequency words do not focus on concepts or skills but are typically listed in order of how often they appear in text.

macron. A straight-line diacritic placed over a vowel grapheme to indicate that it makes a long vowel sound (ā, ē, ī, ō, ū).

mapping. The process of identifying the sounds (phonemes) in a word and matching them to the appropriate letters (graphemes).

morpheme. The smallest meaningful unit of a language. Morphemes can include bases, suffixes, and prefixes. An example of a morpheme could be "face," "ing," or "re."

MSV (three-cueing system). See three-cueing system below. The three cues are M = meaning, S= Syntax, and V= Visual.

National Reading Panel (NRP). A United States government body formed in 1997 to assess the effectiveness of different approaches used to teach reading. The results were published in the year 2000 and have had a significant impact on reshaping the teaching of reading in North America.

nonsense words. Words that do not align with any words found in the language spoken by the reader. Nonsense words are used to check a reader's understanding of a phonics concept being taught and/or reviewed.

onset and rime. A term used to describe the phonological units of a spoken syllable. In a syllable or single-syllable word, the initial sound is the onset, and the remaining portion of the syllable is the rime (not to be confused with "rhyme"). The single-syllable word "chin" has the onset "ch" and "in" is the rime. Not all words have an onset (e.g., "end").

oral language. Oral language, sometimes called spoken language, includes both speaking and listening. Oral language skills are foundational for both word reading and comprehension (SVR).

orthographic lexicon. A bank of stored words in the brain that can be instantly retrieved, identified, and spelled correctly.

orthographic mapping (OM). The mental process of storing words in the brain for immediate and effortless retrieval. The sound of a word, along with its spelling and meaning, contributes to word storage.

phoneme. The smallest sound part in speech. The word "fin" consists of three phonemes: f-i-n.

phoneme manipulation. When students work with individual sounds within a word it is called phoneme manipulation. It may include segmenting, blending, deleting, adding, or substituting phonemes both orally and in writing.

phoneme-to-grapheme spelling. The method to develop and practice spelling skills. Students identify the individual sounds or phonemes in a word and write the correct letter/s or grapheme/s to represent those sounds.

phonemic awareness (PA). The ability to identify, isolate, and manipulate individual sounds in spoken words.

phonics. A method of teaching reading where readers learn to match a spoken sound with a symbol/s using an alphabetic system. Readers can then use this knowledge to write.

phonological awareness. Phonological awareness is an umbrella term that focuses on the sound structure of spoken language. It can include the ability to identify, isolate, and manipulate sound at the sentence, word, and phoneme level. It includes syllables, rhymes, onset and rime, etc.

Pig Latin. Pig Latin is a word play activity with the English language wherein the speaker places the first sound in a word at the end and adds the vocalic syllable /ā/. The names Heather and James would be Eatherhay and Amesjay in Pig Latin.

prefix. A word part added to the beginning of a base or word to add to or modify its meaning. For example, "un" added to the beginning of "happy" means "to not be happy."

progress monitoring (formative assessment). Assessment that is implemented during the independent practice of new concepts to check if students have mastered the target concept or require additional instruction and/or practice.

reading comprehension. An internal process that enables the reader to accurately understand and interpret what is written.

reading intervention. Strategies and time dedicated to target and support the learning of students who struggle with learning to read. Intervention can be done in or out of the classroom and either one-on-one or with a small group of students.

rhyme. The repetition of a similar sound at the end of two or more words (e.g., "cart," "dart," "heart").

Right to Read inquiry report. In October 2019, the Ontario Human Rights Commission announced a public inquiry into concerns around the human rights issues that affect students with reading disabilities in Ontario's education system. Results of the inquiry were published in March 2022, stating that children with reading disabilities have the right to be taught reading in a way that aligns with what neurological researchers understand about how the brain learns to read.

running record. A tracking system that is used when a student is reading a passage or book to assess decoding accuracy. The assessor notates errors in word decoding, repetition of words and phrases, missing or added words, etc. Scores from running records are used to assess progress, accuracy, and achievement in reading fluency.

scaffolding. A process in lesson delivery whereby the teacher provides multiple access points for learners. A lesson may have a variety of activities or learning modalities for students with a wide range of skills.

Scarborough's Reading Rope. A visual graphic created by Hollis Scarborough to help the viewer understand the components of decoding and language comprehension necessary for skilled readers.

schwa. An unstressed central vowel (sounding similar to /ŭ/) that is represented by the symbol /ə/ in the International Phonetic Alphabet (IPA). The presence or absence of schwa in a word can be dependent on regional dialects.

Science of Reading (SOR). A body of scientifically based research regarding how the brain learns to read. Information gained from this research provides insights into evidence-based strategies for teaching reading.

screen. A short, simple assessment tool to identify a student's knowledge of a specific skill or skill set.

segmenting. Segmenting, or segmentation, occurs when students break words into phonemes, onset and rime, or syllables. This can be done orally or in print.

silent reading. While the term itself indicates reading without speaking the words that are being read, in the classroom setting it indicates a specific time period in the school day where students read independently.

Simple View of Reading (SVR). A reading theory that postulates that "decoding × language comprehension = reading comprehension."

Six Syllable Rules. A set of phonics rules used to guide the breaking down of multisyllable words into single syllables for reading and spelling. Use of the rules helps predict whether a vowel sound is long or short. Examples include open and closed syllables, vowel teams, vowel-r, etc.

SOR. See Science of Reading.

sound wall. A bulletin board display of grade-appropriate words arranged by sound. Besides containing target sounds and words, a sound wall may also contain a key word or picture, a picture of the correct mouth formation when the sound is spoken, and, in the case of vowels, variations in how the sound can be spelled. For example, the word "of" would be found under schwa rather than "o" on a sound wall.

Story Grammar Marker. An oral language manipulative tool designed to support the organization of thoughts and ideas while engaging in narrative telling or retelling.

Structured Literacy. A systematic, explicit, engaging, and success-oriented method of reading instruction that aligns with neurological researchers' understanding of how the brain learns to read. In Structured Literacy, the teacher spends a significant amount of time in instruction and coaching, with a minimal amount of time when students are learning on their own. Structured Literacy instruction is based on ongoing assessment, with continual adjustments made in response to the progress of the students being taught.

suffix. A word part added to the end of a base or word to add to or modify its meaning. For example, "ful" added to the end of the word "joy" means "a state of being filled with joy."

SVR. See Simple View of Reading.

syllable. A unit of spoken language that contains one vowel sound.

syllable boards. Small boards (approximately 3" x 5") with a laminated white surface that can be written on with a dry erase pen and then easily erased for ongoing use. They are commonly used for teaching students how to read and write multisyllable words.

synthetic phonics. A method of teaching reading that starts with the introduction of a few letters and sounds, and quickly moves to blending letters to create words.

10-frame. A grid structure of ten squares arranged in two rows of five that is used for teaching math. The grid is used with counters to represent groups or partial groups of ten. This structure can be used in reading instruction with the top line of the grid being used to count the number of phonemes in a word. Under each counter, students can write the letter or letters that represents each identified sound.

three-cueing system. An approach to reading in which reading skills are taught and assessed by a student's use of meaning (M), syntax (S), and visual cues (V).

tricky word. A word that is not easily decoded without a mature understanding of phonics rules and patterns (temporarily irregular). Students are taught these words early in the reading process, by a combination of decoding and memorization because they encounter them often in early text. As students learn more of the rules and patterns of English, many of the sound spellings do not need to be memorized anymore and they are no longer considered tricky (or irregular).

Ubbi Dubbi. A word play activity using the English language where "ub" is added before each vowel sound in a syllable. In Ubbi Dubbi, "Good day" would be "Gubood dubay."

umlaut. A diacritic of two dots placed over a vowel grapheme (ä, ü, ï, ö, ë, ÿ) to indicate it makes a more central or front articulation. For example, "ä" indicates the /aw/ sound, as in "water."

V. A common symbol used in phonics to represent one vowel.

VC. A common symbolic reference used in phonics referring to a word or syllable that begins with one vowel followed by one consonant (e.g., "it" or "er")

virgules. Diagonal lines that denote the sound of a letter or letters (e.g., /ă/, as in "cat", /ā/, as in "mate," or /ä/, as in "water").

vocabulary. All the words that exist in a particular language or subject, or all the words used by a person or group of people.

vowel. A speech sound that is made with the vocal tract open.

vowel team. Two or more letters that work together to create one vowel sound (e.g., "ai" says /ā/). A vowel team may include consonants such as vowel teams "igh" (/ī/) as in "high" or "ow" (/ō/) as in "low."

whiteboards. Small boards with a laminated white surface that can be written on with a dry erase pen and then easily erased for ongoing use. In reading instruction, they are commonly used for teaching a variety of encoding strategies.

whole language instruction. Reading instruction based on the premise that, like speaking, learning to read English comes naturally for young children. Books used to teach whole language reading are typically repetitive and predictable to support understanding of the text. Word accuracy is not a focus, allowing children the freedom to improvise the telling of the story. The underlying goal of this reading approach is to foster a love of reading.

word chains. An encoding activity where students create a chain of words by selecting and changing one letter or sound in the previous word to create a new word. A sample word chain might be flat—slat—slit—slip.

word ladders. An encoding strategy where students generate new words by changing one letter in an existing word. The activity is focused on a printed ladder with a key word written on either the top or bottom rung. If the key word is written at the bottom of the ladder, students work their way up the ladder by writing a new word (with one letter or sound changed) on the rung above.

word sort. A reading activity where students divide words into groups based on a targeted phonics concept.

word wall. A bulletin board display of grade-appropriate words arranged by initial letter. Word walls are designed to support student spelling. For example, the word "giraffe" would be found under the consonant "g" and the word "one" would be listed under "o."

Resources We Recommend

Our Favorite Assessment Screens

Acadience Reading K-6
Acadience Reading K-6. (2022). Retrieved June 18, 2022, from https://www.
   voyagersopris.com/product/assessment/acadience-reading/overview
Formally known as DIBELS Next literacy assessment, Acadience is a comprehensive assessment for predicting and identifying reading difficulties. It comes with extensive free training.

CORE Knowledge Foundation
CORE Knowledge Foundation. (2022). Retrieved May 21, 2022, from https://
   www.coreknowledge.org
A wide variety of free assessment material. You will need to register your name and email to access free material.

Developmental Spelling Test (DST)
Cowichan Valley School District. (Spring 2019). Early success screen:
   Kindergarten to grade 3. Retrieved May 21, 2022, from https://sd79.bc.ca/
   wp-content/uploads/Early-Success-Screen-2019-1.pdf
The DST is a comprehensive spelling screen with clear scoring guidelines.

LETRS: Language Essentials for Teachers of Reading
Region 10 Educational Service Center. (2022). *LETRS1 phonics and word
   reading survey administration and scoring record.* Retrieved May 17, 2022,
   from https://www.region10.org/r10website/assets/File/Phonics%20and%20
   Word%20Reading%20Survey%20Louisa%20Moats.pdf
The LETRS Phonics and Word Reading Survey screen is provided to participants in the LETRS training program and is available through Lexia Learning at https://www.lexialearning.com/letrs. Districts offering LETRS training will often post this screen on their websites as it can be shared for classroom use (not marketed or sold). An example retrieval site is listed above.

The PAST
The PAST Phonemic Awareness Screen by David Kilpatrick in available in *Equipped for Reading Success* (see References). It includes four parts (Forms A, B, C, and D) so that it can be administered several times throughout the same school year, providing progress monitoring for teachers.

Words Their Way Spelling Assessment

Bear, D.R., Invernizzi, M., Templeton, S. & Johnston, F. (2020). *Words their way: Word study for phonics, vocabulary, and spelling instruction.* 6th Edition. New York, NY: Pearson Publishing.

An elementary and upper-level spelling assessment tool that can be found in many of the Words Their Way books.

Phonemic Awareness Resources

Heggerty Phonemic Awareness Curriculum

Heggerty. (2022). *Phonemic awareness: Kindergarten curriculum 2022.* Retrieved May 20, 2022, from https://heggerty.org/curriculum/kindergarten

Week-by-week phonological lessons for prekindergarten through primary classrooms. Although the program is based on a whole year of explicit PA instruction, three months of daily explicit instruction should be adequate for typically developing readers. Following that, PA instruction should be linked to text and embedded in instruction, with isolated explicit instruction for those with unfinished PA learning. Lessons are available in book and video format.

One Minute Phonemic Awareness Activities

The second half of *Equipped for Reading Success* (see References) offers an excellent sequence of one-minute activities for developing phonemic awareness skills and we often recommend this resource for students struggling with phonemic awareness in grades 2 and up.

Fluency Phrases

Letters and Sounds Fluency Phrases

Letters and Sounds. (2022). *Phase 2- captions.* Retrieved May 20, 2022, from https://letters-and-sounds.com/wp-content/uploads/2021/06/p2cap1.pdf

Fluency phrase cards (called Captions) are available for free on the Letters and Sounds website. Caption sets can be found under each phase, starting with Phase 2.

Dr. Edward Fry's Instant Phrases

These short phrases include a phrase for each of the 600 words in the Fry Word List. They are available for free on Tim Rasinski's website (see Websites to Explore).

Decodable Passages

Besides the sites listed below, many excellent reading instruction programs, such as Wilson for Reading, 99% Group, and Really Great Reading, contain decodable passages and phrases for instruction and practice.

CORE Knowledge Foundation

CORE Knowledge. (2022). *Curriculum.* Retrieved May 15, 2022, from https://www.coreknowledge.org/curriculum/download-curriculum

Free decodable passages and activities. You will need to sign up for their free login to access texts.

Developing Fluency Activity Package

Orton Gillingham Online Academy. (2017). *Developing fluency activity package.* Retrieved May 20, 2022, from https://www.ortongillinghammoodle.com/course/index.php?categoryid=1

This comprehensive package includes informal assessments, fluency passages, and student workbooks. The package aligns with the blueprints for grades 2 and 3 in this book. To purchase, the user must create an account or enter the site as a guest. We also use their package for Spelling Rules and Syllable Patterns.

West Virginia Phonics

Tools 4 Reading. (2022). *Tools for teachers: West Virginia phonics.* Retrieved May 22, 2022, from https://www.tools4reading.com/tools4teachers

Now available on the Tools 4 Reading website, West Virginia Phonics contains a large range of decodable passages at the end of each lesson plan. This free resource is organized around explicit phonics instruction. You will need to sign up for the free login on the Tools 4 Reading website to access the material.

Decodable Books

CORE Knowledge Decodable Books

CORE Knowledge Foundation. (2022). *Curriculum.* Retrieved May 15, 2022, from https://www.coreknowledge.org/curriculum/download-curriculum

Free decodable readers with older characters (e.g., the grade 1 level reader *Snap Shots* has two ten-year-old characters). You will need to sign up for their free login to access texts.

Fly Leaf Decodable Books

Fly Leaf Publishing. (2022). Online materials portal for instructors. Retrieved May 21, 2022, from https://portal.flyleafpublishing.com/instructional-resources/

Decodable books for purchase and free e-books and Smartboard files. We recommend the Emergent set of forty books.

Heggerty Decodable Readers

Heggerty. (2022). *The frog series.* Retrieved May 21, 2022, from https://heggerty.org/decodable-books/

Heggerty Decodable Readers consists of two series: the Frog Series and the Toucan Series. The Frog Series includes a variety of animal characters while the Toucan Series has older characters with multicultural representation, making it appropriate for older readers.

Institute for Multi-Sensory Education (IMSE)

Institute for Multi-Sensory Education. (2022). *IMSE decodable readers: Set two PDF (2021 Edition).* Retrieved May 5, 2022, from https://imse.com/products/2423/

IMSE offers three series of decodable readers that can be purchased for a modest price as books or as a PDF download. These books follow the Orton Gillingham phonics scope and sequence, which does not fully align with the scope and sequence we use in grade 1. We like the later two sets of readers as they focus on key concepts covered in grades 2 and 3 in our scope and sequence. This is an inexpensive way to boost your decodable library. If you purchase the PDF, photocopies can be sent home without being concerned about lost or damaged books.

Meg and Greg Books

Orca Two Read. *Meg and Greg*. Retrieved May 21, 2022, from https://orcatworead.com/

These three books all have graphic-novel-styled text on one page and traditional text on the other. They are designed for shared reading with a struggling reader and a stronger reader between the ages of six and nine. We also like them as a bridge from graphic novel reading to text reading. The stories are organized around a small selection of phonics concepts.

Phonics Play Comics

Phonics Play. (2022). *Phonics Play Comics*. Retrieved June 27, 2022, from https://phonicsplaycomics.co.uk/comics.html

These are short decodable comics. They are two pages long each and follow a well-laid-out scope and sequence of skills. These comics are available for free on their website.

Pip and Tim

Little Learners Love Literacy. (2022). *Decodable books*. Retrieved May 20, 2022, from https://www.littlelearnersloveliteracy.com.au/blogs/decodable-books

This excellent series of books, apps, and games moves slowly to provide adequate practice with new concepts. This Australian series follows an explicit scope and sequence. For North American ordering, materials can be purchased through the Reading League.

Primary Phonics

Makar, B.W. (2022). *Primary phonics*. Retrieved May 21, 2022, from https://eps.schoolspecialty.com/EPS/media/Site-Resources/Downloads/program-overviews/21747413-II_Primary-Phonics-brochure_Final_HS.pdf

This recently updated series may be old but it has an excellent skill progression, inexpensive pricing, and accessibility for young readers.

Whole Phonics

Whole Phonics. (2022). *Level 1-3 complete set, readers*. Retrieved May 20, 2022, from https://whole-phonics.com/en-ca/collections/view-all

All three leveled series contain colorful and appealing books for young readers. Two additional levels are scheduled for release in 2023.

References

Recommended Reading

Archer, A., Flood, D., Lapp, J., and Lungren, L. (2001). *PHONICS for reading*. Victoria: Hawker Brownlow Education.

Armbruster, B., Lehr, F., and Osborn, J. (2001). *Put reading first: The research building blocks for teaching children to read*. Retrieved March 20, 2022, from https://www.nichd.nih.gov/publications/product/239

Blevins, W. (2017). *A fresh look at phonics*. Thousand Oaks: Corwin Literacy.

Dehaene, S. (2021). *How we learn*. New York, NY: Penguin Books.

Dehaene, S. (2009). *Reading in the brain: The new science of how we read*. New York, NY: Penguin Books.

Ehri, L. (2014). *Orthographic mapping in the acquisition of sight word reading, spelling memory and vocabulary learning, scientific studies of reading.* Retrieved March 15, 2022, from https://www.readingrockets.org/research-by-topic/orthographic-mapping-acquisition-sight-word-reading-spelling-memory-and-vocabulary

Eide, D. (2011). *Uncovering the logic of English.* Rochester: Pedia Learning Inc.

Gough, P., and Tunmer, W. (1986). "Decoding, reading, and reading disability." *Remedial and Special Education, 7,* 6–10.

Johnston, R., and Watson, J. (2014). *Teaching synthetic phonics in primary schools.* Thousand Oaks: Sage Publishing.

Kilpatrick, D. A. (2016). *Equipped for reading success.* Syracuse: Casey & Kirsch Publishers.

Kleiber, H. K. (2003) *Specific language training.* Greenville, SC: VC Educational Consulting.

Moats, L. (2020). *Speech to print: Language essentials for teachers* (3rd edition). Baltimore: Brookes Publishing.

Rymanowicz, K. (2017, April 03). *Children and empathy: Reading to learn empathy.* Retrieved April 15, 2022, from https://www.canr.msu.edu/news/children_and_learn_empathy

Scarborough, H. S. (2001). *Connecting early language and literacy to later reading (dis)abilities: Evidence, theory, and practice.* In S. Neuman and D. Dickinson (Eds.), *Handbook for research in early literacy* (pp. 97–110). New York, NY: Guilford Press.

Seidenberg, M. (2018). *Language at the speed of sight: How we read, why so many can't, and what can be done about it.* New York, NY: Basic Books.

Willingham, D. (2017). *The reading mind: A cognitive approach to understanding how the mind reads.* Hoboken: Jossey-Bass.

Wolf, M. (2008). *Proust and the squid: The story and science of the reading brain.* New York, NY: Harper Perennial.

Wolf, M. (2016). *Tales of literacy for the 21st century.* Oxford: Oxford University Press.

Blog

Shanahan, T. *Shanahan on literacy.* https://www.shanahanonliteracy.com/blog
A balanced and thoughtful approach to all things reading. Shanahan responds to questions from teachers about emergent reading issues.

Websites to Explore

Institute for Multi-Sensory Education (IMSE): https://imse.com/
A wealth of resources and professional development opportunities.

Kendore Learning: https://kendorelearning.com/
Excellent resources, workshops, and webinars throughout the year.

Really Great Reading: https://www.reallygreatreading.com/
Programs and professional development.

Sightwords.com: https://sightwords.com/sight-words/flash-cards/
Free flash-card generator that contains a dot and arrow under each word.

Syllables Learning Center: https://syllableslearningcenter.com/
Excellent resources and workshops. Free webinars several times a year.

Tim Rasinski: http://www.timrasinski.com/
A wealth of resources, especially regarding fluency instruction.

Tools 4 Reading: https://www.tools4reading.com/
Educational and sound wall materials, and professional development that aligns with SOR.

Podcasts to Explore

EDVIEW 360 from Voyager Sopris
Science of Reading: the Podcast from Amplify

Social Media to Explore

Twitter
#thisishowweteachreading

Tik Tok
@thisishowweteachreading

Instagram
@this.is.how.we.teach.reading

Facebook
Orton Gillingham Continued Learning
Orton Gillingham Teachers
Reading Specialists and Literacy Coaches
Science of Reading: Book Study
Science of Reading: The Community: This group is managed by Amplify Education.
Small Group Reading Intervention
The Science of Reading — What I Should Have Learned in College: There are a variety of Science of Reading Facebook pages. This is one of the original sites and probably the most popular. There are many regional and grade-specific sites created as a result of this page.
This Is How We Teach Reading
Wilson Reading System: Tips and Tricks

Summary of Concepts and Tricky Words Sets Taught in K–3

Kindergarten

concepts of print	page 75
phonemic awareness	page 75
letter names and sounds: a, s, t	page 75
letter names and sounds: p, n	page 79
letter name and sound: i	page 82
letter names and sounds: c, d	page 83
letter name and sound: o	page 84
letter names and sounds: g, m	page 85
letter name and sound: e	page 86
letter names and sounds: k, r (+ spelling rules for c/k)	page 87
letter name and sound: u	page 88
letter names and sounds: h, b (+ b vs. d)	page 90
letter names and sounds: f, l	page 91
letter names and sounds: j, v	page 92
letter names and sounds: w, x	page 93
letter names and sounds: y, z	page 93
letter names and sounds: q/qu	page 94
tricky words: set 1	page 96

Grade 1

Grade 2

Grade 3

Acknowledgments

Thank you to Pembroke Publishers and Mary Macchiusi for publishing our book. We are grateful that you were able to see our vision and gave us the opportunity to fulfill it. We have appreciated your expertise and knowledge throughout the process of publication. From idea, to manuscript, to completed book, to marketing, and beyond, you have graciously guided us through the development of this teaching resource. We also thank you for sending us our wonderful editor, David Kilgour.

David, we have appreciated your love of phonics and the many hours you spent wading through all the technical pieces in the concept pages. Your sense of humor and patience in teaching us the ins and outs of editing have been fantastic.

Edith Martyn, long before we met you, we had heard about you and your passion for ensuring children are explicitly taught how to read. Thank you for looking through the early drafts of our scope and sequence and the research behind how children learn to read. We knew that if anyone had a firm understanding of this research and educational processes, it would be you. Your passion for supporting children and teachers on their reading journeys remains as strong as ever.

The phonics boxes we use are the brainchild of mentorship time with Heather, Alison Carmichael, and Cara Bowley. Cara and Alison, your understanding of how to teach reading, the challenges of working with a wide range of readers, and what needs to be available for teachers has created a tool that has resonated with every teacher we share it with! Our conversations about scope and sequence, as we have built the boxes, have been invaluable.

We especially want to thank our many colleagues, administrators, and teachers across the globe who work tirelessly for children. Assessing, preparing lessons, teaching, and building strong programing are only a small part of what you are asked to do on a daily basis. It is with you in mind that we have written this book. If it makes your job even a little bit easier, then we know we have succeeded.

H.W. and C.A.

Cinta, I could not have asked for a better partner to do this work! Your knowledge and experience show on every page. Covid-19, shingles, IEPs, an LST manual, and student reports have made the past eight months a wee bit insane and yet here we are at the end of our book!

Tracy Pederson and Esther Shatz, it was your concerns about what was not happening with reading instruction that have ignited far-reaching foundational shifts. We are no longer changing the lives of children "one reader at a time."

Thank you to my husband, Lorne, who truly understands my passion for students and teaching. — *Heather*

Heather, thank you for inviting me to be your partner in this journey. Your knowledge and your passion for teaching children to read are an inspiration. You have taught me so much and I am grateful to have shared in this work with you. Thank you to my school administrator, Lisa Scheck, for your encouragement and care every day at work. Your eagerness to be involved in helping our students learn to read by supporting teachers and acquiring the needed resources has helped to make it happen for many children. — *Cinta*

Index

....